Living in Truth Day by Day

A Women's Devotional

Living in Truth Day by Day

A Women's Devotional

Rae Lynn DeAngelis

His word press

Living in Truth Day by Day
A Women's Devotional

Printed in the United States of America
ISBN: **978-0-9885036-0-1**

Learn more information at:
LivingInTruthMinistries.com

Acknowledgements

Lord, I thank you for the wonderful treasures in your Word and for your unconditional love and amazing grace. Most of all, I thank you for Jesus—the author and perfecter of my faith.

Gerry, thank you for your love and support as I follow God's call on my life. You are my best friend and the love of my life. I look forward to growing old together. The best years are yet to come!

Heather, thank you for helping me prepare this manuscript for print. Not only are you a wonderful daughter, but you are a treasured friend and sister-in-Christ. It is such a joy to see you grow in your relationship with Jesus! Your obedience to God's call on your life is an inspiration.

Ben, I am so proud of the young man you have become and look forward to seeing what God has in store for your life. You have wonderful, adventurous years ahead. "Trust in the Lord with all your heart and lean not on your own understanding. In all your ways acknowledge him and he will make your path straight." (Proverbs 3:5-6)

A special thanks to S'ambrosia, my editor. Your insight and encouragement has spurred me on to greater heights as a writer.

Introduction:
Living in Truth Day by Day

In the 1970's film *Adventures of the Wilderness Family,* a young couple gathered their children and few meager belongings and moved to the wilderness, far from the hustle and bustle of suburban mayhem. In the middle of no man's land, these pioneers completely secluded themselves from modern-day culture. Their only access to the contemporary world was by seaplane. This brave, industrious family engineered their home from the provisions of nature and lived off the land through gardening, fishing, and hunting. It was a hard life—but uncomplicated.

Living in a remote part of God's country with no worldly distractions sounds somewhat tempting to me, but would I actually do it? Probably not. I've grown a little too accustomed to modern-day conveniences like running water and electricity. So what is it about this way of life that intrigues me?

I suppose it's the fact that these people were insulated from the worldliness of their culture. Without all the distractions, they could devote themselves to the things most important in life. "Turn my eyes away from the worthless things; preserve my life according to your word." (Psalm 119:37)

Christians are called to be set apart—to live differently than the rest of world—but we are not called to completely separate ourselves from the world. If we, like the Wilderness Family, lived in a remote part of the world away from others, we could not possibly fulfill the great commission to go and make disciples of all nations. (Matthew 28:18)

God calls us to live in the world but not be of the world. "Religion that God our Father accepts as pure and faultless is this... to keep oneself from being polluted by the world." (James 1:27)

Influencing a culture that rejects God and His ways is challenging to say the least. With the many temptations around every corner, we must fight against the effects of worldly sin and corruption in our lives each and every day.

How is it possible to keep pure devotion to God in a predominantly secular culture? We must "set apart" Christ as Lord and allow Him to reign in our lives. When we surrender to God's higher ways through the power of the Holy Spirit, we have the ability to overcome worldly enticements.

God has given us His great and precious promises to teach, correct, and train us in His righteousness. Jesus said, "Sanctify them by the truth; your word is truth." (John 17:17) Scripture enlightens our path and directs our steps towards God's everlasting ways. No matter what we face in life, we can go to the Bible and find strength, hope, and encouragement.

In light of this truth, let us run with perseverance the race marked out for us, never forgetting that Jesus is Lord. He is our ever-present help in times of trouble.

Sweet sisters, as daughters of the King, clothed in His majesty, you and I have been set apart for Kingdom living, a position that comes with great responsibility. Are you ready to jump all the way in? I know that I am!

Let's do our best to live in God's truth day by day.

Restoration Not Renovation

One of my favorite television programs is *Rehab Addict*. The creative show title caught my attention one day when I was scrolling through the menu screen. Interestingly enough, the show has nothing to do with rehab centers. It's actually a home renovation program.

The show's restoration "junkie" prides herself in the fact that she doesn't simply renovate houses—she restores homes to their former glory. New life is poured into these dwellings through blood, sweat, and tears. It is a slow and painful process, but her hard work pays off in the end. After months of scraping away old paint, ripping up old flooring, and patching cracked walls, beauty emerges from the wreckage. What was once covered by decades of fad and fashion suddenly sparkles like new.

I have learned that God is also in the business of restoration. He goes to great lengths to rehabilitate us back to our former splendor. "…you knit me together in my mother's womb. I praise you because I am fearfully and wonderfully made;" (Psalm 139:13b-14a) "My frame was not hidden from you when I was made in the secret place, when I was woven together in the depths of the earth. Your eyes saw my unformed body; all the days ordained for me were written in your book before one of them came to be." (Psalm 139:15-16)

Our Lord loves variety and sees beauty in diversity. No two people are exactly the same—not even twins. We are born into this world unique. Over time, however, Satan convinces us that our differences are actually flaws. We buy into worldly lies that say we need to look and be a certain way.

The result?

We spend an enormous amount of time, money, and energy trying to cover up that which God has already made beautiful. God says, "Do not conform to the pattern of this world, but be transformed by the renewing of your mind." (Romans 12:2a)

I spent many years feeling unhappy with the way I looked and wasted an incredible amount of time conforming to the pattern of this world. Unfortunately, no matter how much weight was lost or makeup was applied, I still didn't feel beautiful.

When God purchased my life with the precious blood of His Son, the restoration process began. It is taking some time to scrape away the many layers of worldly influence (both inside and out), but day by day and truth by truth, God is restoring me into the unique vessel He created me to be.

"You were taught, with regard to your former way of life, to put off your old self, which is being corrupted by its deceitful desires; to be made new in the attitude of your minds; and to put on the new self, created to be like God in true righteousness and holiness." (Ephesians 4:22-24)

Like Nicole Curtis' renovated homes, by the end of our restoration process, may the glory of God's Son make us sparkle like new!

Finding Your Way

Each episode of Discovery Channel's *Man vs. Wild*, Bear Grylls is dropped into extreme locations around the world to teach his audience practical, life-saving techniques. His proven methods prepare potential adventurers to battle the elements of nature until they can find their way out of the landscape's harsh conditions, back to safety.

In one particular episode, Bear entered a remote rainforest far from the comforts of advanced civilization. Because of the tall trees and thick undergrowth, even this survival expert became disoriented and confused about the way he should go. Thankfully, he didn't panic. Instead, he climbed a tall tree to gain better perspective of the surrounding landscape. From his elevated viewpoint, a clearly marked path out of the jungle became obvious.

Sometimes in life we too can become confused about which way to go, especially when faced with life's difficult challenges.

So, how do we find our way out of the wilderness?

To find our way through life's harsh conditions, we must climb to new heights with Jesus Christ and view things from His higher perspective.

"If I rise on the wings of the dawn, if I settle on the far side of the sea, even there your hand will guide me, your right hand will hold me fast..." (Psalm 139:9-10)

One thing is for sure—we are not on this path alone. We have a trusty travel guide (the Holy Spirit) and a reliable road map (God's Word) to help us find our way out of the wilderness. I don't know about you, but I would never consider taking a journey without these trustworthy survival tools.

"Send forth your light and your truth, let them guide me; let them bring me to your holy mountain, to the place where you dwell..." (Psalm 43:3)

"Whether you turn to the right or the left, your ears will hear a voice behind you, saying, 'This is the way; walk in it.'" (Isaiah 30:21)

A clear and discernible path *will* emerge when we view our position from higher ground.

Keep Pressing On

Have you ever noticed how difficult it can be to move forward while looking back? I learned this lesson the hard way.

While I was walking out to my garage to get something, my husband asked me a question. I looked back to answer him but continued walking forward. The next thing I knew I was face down on the garage floor.

Through this painful and slightly embarrassing fall, God taught me a profound life lesson. Moving forward while looking back will not only hinder our progress, but it will oftentimes cause us to stumble and fall.

"Forgetting what is behind and straining toward what is ahead, I press on toward the goal to win the prize for

which God has called me heavenward in Christ Jesus."
(Philippians 3:13-14)

I am reminded through this Scripture that moving forward isn't an easy thing to do. The very words that the apostle Paul uses to describe the method of moving forward imply that it takes a deliberate action. He uses words like *pressing on*, *straining toward*, and *taking hold*.

It implies hard work and perseverance. "Not that I have already obtained all this, or have already been made perfect, but I press on to take hold of that for which Christ Jesus took hold of me." (Philippians 3:12)

Is the road to progress getting a little difficult to travel? Are you at a place in your Christian walk where you could use a little pep talk?

Take Paul's advice. Forget the past, press forward, and keep your eyes fixed on Jesus. Not only will He guide your steps, but He will keep you on the right path and clear the trail up ahead. *Keep pressing on!*

The Spirit's Nudging

One day while heading to school, our son's check engine light suddenly appeared on the dash of his car, signaling he had a problem. The vehicle seemed to be running fine, yet the warning light remained. The manufacturer put this internal detection device in the car's mechanical system to alert the driver to impending problems.

It's true that we could have hired any mechanic to fix the car, but we decided it would be better yet to take the vehicle to the manufacturer who designed the car. Certainly they would better understand all the intricate workings of our son's vehicle.

God is our Creator—our Designer. He knows every detail of our mind, body, and soul. All of our hopes, dreams, and fears are under His watchful eye. When internal malfunctions arise in our lives, we need to go to the One who created us in order to get an accurate diagnosis of the problem.

God placed an internal "mechanism" in our spirit that cautions us when something isn't quite right. Unfortunately, we too often ignore the Holy Spirit's prompting and continue speeding down the highway of life as if there's nothing wrong.

When a warning light comes on in the form of the Spirit's nudging, we must not ignore it. We should go to the Father and seek His guidance. After all, God knows all the intricate workings of our lives and can direct our steps towards His good and perfect will.

> You have searched me, LORD, and you know me. You know when I sit and when I rise; you perceive my thoughts from afar. You discern my going out and my lying down; you are familiar with all my ways. Before a word is on my tongue you, LORD, know it completely. You hem me in behind and before, and you lay your hand upon me. (Psalm 139: 1-5)

God knows everything there is to know about you and me. Therefore, when the Holy Spirit's conviction indicates looming danger, don't ignore the Spirit's nudging. It just might be God's warning device to keep us from bigger problems in the future.

His Chosen Ones

I dreaded the times when my teacher asked team captains to choose players for gym activities. I wasn't very athletic so of course I was one of the last ones to be picked. It was hard to be one of the last ones standing, waiting to be chosen. It seemed to confirm that which I already felt in my heart—nobody wanted me.

When I first joined organized sports, I spent a lot of time warming the bench. I remember thinking: *If someone would just take a chance on me and give me an opportunity to play, maybe I could improve my skills and become a more valuable player to the team.*

Taking a chance on an awkward kid who was uncomfortable in her own skin was highly unlikely.

I wasn't a fast runner or an aggressive player, but I was a good defender and had a powerful kick. For this reason the soccer coach started grooming me for the positions of full back and goalie. When I realized the coach had confidence in me, I began believing in myself. Eventually, I became a decent little soccer player.

Sometimes it just takes one person to believe in you for you to live up to your full potential. Even if man does not believe in you, God believes in you, and He greatly desires for you to be part of His team. You don't have to stand there waiting to be picked. You are already chosen!

You were hand-picked by God to fulfill a specific role in His bigger plan and purpose. "In him we were also chosen, having been predestined according to the plan of him who works out everything in conformity with the purpose of his will...." (Ephesians 1:11)

"For you are a people holy to the LORD your God. The LORD your God has chosen you out of all the peoples on the face of the earth to be his people, his treasured possession." (Deuteronomy 7:6)

God believes in you. *It's time to start believing in yourself!*

"Remember me, O LORD, when you show favor to your people, come to my aid when you save them, that I may enjoy the prosperity of your chosen ones, that I may share in the joy of your nation and join your inheritance in giving praise." (Psalm 106:4-5)

Deeply Rooted

I dropped my friend off at her house after spending the day together. As I began backing out of her driveway, I noticed something strange out of the corner of my eye—a huge oak tree was uprooted, lying on its side.

We quickly determined that a summer storm must have rolled through the neighborhood while we were gone. Strangely, other than a few scattered tree limbs and leaves dotting the ground, the large oak appeared to be the only casualty.

The next day, a tree cutting service came to remove the fallen relic from my friend's yard. She asked the specialist why this tree had been the only one affected by the storm. His answer was surprising. He said that because of the elevation of the land, the tree had a constant source of water. The oak never had to develop deep, strong roots because the water was easily accessed near the surface. The bundle of roots pulled up from the ground was the extent of the root system for the entire tree. It was only a matter of time before a strong wind was able to blow it over.

The condition of my friend's tree warrants reflection. Are we developing strong spiritual roots, or are we simply gathering what we can access near the surface of our lives (attending Sunday worship service or listening to Christian music)?

It's amazing what we can learn through the simple analogy of a tree. In nature, in order for a seed to mature into a tree, it must first grow roots. Tiny fibers sprout from the seed and descend into the soil where they can access essential nutrients and life-giving water. As the sapling grows above the ground, the roots below must expand in proportion. Roots act as an underground storage tank to aid the tree when water is scarce. Although most roots are unseen, they are invaluable to a tree's ability to thrive.

In the same way, our spiritual roots provide stability and enable us to grow, mature, and eventually become beautiful displays of God's splendor. "...They will be called oaks of righteousness, a planting of the Lord for the display of his splendor."(Isaiah 61:3b) "[The cedar] was majestic in beauty, with its spreading boughs, for its roots went down to abundant waters." (Ezekiel 31:7)

Developing strong spiritual roots today better prepares us to withstand the storms of life tomorrow.

When Pressure Builds

"The words of the reckless pierce like a sword, but the tongue of the wise brings healing." (Proverbs 12:18)

It was time to replace our hot water heater along with some other plumbing fixtures in the house. Mineral deposits built up over time had caused damage to our home's pipes, faucets, fixtures, and appliances. Because of scale build-up, water became restricted from flowing freely. As a result, the shower nozzle became clogged. The pressurized flow during a shower actually stung when it hit our skin. Two water heaters in seven years revealed a serious problem. It was time to invest in a water softener system.

After the system was installed, scale deposits began to break away, allowing the flow of water to pour through the pipes unrestricted. The resulting water flow felt soft in more ways than one—gentle and soothing.

Life can be hard, leaving its dirty residue behind. Bitterness, anger, resentment, and stress can build up in our hearts, creating pressure inside. Before we know it, words spew from our mouths and sting others, inflicting pain and heartache where ever they fall.

"For out of the overflow of his heart his mouth speaks." (Luke 6:45b)

When stress builds and pressure releases, it's difficult to keep the overflow from affecting those around us.

"They sharpen their tongues like swords and aim cruel words like deadly arrows." (Psalm 64:3)

Like a water softening system, daily time spent with God and His Word washes away the gunk from our system. God removes the ugly residue in our hearts and makes us purified vessels through whom His living water flows.

"Gracious words are a honeycomb, sweet to the soul and healing to the bones." (Proverbs 16:24)

"Whoever believes in me, as Scripture has said, rivers of living water will flow from within him." (John 7:38)

Stuck in a Rut

Our family had made plans to go boating up the river with some friends. My husband Gerry and I have a checklist of responsibilities to keep our boating trips running smoothly. He backs up the trailer while I take the helm of the watercraft. Then, while Gerry is busy parking the vehicle and boat trailer, I pull around to the nearest dock so that everyone can climb aboard.

This particular day I sat in the boat watching my husband navigate the already crowded parking lot. After spying an open space, he decided to take a short cut through a small grassy area (a maneuver he had done many times before with no problem). Unfortunately, heavy rains from the night before had left the ground saturated. As the SUV hit the grass, all four tires sank into the mud and began spinning. My husband was stuck in a rut.

I called out to him, asking if he needed help, but he shook his head no. He was determined to get out of his predicament alone. I watched helplessly as he rocked the vehicle to and fro, trying to break free from his muddy furrow, but no amount of rocking worked.

I called out to him again, "Are you sure you don't need a little push?" Throwing his hands up in surrender, he finally agreed to accept help. A couple of the guys with us offered their assistance, and after a few energetic shoves in the right direction, the car and trailer were back on solid ground.

Spiritually speaking, have you ever found yourself stuck in a rut, unable to progress in your journey with God? It can happen to anyone—even the strongest Christian.

While it's true that anyone can get stuck in a rut, we are not supposed to remain there. Like my husband, we must acknowledge our need for help. With help from the Holy Spirit, friends, and family, God nudges us back onto solid ground.

"The LORD is faithful to all his promises and loving toward all he has made. The LORD upholds all those who fall and lifts up all who are bowed down." (Psalm 145:13b-14)

Don't waste precious time struggling in a rut alone. Call out to God and wait for His team of support. Before you know it you'll be moving forward again, steady and strong.

"I guide you in the way of wisdom and lead you along straight paths. When you walk, your steps will not be hampered; when you run, you will not stumble." (Proverbs 4:11-12)

"If the LORD delights in a man's way, he makes his steps firm; though he stumble, he will not fall, for the LORD upholds him with his hand." (Psalm 37:23-24)

Don't Drink the Poison

"Bitterness is like drinking poison, expecting someone else to die from it." ~Shelley Hitz, *Forgiveness Formula*

Bitterness results from unforgiveness and slowly destroys relationships. It's something we must continually guard ourselves against. Because we live in a fallen world—people are going to hurt us.

We all struggle to forgive those who have hurt us, but we need to remember that forgiveness is a choice. It's a process that involves letting go of the wrong done to us, rejecting the right to get even, and placing judgment into the hands of a righteous Judge. We have a Judge who arbitrates fairly. We can trust Him to do what is best. "Will not the Judge of all the earth do right?" (Genesis 18:25c)

Even as Jesus was being led like a lamb to the slaughter, he provided a great example of what it looks like to place judgment into God's hands.

"When they hurled their insults at him, [Jesus] did not retaliate; when he suffered, he made no threats. Instead, he entrusted himself to him who judges justly." (1 Peter 2:23)

Sometimes God asks us to take a tough stand, and sometimes He asks us to be silent. This Scripture is not suggesting that we become doormats for others to trample, but it does remind us to seek the Lord's guidance so we can determine how to handle each situation.

Forgiveness takes time. It doesn't happen overnight. Forgiveness is not a one-time declaration either—sometimes we must forgive over and over. If we don't continually forgive, bitterness will creep in and spread across our heart.

"Then Peter came to Jesus and asked, 'Lord, how many times shall I forgive my brother when he sins against me? Up to seven times?' Jesus answered, 'I tell you, not seven times, but seventy-seven times.'" (Matthew 18:21-22)

We may think that we are punishing the other person by holding a grudge. But in reality, we're only hurting ourselves. Pent-up bitterness eats away at us like cancer, making us, and everyone around us, miserable. Being unwilling to forgive others creates a barrier for our own forgiveness. Oftentimes the person we're holding a grudge against has no idea how we truly feel.

Being unwilling to forgive means that we hold everyone around us to a standard of perfection—something we ourselves will never achieve. ~Gary L. Thomas

"If we claim we have not sinned, we make him out to be a liar and his word has no place in our lives." (1 John 1:10)

"Forgive, and you will be forgiven." (Luke 6:37b)

Fed by God

"Meanwhile his disciples urged him, 'Rabbi, eat something.' But he said to them, 'I have food to eat that you know nothing about.'" (John 4:31-32)

I don't know how you deal with the pressures of life, but one of the ways that stress affects me is through my appetite. When I'm going through something really difficult, the last thing I want to do is eat.

God designed our bodies to require the physical nourishment that food provides. But what happens when we just can't eat?

I recently learned what Jesus was talking about when He said He had food to eat that his disciples knew nothing about. When I couldn't eat because of the stress and turmoil caused by a difficult situation, God sustained me with food for the soul. He filled my spirit and gave me strength to face each difficult moment as I needed.

"Then Jesus was led by the Spirit into the desert to be tempted by the devil. After fasting forty days and forty nights, Jesus was hungry. The tempter came to him and said, 'If you are the Son of God, tell these stones to become bread.' Jesus answered, 'It is written: 'Man does not live on bread alone, but on every word that comes from the mouth of God.'" (Matthew 4:1-4)

Sometimes the Spirit of God leads us to desert experiences for a period of time. I'm not sure what my time in the desert represented, but I can tell you how I was able to get through it. Like Elijah, I was fed and sustained by God. "Then the word of the LORD came to Elijah: 'Leave here, turn eastward and hide in the Kerith Ravine, east of the Jordan... I have ordered the ravens to feed you there.'" (1 Kings 17:2-4)

When we grow especially weary, God sends us ravens (friends and loved ones), to help nourish us by speaking truth into our hearts.

One day during a particularly difficult time, my sister-in-law called and read something from her Bible study. She said the Lord had convicted her to share it with me. The message she shared spoke directly to my heart. It was undeniably God providing nourishment for my spirit.

Our times in the desert are no picnic for sure, but God will sustain us, care for us, and make us stronger than before. And when we grow weary and can't go on, God sends us a raven to provide spiritual nourishment until we can thrive on our own again.

"Now he who supplies seed to the sower and bread for food will also supply and increase your store of seed and will enlarge the harvest of your righteousness." (2 Corinthians 9:10)

Fear Not

Each of us struggle through life in one way or another. Where I struggle most (falling prey to Satan's lies), is in my desire for the approval of others. My compulsion to please others was so strong that it became the driving force behind my twenty-five year bondage to an eating disorder called bulimia. In an effort to find love and acceptance, I took drastic measures to become what I thought others wanted me to be—thin.

Thankfully God helped me overcome the stronghold of bulimia through the truth of His Word, and I now believe my value comes from God—not man.

"Am I now trying to win the approval of men, or of God? Or am I still trying to please men? If I were still trying to please men, I would not be a servant of Christ." (Galatians 1:10)

Although I have journeyed a long way in this area, approval seeking continues to be an area of weakness that is entrenched in my personality. I sometimes even slip into old patterns of behavior without realizing it. Suddenly I find myself bending over backwards to please someone at the expense of my own happiness.

Why do I continually fall prey to this trap?

At the very core of my weakness is FEAR. Fear of disappointing others. Fear of not measuring up. Fear of becoming invisible, and fear of not being loved.

FEAR - False Evidence Appearing Real

Fear opens the door for Satan's deception and clears the path to our own destruction. "Fear of man will prove to be a snare, but whoever trusts in the Lord is kept safe." (Proverbs 29:25)

More than any other command in the Bible, God tells us to fear not. If God commands us to "fear not" it must be possible to accomplish.

So, how do we remove fear from our lives?

God provides the answer through the truth of His Word. "In God I trust; I will not be afraid." (Psalm 56:11a) "Perfect love drives out fear…" (1 John 4:18b)

Fear of man proves to be a snare, but trust in the cross sets us free.

TRUST – Totally Renouncing Unbelief Standing on Truth

Therefore sisters... "Trust in the Lord with all your heart and lean not on your own understanding; in all your ways submit to him, and he will make your paths straight." (Proverbs 3:5-6)

Motivation to Change

S ometimes pain is the result of living in a fallen world. Other times pain is the result of living with the consequences of our own actions or neglect. Both are difficult to endure.

"No discipline seems pleasant at the time, but painful. Later on, however, it produces a harvest of righteousness and peace for those who have been trained by it." (Hebrews 12:11)

Pain can be good when it motivates a person towards positive change, but it can be especially tough to watch people suffer as a result of their mistakes. While it's tempting to want to ease another's distress by somehow fixing their problems, we must resist that temptation. After all, people learn through their mistakes.

Dr. Henry Cloud says, "To rescue people from the natural consequences of their behavior is to render them powerless." That certainly puts things into a different perspective.

We need to encourage others to accept responsibility for their own actions and do what they can to change for the better. And we need to do the same when we're the ones on the receiving end of discipline.

Sometimes God uses painful life experiences to direct our steps towards His best for us, and sometimes He uses them to draw us closer to Him. Either way, God's discipline is intended to bring about positive change and is always done in love.

Practice Makes Perfect

"I know, my God, that you test the heart and are pleased with integrity." (1 Chronicles 29:17a)

Have you ever noticed that when we ask for patience, God provides ample opportunities to practice the virtue? In the same way, if we pray for peace, chaos abounds. When we start praying for a humble heart, pride rears its ugly head again and again. As the saying goes… *be careful what you wish for.*

When we pray for these virtues, God tests us to see if we really mean what we say. These tests are not for His benefit. (He already knows the outcome.) Rather God tests us so that we can gauge our own progress and strengthen our resolve. "In this way I will test them and see whether they will follow my instructions." (Exodus 16:4)

It is easy to pray for change, but God seldom modifies our character overnight. Change is usually the result of test after test. "Remember how the LORD your God led you all the way in the desert these forty years, to humble you and to test you in order to know what was in your heart, whether or not you would keep his commands." (Deuteronomy 8:2)

Do you remember taking the SATs in high school? You could take the test as many times as you wanted, as long as you were willing to invest the time and energy necessary to prepare. By taking the exam over and over, you could learn from past mistakes and improve your score for the next time.

Like taking the SATs, with each of God's tests, we learn and grow. Where we see past mistakes, we can change our response for the future. God wants nothing less than our very best. "But he knows the way that I take; when he has tested me, I will come forth as gold." (Job 23:10)

Consider the refining process of precious metals. The refiner turns up the heat, causing the impurities inside the metal to rise to the surface. Here unwanted fragments are easily skimmed away. With each test we face in life ugly sin rises to the surface and is purged from our lives.

"This third I will bring into the fire; I will refine them like silver and test them like gold. They will call on my name and I will answer them; I will say, 'They are my people,' and they will say, 'The LORD is our God.'" (Zechariah 13:9)

As we persevere through the trials of life, taking test after test, we will begin to reflect our Refiner more clearly.

Keep taking the test. After all, practice makes perfect.

Roller Coaster of Life

At a local amusement park called Kings Island, two roller coasters race side by side in a desperate dash for the finish. When the ride first opened over forty years ago, it was designed to have two forward moving coasters. But after innovative rides came on the scene with more thrilling attractions, a change was made—one of the twins would barrel down the track backwards.

Waiting to take the challenge for the first time, I could feel my stomach twisting itself into knots. I knew that I had to conquer my fear of riding a roller coaster backwards at breakneck speed, but how could I prepare myself for each plunge, twist, and turn when I couldn't see where I was going? I was at the mercy of the unknown. The thought of experiencing this thrill ride backwards awakened both excitement and trepidation.

Being young has its advantages. The promise of a thrill ride outweighed common sense. With my heart thumping wildly in my chest, all I could do was hope and pray the person who engineered the ride knew what he was doing. "Now faith is being sure of what we hope for and certain of what we do not see." (Hebrews 11:1)

Faith is kind of like that backwards roller coaster. We can't always see where we are going to adequately prepare for what comes next in life, but as long as we have faith, we don't need to. All we really need is a trustworthy Engineer who is able to keep us on the track during life's challenging ups and downs.

And that's just what we have. God sees every detail of our lives long before we get there. We don't need to see— we just need to trust.

Life is a wild ride. I don't know about you, but I'm keeping my eyes on the One who monitors every plunge, twist, and turn of my life. "'You of little faith, why are you so afraid?' Then [Jesus] got up and rebuked the winds and the waves, and it was completely calm." (Matthew 8:26)

Heaven Awaits

While sitting in a lakeside gazebo with my sisters-in-Christ, I was reminded of the many blessings in my life. While we studied God's Word, the sun was shining, a warm breeze was blowing, and the frogs were singing. It was a beautiful day.

As I sat listening to each woman share her insights from God's Word, I couldn't help but wonder. Is this a preview of what heaven will be like? Will we sit around in the splendor of heaven sharing and digesting the teachings that the Lord has given us?

Undoubtedly, heaven will be much grander than anything we can imagine, and yet there are times when God opens our spiritual eyes and reveals tiny glimpses of His glory here on earth. Through these moments, He provides a foretaste of that which is waiting for us in heaven.

Then the angel showed me the river of the water of life, as clear as crystal, flowing from the throne of God and of the Lamb down the middle of the great street of the city. On each side of the river stood the tree of life, bearing twelve crops of fruit, yielding its fruit every month. And the leaves of the tree are for the healing of the nations. No longer will there be any curse. The throne of God and of the Lamb will be in the city, and his servants will serve him. They will see his face, and his name will be on their foreheads. There will be no more night. They will not need the light of a lamp or the light of the sun, for the Lord God will give them light. And they will reign for ever and ever. (Revelation 22:1-5)

I envision that heaven will include the very best we experience here on earth but be even more magnificent. My spirit soars when I experience a beautiful sunrise, a melodious song, or a tranquil day spent with family and friends. These precious moments on earth are just a foretaste of heaven. This world is not our home. For this reason we have a longing in our soul for our real home— Heaven.

One day all God's people will dwell together on the New Earth, and our spirits will be filled with the richness of God's glory. We will stand in heavenly awe, covered with eternal goose bumps, taking in the splendor the Lord has waiting for us. "No eye has seen, no ear has heard, no mind has conceived what God has prepared for those who love him, but God has revealed it to us by his Spirit." (1 Corinthians 2:9-10) Until then, we must settle for this temporary dwelling, a place where our souls are quelled by the mere glimmer of His glory and presence.

New Route... Recalculating!

"If you want to make God laugh, tell Him your plans."
~Anonymous

Before leaving for vacation, my husband and I both make lists of what we need to do and bring. After more than twenty-five years of marriage, we have our vacation routine down pat. Among other things, my husband's job is to make sure we have our travel route carefully mapped out. With the invention of GPS, the task has become much easier. He types in the address of our destination and the mystery lady communicates instructions along the way.

During our vacation adventure to Hilton Head, South Carolina, we were on the road by the wee hours of the dawn. Within a few hours, my husband cheerfully reported that we were ahead of schedule.

Just when we thought we were making good time, we learned that I-75 south bound was completely closed down because of a chemical spill. Detour signs directed us to the next exit which made little "Miss GPS" extremely flustered. As we followed detour sign after detour sign, she kept repeating, *"New route—recalculating!"* Annoyed, we eventually turned her off.

When a major highway closes down, it's a traffic jam waiting to happen. We found ourselves inching along a two-lane country road, bumper to bumper, traveling at a snail's pace. (We were rapidly falling behind schedule.)

Thankfully, my husband never goes anywhere without his trusty Atlas. As soon as the opportunity presented itself, we made a U-turn and headed back towards town.

Stopping at a gas station, we stretched our legs, got a snack, and mapped out a new route. Gerry discovered another country road that would eventually take us past the chemical spill. Two hours later, we were back on I-75, heading towards our destination.

Sometimes life takes us through one detour after another. Perhaps you've noticed that we rarely see things turn out exactly as we had planned. I believe God uses life's little diversions to direct us toward His ultimate plan for our lives.

"'For I know the plans I have for you,' declares the LORD, 'plans to prosper you and not to harm you, plans to give you hope and a future.'" (Jeremiah 29:11)

Looking back, the two hours spent taking the detour were actually a lot of fun. In fact, it became one of the highlights of our trip. As we wound our way through the country roads, we laughed, joked around, and saw some beautiful scenery along the way.

Just like our detoured excursion, sometimes life's little diversions are the most exciting part of the journey.

"O LORD Almighty, blessed is the man who trusts in you." (Psalm 84:12)

A Team Sport

"The body is a unit, though it is made up of many parts; and though all its parts are many, they form one body. So it is with Christ." (1 Corinthians 12:12)

My closest friends know that I'm absolutely crazy about football. I fell in love with the sport as a teenager; however, my love affair with the game began a bit unconventionally.

It all started with a little handheld electronic football game that my dad received for Christmas one year. As electronic games go it was certainly primitive—especially by today's standards. Team members were represented by little dashes on the screen. The object of the game was to get your dash past the other dashes and score a touchdown. It was with this little electronic device that I learned the mechanics of football and grew a passion for the sport.

Ever since then football season has been an eagerly anticipated time of year in our home. Thankfully, my husband and I share a common zeal for the game. Sundays after church are spent in front of the television set watching our favorite teams play.

Football is a complex sport. It's one of the reasons I love it. Just when I think I have the game all figured out, some penalty takes place, and I'm learning a rule I never knew before.

In football no two games are alike. The best and most productive games occur when each player performs his job to the best of his ability with everyone working together as a team.

Christianity is a lot like football. Working together we must push through obstacles great and small to advance God's Kingdom here on earth. The stakes are high, but the reward is great. One yard at a time we need to keep moving forward. Whether we're running the ball up the field or clearing the path for others to follow, we each have a job to do. Let's do it to the best of our ability.

"Now you are the body of Christ, and each one of you is a part of it." (1 Corinthians 12:27)

"Therefore, since we are surrounded by such a great cloud of witnesses, let us throw off everything that hinders and the sin that so easily entangles, and let us run with perseverance the race marked out for us." (Hebrews 12:1)

Adopted As His Own

When I was a child, I found out that one of my best friends was adopted. At the time I didn't really understand the whole concept of adoption, but I do remember being very curious about the whole thing. Even though I was intrigued about her adoption, I didn't ask my friend a lot of questions because I wasn't sure how she felt about it.

The Bible tells us that we have been adopted as sons and daughters of the King. What a wonderful truth. The subject of adoption has been on the forefront of my mind because the theme repeatedly pops up during my study and devotion time.

With thoughts of spiritual adoption fresh on my mind, I began to wonder about my friend's natural adoption. How did she feel about it? Did she ever wonder about her birth parents or attempt to find out who they were? Since she and I are still friends today, I decided to give her a call. She graciously consented to answer a few of my questions.

I asked my friend how old she was when she found out that she was adopted. She said, "As far back I can remember it was something I knew. My parents never tried to keep it a secret or anything. It was talked about as a matter of fact, so I can't really pinpoint a specific time."

When I asked my friend how she felt about her adoption, her response was very interesting. She said, "I never really questioned being adopted or had any adverse feelings about it until a few kids in the neighborhood began to tease me. It was only then that I began question my adoption and wonder about my birth parents."

It seems that through the loving lens of her adoptive parents, my friend saw herself as she truly was—a cherished member of the family. But once she was exposed to negative comments from ill-informed peers, her perception became skewed and feelings of uncertainty began to emerge.

A similar transfer takes place when it comes to accepting our position in the family of God. Receiving God as our Heavenly Father and believing He has adopted us as His very own requires childlike faith. As long as we have childlike faith, we will never doubt our inheritance. We only begin to doubt our inheritance when worldly influence obscures our view.

Is it possible for us to possess childlike faith and *never* question our heritage as children of God? The answer is yes, so long as we continue perceiving our honored position through the loving lens of our adoptive Father.

"Your statutes are my heritage forever; they are the joy of my heart." (Psalm 119:111) "In love he predestined us to be adopted as his sons through Jesus Christ, in accordance with his pleasure and will— to the praise of his glorious grace, which he has freely given us in the One he loves." (Ephesians 1:5-6)

My friend's adoptive parents may not have given birth, but they sure did give her a wonderful life.

Childlike Faith

One evening our family went to see a Christian illusionist at a local church. Most of the kids sat up front on the floor so they could see. Near the end of the performance the illusionist offered an invitation to accept Jesus as Lord and Savior. He asked everyone in the room to close their eyes, bow their heads, and pray in their hearts the words that he spoke.

At the end of the prayer (while everyone's eyes were still closed), the illusionist asked those who had accepted Jesus for the first time to raise their hands. He then verbally acknowledged that several hands had gone up.

Upon asking the audience to open their eyes he said, "I know this is going to be difficult for some of you and will take a lot of courage, but in a moment, I'm going to count to three. When I do, I would like to ask everyone who raised their hands to please stand up and make your declaration publicly known to this congregation. We would like to pray for you and give you an opportunity to speak with someone about your decision today. We have people waiting in the other room who are ready to help you understand what this commitment means and help you grow in your newfound faith and relationship with God."

The illusionist/evangelist spent a few minutes talking about the importance of making a public declaration when we accept Christ into our lives and expressed how we shouldn't be ashamed to share the decision we've made with others.

Recognizing how much courage it would take to stand in front of everyone, I wondered how many would actually stand up. The tension could be felt in the room as the illusionist began to count... *one... two... three.*

When he got to number three, I was blown away. Eighty percent of the kids sitting up front eagerly stood.

How encouraging it was to see these young people in total abandonment making their decision known to everyone in the room. The following passage came to my mind: "...Jesus called the children to him and said, 'Let the little children come to me, and do not hinder them, for the kingdom of God belongs to such as these.'" (Luke 18:16)

I wondered if I would have been as bold as these young people. God used this experience to speak to my heart. It was a vivid reminder that I need to be more childlike in my faith. We are all called to demonstrate this kind of simple faith—faith that totally trusts, has no doubts, and surrenders in complete abandonment to Jesus Christ—just like a child.

"Truly I tell you, anyone who will not receive the kingdom of God like a little child will never enter it." (Luke 18:17)

Saying Goodbye

It was a very sad day when we had to say goodbye to our dear, sweet golden retriever. Faithfully, our canine watched over the family. Dutifully and tirelessly, he followed me everywhere I went. Quite literally, he never let me out of his sight.

It was his responsibility (or so he thought) to be my protector and guardian, and I must say, he took his job very seriously. Even up to the very end, Boe lumbered up the stairs behind me, lying at my feet as I worked in the office. I attempted to keep him downstairs, since it was getting difficult for him to navigate the steps, but he would have none of it. He simply had to be by my side, no matter what.

Our faithful companion was always waiting to greet our family at the door. We couldn't have asked for a better pet. The fourteen years he devoted to our family were such a blessing. The void in our hearts, after his departure, was as big as a canyon. He is greatly missed.

"There is a time for everything, and a season for every activity under heaven: a time to be born and a time to die… a time to weep and a time to laugh, a time to mourn and a time to dance." (Ecclesiastes 3:1-2; 4)

I don't know how you feel about pets and their value in this world, but I happen to believe that dogs can teach us much about the character of God. I'm not building a theology here—just making an observation. Yes, dogs are animals, but God created them. Throughout creation we see glimpses of God in His magnificent handiwork. Our canine friends are no exception.

The Lord placed some great qualities in the nature of dogs. They are extremely loyal and offer unlimited forgiveness. Even the tiniest of breeds are brave protectors. And last, but certainly not least, dogs offer unconditional love.

Let's see... extremely loyal, unlimited forgiveness, fierce protection, unconditional love. Sounds a lot like the God I have come to know.

Could it be that God placed these character traits in our canines so that we could get a little glimpse of Him each and every day? After all, God spelled backwards is dog.

Our sweet Boe left an indelible mark on our hearts. We were very grateful for his presence in our lives, and he is greatly missed.

A Daunting Challenge - Part I

Several years ago, I had a conversation with my mom about homeschooling—a subject that was heavy on my heart. Since my mom had learned a lot about homeschooling through *Focus on the Family* (a ministry that supports Christian family values), I wanted to know her thoughts on the subject. Given the circumstances and based on what she had learned, she believed homeschooling was a viable option for our family.

Although our, then eleven year-old daughter, was a 'straight A' student, her self-esteem was on a steady decline. The negative influence of peers had amplified the problem to the point that my husband and I grew concerned for our daughter's well-being. Heather was miserable at school and often begged to be homeschooled.

If we were to homeschool our daughter, we would need to homeschool our son as well. The prospect of homeschooling two children was a daunting challenge, especially since I didn't have a college degree.

I appealed to my mom for help. "Mom, I don't know a thing about homeschooling. I wouldn't even know where to begin."

I was desperate to rebuild our daughter's self-esteem but felt extremely inept to tackle something as extreme as teaching our children at home. Perhaps there was another way.

My mom offered some great advice. "Rae Lynn, you need to pray about it. Maybe you can talk with someone who already homeschools and see if they can point you in the right direction."

My mom's recommendation was just what I needed to hear. But who could I ask? I didn't know anyone who homeschooled their kids.

Later that same day I had to pick up the kids from school because Heather had an allergist appointment. While I waited in the main office for them to be released, my heart grew heavier still. Overwhelming thoughts of the homeschooling situation swirled around in my mind. *Who was I kidding? I couldn't teach our kids.*

It seemed to be a hopeless situation, but then I remembered my mom's advice. *Rae Lynn, you need to pray about it.* Closing my eyes, I sent a silent prayer up to God, pleading for His help. *Lord, I don't know what to do. I desperately need your help. Please give me direction.*

"Ask and it will be given to you; seek and you will find; knock and the door will be opened to you. For everyone who asks receives; he who seeks finds; and to him who knocks, the door will be opened." (Matthew 7:7-8)

When I opened my eyes I noticed a woman sitting across the room with her son. She was filling out some paperwork. Recognizing who she was, I called out to her, "Oh my goodness! Ann, is that you?" She looked up, seemingly surprised that someone knew her. "Ann, do you remember me? You were my camp counselor back in high school."

When I was a teenager, my best friend had invited me to her church camp. It was one of the greatest experiences of my youth. Ironically, the event took place at a time when my own self-esteem was under attack. That summer, surrounded by caring Christian men and women, I had a deeply moving encounter with God. And Ann (the woman now sitting across from me) was a big part of it.

"Of course I remember you," she replied. "How are you? Wow, it's been a long time!"

We exchanged a few generalities about life, but after our brief exchange, I nodded in the direction of the little boy sitting next to her.

"Does your son go to this school?"

Ann sheepishly answered no but seemed hesitant to offer any more information. Curious to know more, I prodded her a bit further.

"Well if he doesn't go to school here, what school does he go to?"

Ann looked around the office as if seeking approval to answer, and after hesitating a moment longer, she quietly mouthed the words that I will never forget. *"We homeschool."* To be continued…

A Daunting Challenge—Part II

"God, who has called you into fellowship with his Son Jesus Christ our Lord, is faithful." (1 Corinthians 1:9)

My former church camp counselor just told me that she homeschooled her son. I was amazed! Only moments earlier, I had silently prayed for God's direction about homeschooling our daughter and son, wondering if it was a right fit for our family. I felt that God was nudging my heart in that direction, but it seemed like such a daunting prospect, especially since I had no clue where to begin.

"Jesus looked at them and said, 'With man this is impossible, but not with God; all things are possible with God.'" (Mark 10:27)

Earlier in the day, my mom had suggested that I talk to someone who homeschooled their kids to gain some insight and direction concerning our own situation. Since I didn't know anyone who homeschooled, I prayed to God for help. Ask and you shall receive! "And my God will meet all your needs according to his glorious riches in Christ Jesus." (Philippians 4:19)

Reconnecting with Ann became yet another defining moment in my spiritual journey. I was struggling to contain my excitement after her homeschooling declaration, but I knew the school office was not the proper place to discuss such a subject. After we exchanged phone numbers, I told her that I would give her a call later in the week.

Later, when I recounted the events of the day to my mom, she agreed that my chance meeting with Ann was no coincidence. I definitely needed to keep moving forward with this lead until God gave us clear direction about homeschooling our children.

During my phone conversation with Ann later in the week, it became more and more clear; God was indeed directing me to teach our children at home. I still had huge insecurities about the fact that I didn't have a college degree, but my friend quickly put my concerns to rest, reassuring me a college degree was not a requirement for homeschooling. She explained that trusting God and getting connected with the right curriculum and support system would ensure our success. Ann informed me about a homeschooling conference that was coming later that summer and even offered to go with me. She also encouraged me to attend a homeschool support group with her so I could begin to network with other homeschool moms.

Over the next several months, I gleaned as much information as possible. By the following year we were ready to homeschool. It was an amazing experience for our family. And we couldn't have done it without God!

When Heather and Ben finally re-entered the school system several years later, I knew their years at home had accomplished a lot. Both of our teens entered high school as confident young adults who not only learned how to excel academically, but also soared to new heights socially and spiritually. Our precious years together, learning at home, provided rich growth for all of us.

Perhaps you are facing a daunting challenge, yourself, and feel extremely overwhelmed. Like me, pray to God and seek His will for you. He will direct your every step and provide much needed support and encouragement along the way.

Anchored in the Storm

"We have this hope as an anchor for the soul, firm and secure." (Hebrews 6:19a)

There wasn't a cloud in the sky, and the temperature was just right for spending a fun-filled day boating on the water. Throughout the afternoon, we had a great time water skiing, tubing, and swimming. In fact, we had become so engrossed in the fun that we didn't notice the thick clouds forming off in the distance.

Tired and needing a break from the sun, we headed for a shady cove. With the boat securely anchored it was time to relax for a little while, or so we thought. Our peaceful day was about to take a turn for the worse.

Without warning, the sky grew dark, and a powerful wind plowed through the valley. In the distance, lightning flashed and thunder rumbled, announcing the arrival of a summer storm. We definitely needed to get our boat back to the marina.

In our panic, we almost took off with the boat still tethered to the anchor. Realizing our mistake, my husband turned off the engine and scrambled to the front of the boat. He began pulling with all his might, but the anchor wouldn't budge. Seeing him struggle, the kids and I gathered by his side to offer help. The anchor was obviously caught on something very large at the bottom of the lake, but what?

After several pulls on the rope, we got our answer. Like the scene from a horror movie, a rotted old tree slowly arose from its watery grave. We couldn't believe what we were seeing. Our anchor had attached itself to a fallen tree at the bottom of the lake. Just when my husband was about to cut the anchor line, the tree broke loose, and we were free, heading to safety.

I wonder how many of us go through life thinking we are securely anchored in our faith, only to find in the midst of a storm, we have tethered ourselves to the wrong hold. The storms of life will reveal the foundation of our anchor. But when our faith and hope are in Jesus, we have nothing to fear.

> Then he got into the boat and his disciples followed him. Without warning, a furious storm came up on the lake, so that the waves swept over the boat. But Jesus was sleeping. The disciples went and woke him, saying, 'Lord, save us! We're going to drown!'
>
> "He replied, 'You of little faith, why are you so afraid?' Then he got up and rebuked the winds and the waves, and it was completely calm.
>
> The men were amazed and asked, 'What kind of man is this? Even the winds and the waves obey him!' (Matthew 8:23-27)

The Lord is our refuge and strength, our shelter in the tempest. In Him, we can weather any storm—safe and secure.

God's Pruning Shears

"...Every branch that does bear fruit he prunes so that it will be even more fruitful." (John 15:2)

Perhaps like me you have wondered... *if our lives are bearing fruit, why do we need to be pruned?* Why would God want to cut the branches of our lives that are already producing fruit? Let me share with you how I came to understand the benefit of pruning.

Every summer I plant petunias in the flower boxes of my front windows. When I first plant these blooms, they look puny and sparse. But within a few weeks, the vines grow long and thick, cascading from the window boxes like waterfalls.

One year several weeks after the flowers were planted, I stood outside our house admiring our beautiful flowers. I couldn't believe they were the same sparse saplings we had planted just weeks ago. Seeing how much our plants had grown gave me a sense of pride. "Pride goes before destruction...." (Proverbs 16:18)

The very next morning, when I opened our front window blinds, I received the shock of my life. Our precious flowers were gone—eaten down to little nubs. A wave of nausea hit me as I thought about my friend's recent warning to spray deer repellant on our flowers. *How could I be so careless?* It was a common sight to see deer munching on people's landscaping. I'm not sure what made me think our flowers were different from anyone else's in the neighborhood. It was only a matter of time before the deer discovered the smorgasbord in our window boxes. What bothered me most was realizing the deer had devoured our flowers at their peak.

As days and weeks went by, I began to notice something exciting. The petunias began to bud and flourish again. And to my surprise (in time) they became even more lush and beautiful than before.

I then realized the deer had actually done us a favor. They had pruned our flowers and enabled the plants to produce even more blooms than before. My limited perspective kept me from seeing the true potential of our plants. It wasn't until I saw the lavish new growth that I finally recognized our plants were capable of producing so much more.

The same is true for you and me. God knows our true potential for bearing the greatest possible harvest of fruit. For this reason, we can trust God when He begins pruning certain areas of our lives. God will sometimes prune that which already produces good results in our lives for the purpose of coaxing us to bear even better results someplace else. "No discipline seems pleasant at the time, but painful. Later on, however, it produces a harvest of righteousness and peace for those who have been trained by it." (Hebrews 12:11) "Jesus said, 'You do not realize now what I am doing, but later you will understand.'" (John 13:17)

Painful as it may be to endure, we must surrender our lives to God's pruning shears. When the process becomes a little too painful to bear, just remember our petunias. Lush new growth is just around the corner.

"This is to my Father's glory, that you bear much fruit, showing yourselves to be my disciples." (John 15:8)

Muscles of Faith

A friend shared that she was feeling exhausted in her walk with God. At every turn her family's faith was being tested and frequent life-altering decisions had to be made—decisions that required a great deal of faith and trust in God.

As I sat there listening to my friend share her heart, the Holy Spirit reminded me of a thought provoking quote from author James McDonald: "We must exercise our faith in the Truth of God's Word…. Faith is like a muscle; it gets stronger with use." ~*Lord, Change My Attitude*

I reminded my friend that times of testing can be great opportunities to build stronger faith muscles. I explained that when our faith muscles grow, we feel less exhausted. I then shared with her the following analogy.

When I first began going to exercise classes, I felt completely exhausted. I couldn't always keep up with the instructor and was often unable to complete all the repetitions of a particular exercise set. However, the longer I persevered in going to class, the stronger my muscles grew and the less fatigued my body felt afterwards. It was a slow progression—one that I hadn't really even perceived was taking place, until one day I was able to do all the repetitions and could to keep up with the instructor. I was tempted to think the instructor wasn't being as tough on us anymore, but that wasn't the case at all. In reality my muscles had grown stronger and were better able to handle the extra stress.

I shared with my friend that we strengthen spiritual muscles in much the same way. As we grow in our walk with God, we have more and more opportunities to put our faith into action. As we overcome each challenge in our faith journey, we are better equipped to handle future problems.

"He holds success in store for the upright; he is a shield to those whose walk is blameless, for he guards the course of the just and protects the way of his faithful ones." (Proverbs 2:7-8)

If we want to be more spiritually fit, we must exercise our faith regularly.

Feelings Are Deceptive

"I have been told many times, 'Beth, I can't change the way I feel.' But we can change the way we think, which will lead to a change in the way we feel. That's the essence of the renewed mind." ~Beth Moore, *Patriarchs*

If there is one thing I've learned about myself it's that I cannot trust my feelings. I'm hyper-sensitive and wear my feelings on my shoulders. Therefore, I can't allow my emotions to control my actions or reactions.

Since feelings are often deceptive, we must cultivate a renewed mind through the daily application of God's Word.

How do we accomplish this?

God has taught me a very effective means for renewing the mind. I write Scriptures that hold special significance for me on index cards and read through them every day. Over time these Scriptures are committed to memory and become a fundamental part of my core beliefs.

My index card booklets, now containing more than five-hundred Scripture verses, have been life savers for me, especially when feelings begin to lead me down a crooked path. God always sets me straight through the truth of His Word.

When I'm feeling fat and ugly:

"Listen, O daughter, consider and give ear: Forget your people and your father's house. The king is enthralled by your beauty; honor him, for he is your lord." (Psalm 45:10-11)

When I feel afraid:

"This is what the LORD says to you: 'Do not be afraid or discouraged because of this vast army. For the battle is not yours, but God's.'" (2 Chronicles 20:15b)

When I feel worried:

"Therefore do not worry about tomorrow, for tomorrow will worry about itself. Each day has enough trouble of its own." (Matthew 6:34)

When I feel like giving up:

"Let us not become weary in doing good, for at the proper time we will reap a harvest if we do not give up." (Galatians 6:9)

When I'm full of doubt:

"For the LORD will be your confidence and will keep your foot from being snared." (Proverbs 3:26)

When I'm feeling defeated:

"So do not throw away your confidence; it will be richly rewarded. You need to persevere so that when you have done the will of God, you will receive what he has promised." (Hebrews 10:35-36)

When I feel mistreated:

"And we know in all things God works for the good of those who love him, who have been called according to his purpose." (Romans 8:28)

When our feelings don't line up with God's truth, we can make a conscious choice to deny our feelings and trust God's Word instead. His Word is always trustworthy.

A Slippery Slope

I t's probably safe to say we can all look back on our lives and see where we've made poor decisions. Sometimes, one poor decision leads to another, and it's not until we hit rock bottom that we realize the height from which we have fallen.

The Bible is full of examples of individuals who made poor decisions. God preserved these historical events in His Word so that we could learn through the mistakes of others.

David's midnight stroll on a rooftop led to lust, infidelity, pregnancy, murder, and the untimely death of his child.

Jonah's disregard for God's command to preach to the Ninevite people landed him in the belly of a great fish.

The Israelites' lack of faith to capture the Promised Land led to their forty year wanderings in the desert.

Sarah's decision to use her maidservant Hagar to help God fulfill His promise to give Abraham a son led to her broken heart and dysfunctional family.

"There is a way that seems right to man, but in the end it leads to death." (Proverbs 14:12)

God promises to provide a way out when we find ourselves in the middle of temptation. The question is— are we willing to accept His help? "No temptation has seized you except what is common to man. And God is faithful; he will not let you be tempted beyond what you can bear. But when you are tempted, he will also provide a way out so that you can stand up under it." (1 Corinthians 10:13)

If we could just accept God's help when He offers it the first time around, we wouldn't have to fall all the way to the bottom of the slippery slope.

Perhaps you're at a place in life where you're plummeting fast. Look up and call out to Jesus. He's right there waiting to grab your hand.

"I sinned, and perverted what was right, but I did not get what I deserved. "He redeemed my soul from going down to the pit, and I will live to enjoy the light." (Job 33:27-28)

Don't wait until you hit rock bottom. I can tell you from personal experience. The bottom of the pit is a dark and lonely place.

"Yet the LORD longs to be gracious to you; he rises to show you compassion. For the LORD is a God of justice. Blessed are all who wait for him!" (Isaiah 30:18)

Take the hand of Jesus. He will help you up and give you a firm place to stand.

Wait for It

"We tend to want to pick our blessings from the tree while they are still green, yet God wants us to wait until they are fully ripe." ~Streams in the Desert

We live in a world of instant gratification. Americans have especially been groomed to see it, want it, and get it now. We can cook food in record time, travel the world in no time flat, and access information lickety-split. For goodness sake, we can even have fun on demand.

God is not confined by an earthly timetable, yet He rarely does things quickly. I've even heard it said that God is never late, but He is seldom early.

"But if we hope for what we do not yet have, we wait for it patiently." (Romans 8:25)

Because we have been programmed by instant gratification mentality, we have lost much of the joy that comes from anticipation. As a child, I learned that sometimes the expectation of waiting for something is more delightful than the actual experience of receiving it.

My excitement would build before each Christmas or birthday, waiting for that special something. Sometimes I even saved up months of allowance in order to buy a special toy or item of clothing. The anticipation was actually a lot of fun.

Many have the mentality if you want it now—get it now. Unfortunately, we miss the delight of anticipation when we immediately satisfy every longing of the heart.

If you are waiting for something special, I encourage you to enjoy your time of waiting. Joyfully anticipate the wonderful moment when you finally receive your perfectly-timed, fully-ripened blessing.

"But as for me, I watch in hope for the LORD, I wait for God my Savior...." (Micah 7:7)

There is nothing quite like experiencing a blessing that's been given at its God-appointed peak. *Wait for it!*

Your Right Arm

Have you ever heard the expression, *I would give my right arm if I could have_____*? This figure of speech is often used to express how badly a person might want something.

The question begs to be asked. Is there anything we ought to want so badly we would consider actually giving up our right arm to achieve it?

According to Scripture the answer is yes— SANCTIFICATION. "And if your right hand causes you to sin, cut it off and throw it away. It is better for you to lose one part of your body than for your whole body to go into hell." (Matthew 5:30)

I don't know about you, but my right hand is pretty important to me. It aids me in the tasks of everyday life. And yet, Christ declared that if my right hand causes me to sin, I should cut it off and throw it away. So, what did Jesus mean by this statement?

Our Lord was using this analogy to express how important it is to remove that which hinders our walk with God.

> Jesus did not say that everyone must cut off the right hand, but – if your right hand offends you in your walk with Me, cut it off. Your right hand is one of the best things you have, but Jesus says, if it hinders you in following His precepts, cut it off. ~Oswald Chambers, *My Utmost for His Highest*

Larry Alford was nicknamed the one arm bandit. As a promising young golfer, at the age of eighteen, Larry's life suddenly turned upside down when he lost his arm in a tragic automobile accident caused by his own drunk driving. It seemed that his golf career was over, but Larry Alford wasn't about to let his handicap stop him from pressing forward.

After receiving a prosthetic arm, he relearned how to swing a club with such precision that he became an even better golfer than before.

Although Larry continues to golf, the accident caused him to reflect on his values, goals, and priorities. Now he is a motivational speaker and charity event golfer, inspiring many through his ability to persevere and overcome adversity. Larry once shared the following encouraging words with an audience of children who had lost their limbs. "Don't think of your missing limb as something that makes you a lesser person. Think of it as something that can make you stronger."

God only asks us to remove the things from our lives that, when they are absent, ultimately make us stronger and better Christians in the end.

How badly do you want to be sanctified? Metaphorically speaking—*would you give your right arm?*

Change Your Perspective

One of my favorite pastime activities as a child was climbing trees. Our weekend retreat farmhouse was over a hundred years old, and the property was surrounded by large, beautiful trees—perfect for climbing.

There was one tree in particular that I loved to scale and settle atop its branches. It was out in the front yard and towered above the farmhouse, barn, and outbuildings. The trunk had thick, sturdy limbs near the base so that a small person like me could easily make its ascent.

Up and up, I would steadily climb with careful precision. The higher I would go, the more amazing the view. Strangely, my perspective seemed to change while resting at the top. From the ground the farmhouse seemed colossal, but from the treetop it appeared small and insignificant. Serenity enveloped me every time I climbed that tree—it was a spiritual high of sorts—one that I frequented many times during my childhood.

Do problems in your life seem so big and overwhelming that you can't see past them? Perhaps it's time to change your perspective.

Like climbing a tree, our faith in the one true God lifts us to greater heights. As we ascend with the Father, our perspective changes. Our problems become smaller, and our God becomes bigger.

"So we fix our eyes not on what is seen, but on what is unseen. For what is seen is temporary, but what is unseen is eternal." (2 Corinthians 4:18)

We need to remember that no problem on earth is too big for God to handle.

Just make sure you are clinging to the right tree.

"[Christ] himself bore our sins in his body on the tree, so that we might die to sins and live for righteousness; by his wounds you have been healed." (1Peter 2:24)

From Mess to Message

"Before I was afflicted I went astray, but now I obey your word. You are good and what you do is good; teach me your decrees. It was good for me to be afflicted so that I might learn your decrees. The law from your mouth is more precious to me than thousands of pieces of silver and gold." (Psalm 119:67-68, 71-72)

This may sound crazy, but I truly believe it was good for me to be afflicted with an eating disorder because in my desperation to be filled by something, I found the true filling of God through His Word.

Looking back over forty plus years, I can see a common theme in my life—the power of words.

As a child, the careless words of others inflicted wounds to my self-esteem and squashed my spirit.

Distraught, I eventually sought comfort through the control of food.

As an adult, the perfect Word of God became a healing balm to the wounds of my past.

Thankfully, I no longer seek to be filled with food. I seek to be filled with food for the soul—God's Word.

"He heals the brokenhearted and binds up their wounds." (Psalm 147:3)

That which Satan sought to destroy, the Lord has used to make me whole. God has brought beauty from the ashes—His specialty.

> ...He has sent me to bind up the brokenhearted, to proclaim freedom for the captives and release from darkness for the prisoners, to proclaim the year of the Lord's favor and the day of vengeance of our God, to comfort all who mourn, and provide for those who grieve in Zion—to bestow on them a crown of beauty instead of ashes, the oil of gladness instead of mourning, and a garment of praise instead of a spirit of despair. They will be called oaks of righteousness, a planting of the Lord for the display of his splendor. (Isaiah 61:1-3)

God has brought great healing to my soul and turned my mess into a message.

"Instead of their shame my people will receive a double portion, and instead of disgrace they will rejoice in their inheritance; and so they will inherit a double portion in their land, and everlasting joy will be theirs." (Isaiah 61:7)

Lord, thank you for turning my disgrace into everlasting joy. I am eternally grateful!

"How can I repay the LORD for all his goodness to me? I will lift up the cup of salvation and call on the name of the LORD. I will fulfill my vows to the LORD in the presence of all his people." (Psalm 116:12-14)

"I love the LORD, for he heard my voice; he heard my cry for mercy. Because he turned his ear to me, I will call on him as long as I live." (Psalm 116:1-2)

Fearfully and Wonderfully Made

"For you created my inmost being; you knit me together in my mother's womb. I praise you because I am fearfully and wonderfully made; your works are wonderful, I know that full well. My frame was not hidden from you when I was made in the secret place. When I was woven together in the depths of the earth, your eyes saw my unformed body. All the days ordained for me were written in your book before one of them came to be." (Psalm 139:13-16)

God created each one of us uniquely—with careful precision and purpose. Before our mothers were even aware of our existence, God knew every detail of who we would be inside and out. I love how Psalm 139 uses the analogy of God knitting us together.

When I was a little girl, I used to love to watch my grandmother knit. I was amazed at the seemingly effortless way her hands maneuvered the yarn and needles. To my youthful eyes it was magic. In a matter of minutes, an intricate pattern took shape. By the time my grandma completed one of her works of art, her hands had literally touched every fiber and thread of yarn.

The image that David paints of God knitting us together in our mother's womb reveals the careful attention that God pays to each and every one of His magnificent creations. Much thought and attention to detail goes into His handiwork. The human body is a magnificently complex piece of machinery. Biologists are amazed at the complexity of such marvels as DNA, the very blueprint for life, which carries enough information in each cell to fill one thousand books!

Like an intricately designed afghan, we are beautiful works of art, priceless in God's eyes. We are uniquely designed with God's plan and purpose in mind. And because God likes variety, we come in all different shapes, sizes, and colors.

The next time we are tempted to put ourselves down, we need to remember that we were made in the image of God, created to fulfill a special plan and purpose here on earth.

It's time to embrace our unique differences and brilliantly reflect the image of our awesome Designer.

"So God created mankind in his own image, in the image of God he created them; male and female he created them." (Genesis 1:27)

All Sunshine Makes a Desert

"For the sun rises with scorching heat and withers the plant; its blossom falls and its beauty is destroyed." (James 1:11a)

My friend's grandmother used to say, "All sunshine makes a desert." How very true. Although the Midwest provides enough precipitation during the spring, fall, and winter months to keep us from desert-like conditions, in a spiritual sense, we are all in danger of living in a parched environment. The trials and hardships of life can leave us feeling dehydrated and depleted of strength. This is true especially when we attempt to run away from adversities or deny the lessons God may be trying to teach us through them. Difficult as it may be to accept, adversity is a fact of life. Trying times will come, and when they do, they are wonderful opportunities to grow as individuals.

"Let my teaching fall like rain and my words descend like dew, like showers on new grass, like abundant rain on tender plants." (Deuteronomy 32:2)

We may not enjoy going through difficult life circumstances any more than we would enjoy being out in the elements during a powerful storm, but we must remember that the storms of life have a purpose. The soaking rains of tribulation encourage rich, new growth.

"Teach them the right way to live, and send rain on the land you gave your people for an inheritance." (1 Kings 8:36)

The desert life can be brutal. Most wouldn't survive long in the desert wilderness, with its scorching heat and extremely dry conditions. So, the next time you are tempted to wish life could be all sunshine, remember Pearl Landrum's gentle admonition, *"All sunshine makes a desert"*.

Transplanted

When you buy plants from a nursery, the roots are often so thick and tangled that they literally take on the shape of the container. Appearing desperate for more space, a plant is entirely dependent on the gardener to change its environment. Once transplanted, the gardener carefully monitors the plant's progress to ensure it receives the proper amount of water and sunlight—factors essential to the plant's growth and survival.

We depend on God (our Gardner) to place us in surroundings where we have room to grow. Like plants, when the Lord changes our circumstances, we are likely to experience a period of adjustment. During this time, we are under the watchful eye of our Heavenly Father. His desire is to have us flourish in our new environment. Like a plant, "water" and "light" become essential elements for rich, new growth. "That person is like a tree planted by streams of water, which yields its fruit in season and

whose leaf does not wither— whatever they do prospers."
(Psalm 1:3) "Blessed are those who have learned to
acclaim you, who walk in the light of your presence,
Lord." (Psalm 89:15)

There have been times in my life when I felt God
stirring my heart towards change, but I had become a little
too comfortable in my surroundings. As a result, I stayed
in a situation much longer than God originally intended.
Like a plant from the nursery, I became spiritually root-
bound.

> Sometimes we can settle into a spiritual
> comfort zone, unaware that our spiritual
> health may be slowly but surely
> deteriorating. But trying new spiritual
> activities can help our spirits remain whole
> and strong and keep us in touch with God's
> will. When we move beyond our comfort
> zone, we grow. ~*Upper Room*

"By faith Abraham, when called to go to a place he
would later receive as his inheritance, obeyed and went,
even though he did not know where he was going."
(Hebrews 11:8)

Today when I feel that God is nudging me on to
something new, I try to follow Abraham's example of
faith and obedience. *I go so I can grow.*

"The righteous will flourish like a palm tree, they will
grow like a cedar of Lebanon; planted in the house of the
LORD, they will flourish in the courts of our God." (Psalm
92:12-13)

Sinking Sand

Early one morning on vacation, while the family was still sleeping, I tiptoed out of the room and stole a few minutes down by the beach. It was a wonderful chance to connect with God and enjoy His magnificent creation.

Strolling along the seashore, I stopped for a few moments to enjoy the beautiful sunrise. While I was peering across the ocean's expanse, with the waves sweeping over my feet, I began sinking further and further into the substance beneath me. Before long, I was ankle deep in wet sand.

> But everyone who hears these words of mine and does not put them into practice is like a foolish man who built his house on sand. The rain came down, the streams rose, and the winds blew and beat against that house, and it fell with a great crash. (Matthew 7:26-27)

God's Word is the secure foundation that we can count on to hold us up when life's circumstances threaten to bring us down. Waves of uncertainty, hopelessness, grief, and doubt sink us further and further into a pit of despair if we are not standing on the solid promises of God.

Therefore everyone who hears these words of mine and puts them into practice is like a wise man who built his house on the rock. The rain came down, the streams rose, and the winds blew and beat against that house; yet it did not fall, because it had its foundation on the rock. (Matthew 7:24-25)

Whether you're experiencing the high tides or low tides of life, be sure that you are building on the solid foundation of God's Word.

Behind the Scenes

"Now you are the body of Christ, and each one of you is a part of it." (1 Corinthians 12:27)

In my previous devotion, I mentioned my early morning stroll along the beach during a family vacation. After my walk, I went up to the hotel pool area and sat for a spell in one of the lounge chairs, enjoying the moment.

Not many guests were up and about that early in the morning, but there were several employees buzzing around the grounds, working to get things ready for the guests who would be emerging from their rooms very soon. Ironically, I rarely noticed the workers during the daytime hours, but here they were, hustling and bustling in the wee hours of the morning: cleaning the pool, straightening the chairs, folding the towels, preparing the food, and maintaining the grounds to make everything beautiful. The exertion that they poured into each day made our vacation extra special. Their contribution was enormous, yet they received little recognition from the guests for their efforts. In fact, if I hadn't gotten up extra early that day, I probably wouldn't have even acknowledged their existence.

As I began whispering a prayer for these diligent workers, thanking God for their humble service and invaluable contribution towards making our vacation extra special, God reminded me of how all areas of service are important to Him. While some people serve up front and receive much attention, an even greater number of people serve behind the scenes, and their contribution is just as important to the Kingdom of God.

> Your attitude should be the same as that of Christ Jesus: Who, being in very nature God, did not consider equality with God something to be grasped, but made himself nothing, taking the very nature of a servant, being made in human likeness. And being found in appearance as a man, he humbled himself and became obedient to death— even death on a cross! (Philippians 2:5-8)

No matter where God calls us to serve: in our homes, at the office, in a large church, or as the grounds keeper for a large hotel, we should serve humbly with all our heart, giving the Lord and others our very best.

Time to Heal

"My wounds fester and are loathsome because of my sinful folly." (Psalm 38:5)

Late one evening on our vacation, we decided to go for a swim in the pool. Like a child hoping to impress with his skill, my husband Gerry proudly professed that he could swim the length of the pool underwater. Eager to prove his talent, he ducked beneath the surface and began swimming. Not the best idea considering there was little light to illuminate his way. Three quarters of the way across the pool, he bumped into the corner wall and came up holding his forehead, sporting a nasty cut across his nose. The injury was minor, but his pride took a pretty big hit.

Eventually the cut scabbed over. It's wonderful how God designed our bodies with the remarkable ability to heal. Scabs provide protection over an injury, allowing the healing process to take place with no interference.

A couple of days later, however, I noticed his cut was bleeding again. When I asked what happened, he explained that he had picked off the scab because it was bothering him. This became a pattern of behavior over the next couple of days.

How many times do we, figuratively speaking, pick the scabs off old wounds, never allowing them to heal? We allow bitterness, anger, and self-pity to dictate our thoughts, words, and actions, keeping the injury as fresh as the day it occurred. Each time we mentally or verbally re-live a past injury, we pick away the scab that is intended to repair the hurt and delay the healing process even further. "From the sole of your foot to the top of your head there is no soundness— only wounds and welts and open sores, not cleansed or bandaged or soothed with oil." (Isaiah 1:6)

There is a safe place—a sterile environment—where our wounds can heal successfully under the care of the Great Physician, Jesus Christ.

"'But I will restore you to health and heal your wounds,' declares the LORD...." (Jeremiah 30:17) "He heals the brokenhearted and binds up their wounds." (Psalm 147:3)

Do you have festering wounds that are unable to heal? Remember, "by his wounds you have been healed." (1 Peter 2:24)

Sensing God's Presence

Our shark fishing excursion took us out some distance from the harbor where we dropped anchor. After a brief set of instructions from the experts, highlighting the best techniques for baiting your hook and catching a shark, everyone aboard the vessel gathered around the railing, ready to cast their lines. With approximately eighty passengers onboard, we were packed in like sardines.

I am not much of an angler. In fact, I don't even bait my own hook, so I'm a little embarrassed to admit that my seven shark catch was the highest number achieved by anyone that day. What is even more distressing is the fact that our then teenage son didn't catch a single fish.

Although Ben was fishing in the very same place, using the very same bait and getting bites by the very same sharks, his hook consistently came up empty. Why? Apparently he couldn't sense when the sharks were nibbling his bait.

Have you noticed how some people hear God's inaudible voice and sense the Holy Spirit's promptings time after time, while others rarely do?

The same God speaks to all of His children. Yet it is only the expectant, discerning, and sensitive Christian who is able to sense God on a regular basis.

How can we be more discerning?

We must become more conscious of God's leading by tuning in to Him through ongoing prayer, daily meditation, and quality study of His Word. The more time we spend in God's presence, the more likely we are to hear, recognize, and sense His presence in our lives.

"Speak, LORD, for your servant is listening." (1 Samuel 3:9)

God is definitely speaking. The question is... *are we listening?*

"Today, if you hear his voice, do not harden your hearts." (Hebrews 3:15)

Straight Shot

"....in all your ways acknowledge him, and he will make your paths straight." (Proverbs 3:6)

The sand on Hilton Head Island is dense and compact, perfect for riding bikes along the ocean's shoreline. Our family decided to take a long bike ride to the town square where there were shops, restaurants, and even a family friendly water fountain, ideal for cooling down in the southern heat.

Biking up the beach was a straight shot (the quickest route to our destination). But once we began peddling, resistance from the strong winds kept blowing against us, and we were getting tired fast. We peddled with all our might but seemed to move at a snail's pace. What was supposed to be an enjoyable bike ride quickly turned unpleasant. My heaving lungs reached full capacity while my legs felt like limp noodles. At the rate we were traveling, it would take us all day to reach our destination.

Under much duress, we made the impromptu decision to exit the beach using a hotel access ramp so we could travel along the paved bike path instead. Surely the homes and buildings would shield us from the strong winds that were hindering our progress.

It seemed like a good plan. Unfortunately, the only way to get to the main bike path was to follow the road back to our hotel. We actually had to backtrack before moving forward.

It was quickly becoming a journey to nowhere! The road curved in and out so much that it seemed like forever just to get back to our original starting point. We eventually made it to the town square, but it took us a full two hours to get there.

"I guide you in the way of wisdom and lead you along straight paths." (Proverbs 4:11)

Do you ever feel like you're traveling through life with so much resistance that it's wearing you down? You keep trying to move forward, but it seems there's always something working against you. Perhaps you're tempted to get off the beaten path and take an easier route instead.

Like our little biking expedition, just because another way appears easier doesn't mean it is. Honestly, we wasted a lot of time backtracking that day. We could have reached our destination much faster if we had just persevered against the wind and continued moving forward. In fact, we later learned that we were more than halfway to our destination when we had given up and changed routes.

If you are at a place where you're feeling discouraged, ready to give up and take another route, I encourage you to go before the Lord in prayer, and ask for His direction. If He makes it clear that you are on the right path, hang in there. God is with you. He will travel ahead to clear your path and provide much needed strength when you grow weary.

"Listen, my son, and be wise, and keep your heart on the right path." (Proverbs 23:19)

Don't lose hope. *You are almost there!*

Worthy of My Praise

Sometimes the Lord whispers His truths, and other times He shouts them. One particular morning His message came to me loud and clear. *The LORD is great and most worthy of my praise.*

The miracle of Jesus raising Lazarus from the grave was the featured story in my devotion that morning. The author explained how Jesus had given praise and thanks to His Father *before* the miracle took place. "...Jesus looked up and said, 'Father, I thank you that you have heard me.'" (John 11:41b)

My devotion continued, "Praise is actually the most vital preparation to the working of miracles. Miracles are performed through spiritual power, and our spiritual power is always in proportion to our faith." ~*Streams in the Desert*

God spoke to my heart. *Rae Lynn, you need to offer up praise and thanks to me beforehand and <u>believe</u> that I will do as you have asked.*

I had been praying a consistent prayer concerning a strained relationship with a friend. I wanted forgiveness and peace between us.

We may not know the mind of God, but we can certainly know the character of God, because He repeatedly reveals His character through His Word. If our prayers fall within the boundaries of what we know about God's character, then we can rest assured that God will answer our prayers. It may not be in the timing we prefer, or take place in the manner in which we anticipate, but God will certainly come through. "According to your faith let it be done to you." (Matthew 9:29)

"Ask and it will be given to you; seek and you will find; knock and the door will be opened to you. For everyone who asks receives; the one who seeks finds; and to the one who knocks, the door will be opened." (Matthew 7:7-8)

"Which of you, if your son asks for bread, will give him a stone? Or if he asks for a fish, will give him a snake? If you, then, though you are evil, know how to give good gifts to your children, how much more will your Father in heaven give good gifts to those who ask him!" (Matthew 7:9-11)

True to His Word, God eventually brought healing and restoration to my relationship. God is faithful.

"Great is the LORD and most worthy of praise...." (Psalm 48:1)

Through the example of Jesus, let's start giving praise and thanks to God *now* for what we believe He will do *later*.

More than Enough

While growing up, my family was very close to another family. So close, in fact, that our parents purchased a sixty-three acre farm in the country together. Nearly every weekend we would head out to Milan, Indiana and share life together. The memories I carry with me from this time are some of the very best of my childhood. The farmhouse was over 100 years old when we purchased it—so old that it didn't have indoor plumbing. Eventually, we upgraded the place with running water, but for a while we had to use an outhouse. (Let me just say, using an outdoor potty was an experience that made me greatly appreciate the modern efficiency of indoor plumbing.) The farm's wide open space of land gave us suburban folks the chance to experience God's magnificent creation up close and personal.

Between our two families, there were thirteen of us. We were like one big happy family. Extended family and friends would often pop in for a visit right around dinner time. Our moms used to joke and say that Jesus was going to have to perform a miracle so there would be enough food to go around. Feeding our own clan was challenge enough. Feeding unscheduled guests was an even greater task.

Even though our parents were not prepared for more dinner guests, they would never dream of sending people away. They said that God would make sure we had enough to go around. And guess what? He always did. Not only was there enough to go around but we almost always had leftovers.

> As evening approached, the disciples came to him and said, "This is a remote place, and it's already getting late. Send the crowds away, so they can go to the villages and buy themselves some food."
> Jesus replied, "They do not need to go away. You give them something to eat."
> "We have here only five loaves of bread and two fish," they answered.
> "Bring them here to me," he said.

And he directed the people to sit down on the grass. Taking the five loaves and the two fish and looking up to heaven, he gave thanks and broke the loaves. Then he gave them to the disciples, and the disciples gave them to the people. They all ate and were satisfied, and the disciples picked up twelve basketfuls of broken pieces that were left over. The number of those who ate was about five thousand men, besides women and children. (Matthew 14:15-21)

What we have to offer might not seem like much to some, but in the hands of Jesus… *it's more than enough.*

Hidden Treasure

"I will give you hidden treasures, riches stored in secret places, so that you may know that I am the LORD, the God of Israel, who summons you by name." (Isaiah 45:3)

When our kids were little, we hosted treasure hunts for holiday and birthday celebrations. It was a great way to add fun to an already joyful occasion. Each child was given a first clue, which led to another clue, and so on. Delayed gratification was a great way to build anticipation. After all, who doesn't like searching for hidden treasure!

Easter Sunday, the prize was a single egg with money inside. On birthdays, the treasure trove was a goody bag filled with candy and party favors.

Our kids loved the hunt and couldn't wait to see what was awaiting them at the end of their expedition. Gathering clues was like putting together pieces of a puzzle. With each new piece of information, the picture became more and more clear. My husband and I loved hiding the clues, and we greatly enjoyed watching our children's reaction when a new piece of evidence was uncovered, pointing their way to the long awaited treasure.

The study of God's Word is like going on a treasure hunt. There is no greater fortune to be found than that which is buried in the pages of Scripture. It is where God reveals Himself, and we get to discover the great reward of eternal life in heaven with Him. God intentionally buried clues in His Word so that we could experience the great joy of discovering who He is and what a relationship with Him means.

> My son, if you accept my words and store up my commands within you, turning your ear to wisdom and applying your heart to understanding—indeed, if you call out for insight and cry aloud for understanding, and if you look for it as for silver and search for it as for hidden treasure, then you will understand the fear of the LORD and find the knowledge of God. (Proverbs 2:1-5)

God gets great joy from watching His children discover the treasure He has hidden. He loves revealing Himself to us.

You and I have treasure awaiting us at the end of our journey on earth, and it's priceless. God provides the clues, Jesus paid the price, and it's available for the taking. Grab hold of your treasure, and never let go. Seek and you shall find.

"I have not departed from the commands of his lips; I have treasured the words of his mouth more than my daily bread." (Job 23:12)

Food for the Soul

"In fact, though by this time you ought to be teachers, you need someone to teach you the elementary truths of God's word all over again. You need milk, not solid food!" (Hebrews 5:12)

What is the difference between milk and solid food? *Solid food requires chewing.* Perhaps you've heard the expression: I'm going to have to chew on that for a while. In other words, a matter needs further consideration in order to be fully understood.

When we are newer Christians, we are not ready for the deep and meditative teachings of God's Word. Like infants, we need to be fed with easy to understand, straightforward concepts for rapid growth.

"I gave you milk, not solid food, for you were not yet ready for it. Indeed, you are still not ready." (1 Corinthians 3:2)

Although babies grow very rapidly on their mother's milk, their bodies are not designed to thrive on milk forever. Children need more substantial nourishment for further growth and development. In the same way, Christians are not designed to live on spiritual milk forever either. Eventually, we must develop "spiritual teeth" so that we can digest the deeper teachings of God.

> Then we will no longer be infants, tossed back and forth by the waves, and blown here and there by every wind of teaching and by the cunning and craftiness of people in their deceitful scheming. Instead, speaking the truth in love, we will grow to become in every respect the mature body of him who is the head, that is, Christ. (Ephesians 4:14-15)

Are you ready for some meat?
Diligently seek the Lord, and He will give you food for the soul.

God's Holiness

"'Do not come any closer,' God said. 'Take off your sandals, for the place where you are standing is holy ground.'" (Exodus 3:5)

I wonder. Do we truly grasp the greatness of God? Perhaps a fresh perspective concerning God's holiness will provide greater appreciation for the reverence God deserves.

Throughout the Old Testament, God's holiness is emphasized as a common theme. The people of that day understood the magnitude of what God expected in relation to Him. Inside the temple, separated by a curtain, was a place where God's *Shekinah glory* (His divine presence) dwelled. The Holy of Holies (also called the Most Holy Place) was so sacred that it could only be entered once a year by the high priest—and only on the Day of Atonement. During this appointed time, the high priest was permitted to enter the hallowed space of the temple to intercede on behalf of the people and seek God's forgiveness for their sins.

Although it was a great honor to be the high priest, the job came with some serious risks. The Lord gave very specific instructions for entering the Most Holy Place. If the instructions were not followed to the letter, the high priest could be struck dead on the spot. Reverence was of utmost importance.

As a precautionary measure, a rope of bells was attached to the priest's ankle before entering the sacred space. In this way, if the priest was struck down by God because of irreverence, the other priests could safely retrieve the body without meeting a similar end.

The same day that Jesus was crucified on the hill called Golgotha and the very moment that He breathed His last breath, the temple curtain was torn in two and God no longer separated Himself from the common man. Through Christ's death and resurrection, our bodies are now God's dwelling place, and Jesus is our eternal High Priest. Jesus now intercedes on our behalf and makes it possible for us to go directly before God, our Father in heaven.

"Such a high priest meets our need–one who is holy, blameless, pure, set apart from sinners, exalted above the heavens." (Hebrews 7:26)

Although Jesus reconciled us to God when He gave His life as a final sacrifice on the cross, we still need to remember that God is Holy. He still deserves our utmost respect and reverence.

"Holy, Holy, Holy, is the LORD of hosts. The whole earth is full of His glory." (Isaiah 6:3)

"Do you not know that your body is a temple of the Holy Spirit, who is in you, whom you have received from God? You are not your own; you were bought at a price. Therefore honor God with your body." (1 Corinthians 6:19-20)

Remember who God is. Remember what Jesus did. And never take God's holiness for granted.

Wounds That Bleed

While loading my dishwasher one day, I noticed a broken glass on the top rack. I picked up the broken pieces, finished the dishes, and continued cleaning the rest of our house.

My next chore was vacuuming the living room. As I went about the task, I felt something warm and wet on my left hand. Looking down, I noticed my hand was bleeding rather profusely. Apparently, in my attempt to clean up the broken glass, I cut my finger.

Strangely, I didn't realize that I had been cut. In fact, when I saw the blood, I had to stop and think what happened. Once realization set in, I stopped and bandaged my wound to keep the blood from staining our carpet and furniture.

Once again, I am amazed at the spiritual lessons God teaches through everyday life experiences. Like my cut hand, you and I may not realize how bad we've been hurt in life until something unexpected pours out later.

Have you ever reacted to a situation a little more drastically than the circumstances deemed necessary? Perhaps extreme anger erupted from a minor irritation. Maybe bitterness reared its ugly head when forgiveness was the proper reply. Sarcasm or hateful words may have spewed forth like venom when a cool and collected response was the appropriate reaction.

"My friends and companions avoid me because of my wounds; my neighbors stay far away." (Psalm 38:11)

When we respond to a situation radically, we need to ask ourselves if it's possible that a past injury is causing our adverse reaction to the situation.

To some degree, we are all products of our past. Past experiences can become a catalyst for our future responses. We need to ask God to help us identify any open wounds that may be causing our amplified bleeding response.

Do you have un-bandaged wounds that occasionally bleed? Go to the Father, and ask Him to apply His healing balm over your injury. Do it now, before another hostile response leaves a permanent stain on your relationships.

"'But I will restore you to health and heal your wounds,' declares the LORD..." (Jeremiah 30:17)

"...by his wounds we are healed." (Isaiah 53:5)

Break the Silence

"Satan builds his strongholds in the secrets of our lives and reinforces them by our silence. When we break the silence we break the strongholds." ~Jonas Biehler

The first step towards breaking free from my eating disorder was in some ways the biggest and most important—I exposed my twenty-five year secret to a trusted friend. She then encouraged me to share my secret with a group of women in my Bible study group. The more people who knew about my bulimia, the less power Satan had over my life.

Satan lost power. But I gained it.

After my confession I felt support, encouragement, and love pouring through my dear sisters in Christ. I was no longer alone in my battle. Several mighty warriors prayed for me on a daily basis, held me accountable, and spoke truth into my life. In true Christian fashion, they became the hands and feet of Jesus. That's when the real healing began.

After some time, I worked up the courage to tell my husband. This was really hard because he had no idea I had been battling this demon. When I finally confessed what I had been dealing with, he was hurt because I hid it from him for so long. Although hurt, he was also thankful to finally know the truth.

It took some time to rebuild the trust between us. Just because I had exposed my secret didn't mean I was exempt from facing consequences for my actions.

Eventually I shared my secret with others. With each confession I worried what people might think of me, but my fears never materialized. Instead, I was always embraced with love, compassion, and forgiveness.

"Therefore confess your sins to each other and pray for each other so that you may be healed." (James 5:16)

Do you have a secret that you have been carrying for far too long? Don't give Satan control over your life any longer. *Break the silence, and break the stronghold!*

A Clear Vision

"And it will be said: 'Build up, build up, prepare the road! Remove the obstacles out of the way of my people.'" (Isaiah 57:14)

As I jumped in my car, I had a flashback of my driving experience the day before when remnants of a bug storm splattered my windshield, making it difficult to see. Since my attention was repeatedly drawn towards the smeared splotches during my last trip, before I took off down the road again, I grabbed some paper towels and window cleaner and spent the next few minutes cleaning away the sticky mess.

In the grand scheme of life, splattered bugs on the windshield is a minor irritation, but not the only thing obscuring our clear line of vision. Worry, fatigue, stress, fear, strained relationships, and poor health can be just as aggravating. Unfortunately, these types of distractions are not so easily removed. We need more than Windex and paper towels to see clearly again. We need God's help.

"Show me your ways, O LORD, teach me your paths." (Psalm 25:4)

God wants our focus on Him and the road He sets before us, but don't be fooled. Satan will use chaos in our lives to keep us immobilized and ineffective.

Just as windshield wipers aren't very successful when clearing away the sticky mess of bugs, neither are we very effective at cleaning away the worldly distractions through our own merit and strength. God is ready and willing to help us clear away the unwanted fragments, but we still need to ask for His help.

Don't allow annoying diversions to obstruct your clear line of vision any longer. God may not remove our mayhem completely, but He will definitely help us see things more clearly and get us moving in the right direction again.

"You have made known to me the path of life; you will fill me with joy in your presence, with eternal pleasures at your right hand." (Psalm 16:11)

The Sting of Betrayal

"When evening came, Jesus was reclining at the table with the Twelve. And while they were eating, he said, 'I tell you the truth, one of you will betray me.'" (Matthew 26:20-21)

O ur family and friends, no matter how close, will at times disappoint or even fail us. If the Son of God experienced this reality, you can rest assured—so will we.

"For we do not have a high priest who is unable to sympathize with our weaknesses, but we have one who has been tempted in every way, just as we are—yet was without sin." (Hebrews 4:15)

Jesus had the foreknowledge of His betrayer, and yet he still allowed Judas to dip into the same bowl as himself. Our minds have a difficult time comprehending such forgiveness.

Perhaps you can relate to the sudden anguish prompted by someone's betrayal. Judas was someone who Jesus had allowed to get very close. The disciples were Jesus' constant companions. He knew them, and they knew Him.

Betrayal almost always involves a close relationship. In fact, I'm not sure it would even classify as betrayal if it didn't involve a close association.

Like many of you, I can relate to the sting of betrayal. Thankfully, I didn't linger in that frame of mind for long.

God quickly picked me up, dusted me off, and began the process of healing. He revealed, through the truth of His Word, that I needed to forgive my betrayer and move on. The complete healing of my heart hinged upon forgiveness. Knowing this, I spent the next several days soaking myself in God's Word and prayer. I was very hurt and knew it was not within me to forgive—*I needed God's help.*

"The righteous cry out, and the LORD hears them; he delivers them from all their troubles. The LORD is close to the brokenhearted and saves those who are crushed in spirit." (Psalm 34:17-18)

In time, the former sting of betrayal hurt less and less. Eventually, it was gone completely.

When we place things into God's hands, what Satan seeks to destroy, God uses as an opportunity for spiritual growth and maturity.

"Blessed is the man who perseveres under trial, because when he has stood the test, he will receive the crown of life that God has promised to those who love him." (James 1:12)

Any time we allow someone to get close, we risk getting hurt. But if we want to be forgiven for our own grievances, we must be ready to forgive others when they hurt us.

"Then Peter came to Jesus and asked, 'Lord, how many times shall I forgive my brother when he sins against me? Up to seven times?' Jesus answered, 'I tell you, not seven times, but seventy-seven times.'" (Matthew 18:21-22)

"Forgive, and you will be forgiven." (Luke 6:37)

Deepest Despair

O ur closest friends can follow us into the garden of despair. They can hold us, encourage us, and lift us up in prayer. However, there is a point at which even our closest friends cannot cross over. It is in this place that we must enter with only one by our side— God the Father.

> Then Jesus went with his disciples to a place called Gethsemane, and he said to them, 'Sit here while I go over there and pray.' He took Peter and the two sons of Zebedee along with him, and he began to be sorrowful and troubled. Then he said to them, 'My soul is overwhelmed with sorrow to the point of death. Stay here and keep watch with me.' (Matthew 26:36-38)

In our deepest despair, only God is capable of going the entire distance with us. Jesus knew this to be true, which is why He left His friends behind and went further into the garden to be alone to be with His Father.

"Going a little farther, he fell with his face to the ground and prayed, 'My Father, if it is possible, may this cup be taken from me. Yet not as I will, but as you will.'" (Matthew 26:39)

Just as close relationships are established through time spent together, we must invest time alone with God to establish intimacy with Him. In this way, we experience the full benefits of a loving relationship with our Father and receive the true comfort and reassurance that only He can provide, especially during life's grueling moments of darkness.

"Praise be to the God and Father of our Lord Jesus Christ, the Father of compassion and the God of all comfort, who comforts us in all our troubles, so that we can comfort those in any trouble with the comfort we ourselves have received from God." (2 Corinthians 1:3-4)

Like Peter, James, and John, some friends will walk further into the garden of despair than others, but only God can go the entire distance with us. Time alone with our Father will strengthen us for whatever comes our way.

Taste and See

My husband and I were invited to our friend's home for dinner. When we first arrived and stood talking in the foyer, my husband reached into a candy dish, sitting on a nearby table, and popped a few butter mints into his mouth. With a look of shock and disgust, he quickly spit the candy into his hand and turned to our friends who were now laughing hysterically. The butter mints were not mints at all. They were air fresheners. Of course we spent the rest of the evening joking about my husband's "extra fresh" breath. We couldn't resist.

This experience reminds me that looks can be deceiving. Just because something appears to be the real deal doesn't mean it is.

"Taste and see that the LORD is good; blessed is the man who takes refuge in him." (Psalm 34:8)

Before you became a Christian, you likely spent a fair amount of time looking to be filled by something other than God. Initially, you may have thought these things would satisfy the longing in your heart, but instead, you came away feeling even emptier than before.

Satan is a master of disguises. He is very good at making bad things appear good. If we fully comprehended the dangers involved in our times of temptation, it's likely that we wouldn't take the bait.

"Be self-controlled and alert. Your enemy the devil prowls around like a roaring lion looking for someone to devour." (1 Peter 5:8)

After years of struggling with poor body-image and insecurity, I eventually sought to control food and weight gain through an eating disorder called bulimia.

When I first began my eating disorder behavior, I was simply hoping to lose weight. All I knew was the immediate gratification and desired outcome—losing weight. I didn't realize I was heading towards twenty-five years of bondage to bulimia. By the time that I realized I had been duped by Satan's lies, I was powerless to break free on my own.

There is only one type of filling that's always good for our souls—Jesus Christ. Jesus came so that we might have life to the fullest.

> I pray that out of his glorious riches he
> may strengthen you with power through
> his Spirit in your inner being, so that Christ
> may dwell in your hearts through faith.
> And I pray that you, being rooted and

established in love, may have power, together with all the saints, to grasp how wide and long and high and deep is the love of Christ, and to know this love that surpasses knowledge—that you may be filled to the measure of all the fullness of God. (Ephesians 3:16-19)

Make sure that you're reaching out for the real deal. Taste and see; the LORD is good.

God's Got My Back

"Turn to me and have mercy on me, as you always do to those who love your name" (Psalm 119:132)

After my husband left the house for an international trip, the phone rang and awakened me from my morning slumber.

It was Gerry in a panic because he'd left the house without his passport. We only live twenty minutes from the airport, but there wasn't enough time for him to drive home and get back to the airport before his flight.

"Rae Lynn, can you please bring me my passport?" he pleaded.

I quickly got dressed, covered my bed-head hair with a ball cap, and was on the road in record time.

Adhering to my husband's instructions to watch the speed limit signs at the airport, I kept my eye on the speedometer. After navigating through the confusing terminal thoroughfares, I finally saw my husband up ahead on the curb waiting. At the same moment, I noticed a police car to my right. I looked down at the dashboard to make sure that I wasn't speeding. I was actually driving under the speed limit.

I pulled over to the curb and handed my husband his passport, but at the very moment, the police car pulled up behind me with its lights on. With wide eyes, I turned to my husband and assured him I had not been speeding. My heart was pounding so hard in my chest, I could feel the pulse in my neck. I couldn't imagine what I had done wrong.

The officer sauntered up to my car window and informed me of my error, "Ma'am, you ran a stop sign back there."

Apparently, in my fervent search to follow the signs leading to my husband's location, I completely missed a very important sign—STOP.

My husband came to my aid and explained the situation. After pleading our case, the sympathetic officer replied, "Well Ma'am, I'll tell you what. If your license comes back clean and everything else checks out okay, I'll let you go this time."

I assured him my record was not only clean—it was squeaky clean. I never had a ticket in my life. I handed him my driver's license and proof of insurance. After looking them over a few moments he informed me, "Ma'am, this insurance card has expired."

This just wasn't my day!

We spent the next few minutes explaining to the officer how our insurance renewal came in the mail only a few days earlier, but we just hadn't put the new card in the vehicle yet. After a phone call to our insurance company, verifying appropriate vehicle coverage, the policeman finally agreed to let me go with a warning.

"This is what the LORD Almighty says: 'Administer true justice; show mercy and compassion to one another.'" (Zechariah 7:9)

Did I deserve to be punished for my negligence that day? Yes. I broke the law—albeit unintentionally. But thankfully, God sent a compassionate police officer to bestow mercy on me and give me a second chance.

"When a man's ways are pleasing to the LORD, he makes even his enemies live at peace with him." (Proverbs 16:7)

"Do not withhold your mercy from me, O LORD; may your love and your truth always protect me." (Psalm 40:11)

When we find ourselves in difficult situations, I'm glad to know that God's got our back.

United We Stand

"I appeal to you, brothers, in the name of our Lord Jesus Christ, that all of you agree with one another so that there may be no divisions among you and that you may be perfectly united in mind and thought." (1 Corinthians 1:10)

Despite what some may say, I believe this country is still a Christian nation. All over this blessed union, men, women, and children congregate on the weekends to offer up praise and worship to our Lord and Savior Jesus Christ. Some gather in mega churches, while an even greater number gather in small assemblies.

Everywhere you look this great nation is dotted with true believers.

I've had the privilege to attend many different worship centers throughout my lifetime, and it is becoming increasingly clear. *God is much more concerned with the name written on our hearts than He is with the name on our buildings.*

"Jesus answered, 'I am the way and the truth and the life. No one comes to the Father except through me.'" (John 14:6)

We are supposed to be the United States of America, but far too often *divided* more accurately describes us—especially in the church. This country was founded and established on Christian values and principles and everyday life once reflected this reality. But now, secular principles and practices dominate our culture and even our world. *How did we get here?*

It's not because we have less Christians in our country. It's because Christians are less united in our country. We have separated ourselves into our own little buildings, denominations, and beliefs, and as a result, Christians have lost their voice as a whole.

It doesn't matter where each participant attends worship. What matters is the common bond we share as believers in Christ. We are all part of God's Church.

If we as a whole could come together in the name of Jesus Christ and put aside our petty differences, what a difference we could make in the world.

Let's make a commitment to stand together, united in love and empowered by truth, knowing full-well that one day we will be together in heaven, kneeling at the feet of Jesus, filled with inexplicable wonder and awe at His magnificent presence. We better learn how to get along now because eternity is an awfully long time. *United we stand – divided we fall.*

"'As surely as I live,' says the Lord, 'every knee will bow before me; every tongue will confess to God.'" (Romans 14:11)

"If my people, who are called by my name, will humble themselves and pray and seek my face and turn from their wicked ways, then will I hear from heaven and will forgive their sin and will heal their land." (2 Chronicles 7:14)

"Now to him who is able to do immeasurably more than all we ask or imagine, according to his power that is at work within us, to him be glory in the church and in Christ Jesus throughout all generations, for ever and ever! Amen." (Ephesians 3:20-21)

One Church. Under God. Indivisible. With liberty and justice for all.

Revival – Not Survival

"For in the day of trouble he will keep me safe in his dwelling; he will hide me in the shelter of his tabernacle and set me high upon a rock." (Psalm 27:5)

Paging through the menu screen of our television, I stumbled across a program called *Doomsday Preppers*. Curiosity got the best of me, so I watched a few minutes to see what the program was all about.

This so-called "reality show" peeks into the lives of individuals making preparations for the end of the world. Out of obvious fear, they stockpile huge quantities of food and water, weapons, and other tools to insure survival. Some have even built special underground shelters to keep them safe in the event of a catastrophic incident. I'm all for being prepared to face the end of the world. I just go about it a little differently. "The Lord is my rock, my fortress and my deliverer; my God is my rock, in whom I take refuge. He is my shield and the horn of my salvation, my stronghold." (Psalm 18:2)

Why would anyone put their faith into a structure built by human hands when they can rest in the shadow of the Almighty—the One who made the heavens and the earth and all that is in them? "He who dwells in the shelter of the Most High will rest in the shadow of the Almighty." (Psalm 91:1)

The end is coming because the Bible clearly warns us of the fact. But if we are in Christ, we have nothing to fear. Death is merely a pathway leading to eternal life in heaven. The end is really just the beginning.

The Bible says the earth will be burned up and the old order of things will pass away. Why would we want to hold on to this world when what comes next is so much better? "He will wipe every tear from their eyes. There will be no more death or mourning or crying or pain, for the old order of things has passed away." (Revelation 21:4)

We need to prepare for the end by gathering our loved ones and teaching them about Jesus. "Jesus answered, 'I am the way and the truth and the life. No one comes to the Father except through me.'" (John 14:6)

We need to prepare for the end by growing closer to God and learning all we can about Him. "Wisdom preserves those who have it." (Ecclesiastes 7:12b)

We need to prepare for the end by making sure that everyone we know is coming to heaven with us.

Then I saw a new heaven and a new earth, for the first heaven and the first earth had passed away, and there was no longer any sea. I saw the Holy City, the new Jerusalem, coming down out of heaven from God, prepared as a bride beautifully dressed for her husband. And I heard a loud voice from the throne saying, "Now the dwelling of God is with men, and he will live with them. They will be his people, and God himself will be with them and be their God. (Revelation 21:1-3)

Our goal should be revival—not survival.

Speaking Truth in Love

"Love does not delight in evil but rejoices with the truth."
(1 Corinthians 13:6)

There are two powerful means of influence in this world—truth and love. When they work together, the stage is set for radical change.

Have you ever had to speak the truth in love to someone? Not only is speaking the truth difficult, but sometimes, no matter how gently and lovingly we try to voice the words, they are not received in the manner we hope—at least not initially.

"Have I now become your enemy by telling you the truth?" (Galatians 4:16)

Some will not only reject the truth we voice, but they may even reject us for being the vehicle through which the truth was spoken.

Even though someone rejects our words initially, the seeds of truth planted today may bloom at a later time. It takes time for the truth to sink in. It also takes a teachable spirit with a willingness to reflect inward, something to remember when we are on the receiving end of spoken truth. As God's children, we should have a pliable spirit. "Sanctify them by the truth; your word is truth." (John 17:17)

> As the rain and the snow come down from heaven, and do not return to it without watering the earth and making it bud and flourish, so that it yields seed for the sower and bread for the eater, so is my word that goes out from my mouth: It will not return to me empty, but will accomplish what I desire and achieve the purpose for which I sent it. (Isaiah 55:10-11)

Before speaking the truth to someone, we need to check our motives and begin by asking ourselves: *What do I hope to achieve by sharing this information?* If our motives are anything but love, then we need to examine our own heart in the matter.

"Love does not delight in evil but rejoices with the truth." (1 Corinthians 13:6)

I have learned through personal experience, when speaking the truth in love, we must first cover the situation in prayer and seek God's guidance. Then God's Spirit will give us the right words and attitude when the time comes to take action. We also need to ask God to prepare the heart of the one to whom we will speak.

"Instead, speaking the truth in love, we will in all things grow up into him who is the Head, that is, Christ." (Ephesians 4:15)

Truth and love—*together they can change the world.*

The Wrong Way!

I was about seventeen years old when a friend and I spent the entire day at a local amusement park called Kings Island. Reminiscing about the day and feeling extremely grown up because it was our first time to visit the park on our own, we got in our car and headed home.

I will be the first to admit that driving home late at night was a mistake. Somewhere along the way we were supposed to merge onto a different highway, but because I was tired and not fully alert, I missed the sign. We both realized that we were lost when we found ourselves approaching downtown Cincinnati at midnight (the complete opposite direction of where we needed to go). This wasn't good. Neither of us knew how to get home from this part of town, and we were afraid to stop and ask for directions. Downtown. Late at night. Seedy area. Need I say more?

Instead of stopping, we kept driving up and down the one way streets until a familiar highway sign pointed us in the direction of home. I learned a valuable lesson that day. *Pay attention to the signs.*

Spiritually speaking, don't you sometimes wish God would place a great big sign in our path, telling us the exact way we should go?

God does provide direction for our lives. It may not be as obvious as a neon sign, but His directions are just as real. In fact, there are many ways we can receive direction from God, but His primary ways are through His Word and His Holy Spirit. "Your word is a lamp to my feet and a light for my path." (Psalm 119:105) "I guide you in the way of wisdom and lead you along straight paths." (Proverbs 4:11) "Show me your ways, O LORD, teach me your paths; guide me in your truth and teach me, for you are God my Savior, and my hope is in you all day long." (Psalm 25:4-5)

If we are not reading our Bibles regularly or seeking the Holy Spirit's guidance, God might use a person, circumstance, or even adversity to direct our steps.

Sometimes we can be so distracted by life that we miss every one of God's warning signs. It's not until we are knee-deep in trouble that we finally recognize how far off course we have traveled.

If I had paid closer attention to the signs as a teenager, I wouldn't have gone the wrong way in the first place.

"Send forth your light and your truth, let them guide me...." (Psalm 43:3)

The safest place to be is under the umbrella of God's protection—the shelter of the Most High.

Deep Water Faith

Initially my mom's proposition to attend swim lessons resulted in numerous tears and pleadings. Sure, I wanted to know how to swim like my big brother and sister, but learning from a perfect stranger terrified me. Luckily my parents discerned what was truly best and signed me up for swim lessons anyway.

Memories of my swim coach are alive and well in my mind to this day. He was mean! (Or at least that was my five year old perception of him.) He made me swim in deep water—something which terrified me.

The day of our last swim lesson, the coach instructed us to swim the width of the pool all by ourselves in the deep end. The coach threw us into the water. We didn't have a lot of choice in the matter. It was sink or swim. Thankfully, I chose to swim.

Keep in mind that we only had to swim the width of the pool, but somewhere along the way I became disoriented and ended up swimming the entire length of the pool. When I came up out of the water, I was shocked to see where I had landed. What a boost to my confidence!

My little swim lesson became a life lesson.

"The LORD is faithful to all his promises and loving toward all he has made. The LORD upholds all those who fall and lifts up all who are bowed down." (Psalm 145:13b-14)

Similar scenarios have played out in my life over and over. I might become angry, scared, or even frustrated when God calls me to carry out something that I don't feel capable of doing. With grumbling and complaining I try and talk my way out of it, but eventually, God throws me in the deep end and I have a choice—sink or swim.

"The LORD will fulfill his purposes for me; your love, O LORD, endures forever – do not abandon the works of your hands." (Psalm 138:8)

We are often surprised by the end results when God moves us away from our comfort zone. Before we know it, our fears are conquered, and we accomplish more than we ever thought possible.

God uses opportunities such as these to grow and strengthen our faith. What we are powerless to accomplish on our own, we more than conquer through Him who loves us.

"Who is like you, LORD God Almighty? You, LORD, are mighty, and your faithfulness surrounds you." (Psalm 89:8)

"I thank Christ Jesus our Lord, who has given me strength, that he considered me faithful, appointing me to his service." (1 Timothy 1:12)

God continues to stretch us beyond our comfort zone because He wants us to have deep water faith.

Eyes Wide Open

I'm not a very observant person. I have a problem with tunnel vision. This can be a good attribute when trying to focus on something in particular and there are lots of distractions going on. But tunnel vision can also be a challenging trait, especially when I am so focused on something that I become oblivious to important matters around me.

Allow me to explain. While heading to a local flea market, deep in conversation with my friend, a car suddenly laid on its horn. Apparently, my focus was so much on our conversation that I drove straight through a flashing red light! My heart skipped a beat. We were lucky that we didn't get hit.

Sometimes my tunnel vision carries over into my faith walk. I can become so focused on a spiritual dilemma that I forget to rely on God's provisions before me.

We need to remember that no problem coming against us is too big for God to handle. Often, our greatest obstacle to solving the problems coming against us is ourselves. We don't let go long enough for God to handle them.

"For everything that was written in the past was written to teach us, so that through endurance and the encouragement of the Scriptures we might have hope." (Romans 15:4)

God has counsel in His Word for anything we could possibly face in life, including tunnel vision.

When the servant of the man of God got up and went out early the next morning, an army with horses and chariots had surrounded the city. "Oh, my lord, what shall we do?" the servant asked. "Don't be afraid," the prophet answered. "Those who are with us are more than those who are with them." <u>And Elisha prayed, "O LORD, open his eyes so he may see.</u>" Then the LORD opened the servant's eyes, and he looked and saw the hills full of horses and chariots of fire all around Elisha. (2 Kings 6:15-17)

Elisha's servant was overwhelmed by the army before them and became discouraged. Recognizing this, Elisha prayed for God to open his servant's eyes to see the Lord's army of angel's encamped around them, ready to fight.

This biblical account reminds me that the problems before us are never bigger than the Power behind us.

Ah, Sovereign LORD, you have made the heavens and the earth by your great power and outstretched arm. Nothing is too hard for you." (Jeremiah 32:17)

"What, then, shall we say in response to this? If God is for us, who can be against us?" (Romans 8:31)

No more tunnel vision when it comes to God. May our eyes be wide open to what God is doing all around.

Treasure Inside

A dear friend gave me an unexpected gift one day. When I first opened the package, I was delighted to find a little wooden plaque shaped like an apple. It had the following words engraved on the front. *The fruit of the Spirit is LOVE, JOY, PEACE (Gal. 5:22)*

I was blessed by my friend's thoughtfulness and her little reminder about the fruit of the Spirit. When I got home, I laid the trinket on my nightstand until I could find it a more permanent home.

A few days later, I picked up the wooden plaque and began to admire the thoughtfulness of my sweet friend. As I turned the plaque over in my hands, I noticed a separation in the wood along the sides. To my surprise the plaque opened up. Inside was an unexpected treasure—two mirrors—one on either side.

My plaque wasn't a plaque at all! It was a compact mirror for my purse.

If I had set the item on a table somewhere and only admired the outside, I would have completely missed out on the practical, intended purpose of my gift.

The Bible is God's gift to us. It is living and active and offers practical applications for our everyday lives.

"For the word of God is living and active. Sharper than any double-edged sword, it penetrates even to dividing soul and spirit, joints and marrow; it judges the thoughts and attitudes of the heart." (Hebrews 4:12)

"All Scripture is God-breathed and is useful for teaching, rebuking, correcting and training in righteousness, so that the man of God may be thoroughly equipped for every good work." (2 Timothy 3:16-17)

Like my little wooden plaque, an unopened Bible is nothing more than a decorative piece collecting dust in our home. God has hidden wonderful treasures in His Word for us to find. But if we never crack open the manuscript and explore the pages of Scripture we will never receive and experience the riches God has for us.

"I will give you the treasures of darkness, riches stored in secret places, so that you may know that I am the LORD, the God of Israel, who summons you by name." (Isaiah 45:3)

The next time you walk past your Bible, pick it up and think about the One who preserved and protected this priceless treasure. Thank Him for His unbelievable love and thoughtfulness, for the wonderful gift of His Word—the greatest love story ever told.

"In this way they will lay up treasure for themselves as a firm foundation for the coming age, so that they may take hold of the life that is truly life." (1Timothy 6:19)

Take time each and every day to open your prized possession and discover its true intended purpose for your life.

The Bible is not a piece to be admired on a shelf. *It's a treasure to be opened and enjoyed.*

Letting Go

Some days we feel completely out of control. An unexpected illness, difficult relationships, strained finances, loss of a job, stress—even an untidy house can send some of us into a frazzled state of mind.

Our natural tendency is to focus attention on another area of life where we can gain some semblance of control. But for some, the diversion becomes more than a means of distraction. It grows into something dangerous—a stronghold that takes over our life.

Out of control feelings present a real problem for individuals with eating disorders. As a means to cope, anorexics restrict food intake, bulimics binge and purge, and compulsive overeaters consume large quantities of food. These unhealthy patterns of behavior eventually consume a person's life to the point of powerlessness. I know because I lived this way for many years.

Ironically, disordered eating behaviors have little to do with food, even though food becomes the method or drug of choice. The unhealthy patterns of behavior are an attempt to gain control of one's circumstances. I say attempt, because when I was living in bondage to my bulimia, I wasn't in control of my eating disorder at all. It was controlling me.

"Trust in the LORD with all your heart and lean not on your own understanding; in all your ways acknowledge him, and he will make your paths straight. 'Do not be wise in your own eyes; fear the LORD and shun evil. This will bring health to your body and nourishment to your bones..." (Proverbs 3:5-8)

After being set free from bulimia, I learned the secret to finding peace and balance in my life, even when my circumstances spiral out of control. Instead of holding on tighter, I let go completely, surrendering to the ONE who controls everything—God.

> He reached down from on high and took hold of me; he drew me out of deep waters. He rescued me from my powerful enemy, from my foes, who were too strong for me. They confronted me in the day of my disaster, but the LORD was my support. He brought me out into a spacious place; he rescued me because he delighted in me. (Psalm 18:16-19)

Yielding is the most difficult thing to do, yet surrender is where we find true peace, joy, and balance for our lives.

Does a stronghold have a tight grip on your life?

It's time to start letting go.

Devastation Unleashed

W e witness the fury of nature when storms and tornadoes rip across the land, leaving behind trails of destruction in their wake. These tragedies become bold reminders that in a matter of minutes, lives can be changed forever.

Several years ago, I experienced first-hand the damage tornados can leave behind. It was when my husband, daughter, and I were living with my parents, waiting for our home to be built.

After tucking our then two-year-old daughter into bed, I headed downstairs to watch the news with my parents. Forecasters were predicting intense storms moving through the area overnight, but because these kind of spring storms take place every year, I didn't think too much about it. My husband and I went off to bed, but my parents stayed up to watch the news for a while longer. It's a good thing they did.

I had just fallen asleep when my parents yelled upstairs that we needed to get into the basement. A tornado warning had been issued for our area. Loud sirens began to wail, warning our community of imminent danger. Along with the sirens, we could hear howling winds and pounding rains pelting against the window pane. When the electricity shut off, reality set in. This was serious! My husband and I leaped out of bed and ran to get our daughter.

Anxiously, we crouched in the corner of the basement covered with blankets, waiting for the storm to pass. Our daughter started crying sensing something was wrong, but I kept trying to reassure her that everything was okay. In my heart, I wasn't so sure.

Then came dead silence—the calm before the storm. Off in the distance we could hear a faint roaring sound growing louder and louder. It sounded like a freight train gathering up speed to barrel through my parents' home. My husband and father took this as their cue to join us under the blankets. Frantically we prayed over and over... *Please dear God, keep us safe.*

Then, just as quickly as the storm appeared, it was gone. The electricity was out, but we were safe. We went back to bed completely unaware of the devastation surrounding us.

The next morning, the sun crept over the horizon and burst through the trees as if to mock the night before. It was surreal to see clear blue skies after the storm's wrath just hours earlier. As I peered out the window, I began to realize just how lucky we were. Debris scattered across my parent's lawn and a huge tree lay on its side, completely uprooted.

As we walked up the street, our hearts shuddered at the horror. Home after home was ripped apart—half gone. The storm had no respect for man or his property. Clothing was scattered all over—littering the ground and dangling from the trees. Personal items of all kinds were strewn about as if they were nothing. One home was completely obliterated, while another, just yards away, was virtually untouched. It was as if the storm chose its victims one by one.

Nothing can prepare you for that kind of devastation. We were extremely grateful. Only a few shingles were lost from my parent's home.

In the weeks and months that followed, a great outpouring of love and support came from the surrounding communities as people began to rebuild their homes and lives. "They will rebuild the ancient ruins and restore the places long devastated; they will renew the ruined cities that have been devastated for generations." (Isaiah 61:4)

Are you facing a storm in your life? Perhaps you find yourself wandering around in complete shock by the devastation it has left behind. Does it feel like pieces of your life are strewn about for the whole world to see? Things may appear bleak right now, but like the morning after the storm, the sun will shine again. Your life will be restored.

The LORD will guide you always; he will satisfy your needs in a sun-scorched land and will strengthen your frame. You will be like a well-watered garden, like a spring whose waters never fail. Your people will rebuild the ancient ruins and will raise up the age-old foundations; you will be called Repairer of Broken Walls, Restorer of Streets with Dwellings. (Isaiah 58:11-12)

Keep trusting in the Lord. He will help you pick up the pieces and rebuild the ruins of your life.

The Real Deal

"See to it that no one takes you captive through hollow and deceptive philosophy, which depends on human tradition and the basic principles of this world rather than on Christ." (Colossians 2:8)

When we are young, we tend to believe things just because someone tells us it's true. The Bible tells us that we need to be childlike in our faith, but at some point, in order to mature in our Christian faith, we need to carefully examine what we've been taught and determine if it holds together as truth.

As an adult, I began to seek Jesus in a more personal and deliberate manner. I had grown up in the church but eventually realized I needed to discover who Jesus was for myself. Each of us must have our own personal relationship with Jesus. We cannot ride into heaven on the coat-tails of our parents or grandparents. Our faith journey must be our own.

Everything I have learned and continue to learn about Jesus only confirms the truth—that Jesus really is the Son of the Living God. He is who He says He is.

"For everything that was written in the past was written to teach us, so that through endurance and the encouragement of the Scriptures we might have hope." (Romans 15:4)

"All Scripture is God-breathed and is useful for teaching, rebuking, correcting and training in righteousness, so that the man of God may be thoroughly equipped for every good work." (2 Timothy 3:16-17)

The Bereans were acknowledged as a people of noble character because they didn't just accept a teaching as truth when someone said it was so. They first checked everything against the Scriptures to see if what they were being taught lined up with God's Word.

"Now the Berean Jews were of more noble character than those in Thessalonica, for they received the message with great eagerness and examined the Scriptures every day to see if what Paul said was true." (Acts 17:11)

Like the Bereans, we need to investigate the stories about Jesus for ourselves. We need to dig deep into Scripture and see if what we've been taught lines up with what the Bible says. The Bible is truth and has stood the test of time. It is trustworthy and unchanging. God has protected His Word for thousands of years. He did this so that you and I wouldn't have to wonder what is true and what is not—we can read it for ourselves. We can know the truth because it has been preserved for all time.

"Your word, O LORD, is eternal; it stands firm in the heavens." (Psalm 119:89)

Growing Pains

W hen our son was just a little guy, he used to get horrible growing pains in his legs. He'd often wake up in the middle of the night, crying out in extreme pain. My husband and I would hurry into his bedroom, hold him close, and massage his legs until the ibuprofen kicked in.

As parents, we hated watching our little boy suffer. It was such a helpless feeling. The pediatrician explained the reason for his growing pains. His bones were growing faster than his tendons, and the strain was causing him to experience pain and discomfort. There was no real cure. It was just part of the growth process.

I wish I could say that growing pains only happen during childhood, but adults experience growing pains too, especially during times of spiritual and emotional growth.

For example, we experience growing pains every time we step out of our comfort zone and face a confrontational situation with someone. We experience growing pains every time we see our loved ones suffer, or when we ourselves suffer. We experience growing pains while trying to resolve conflict in our lives. And the list goes on.

Even positive events in our lives can cause us growing pains. Being newly married, the birth of a child, working a new job, or reaching a growth spurt in our relationship with God are all situations that can stretch us beyond what feels comfortable.

Much like my son's growing pains, these experiences stretch us beyond the limit of what we could previously tolerate. God watches us go through these distressing times, and although He feels great compassion for our discomfort, He knows it's simply part of the growth process. Like our son's growing pains, the ache is temporary and will subside with time.

When the stress is more than we can bear and we're stretched beyond our limit, like we did for our son, our Heavenly Father will wrap His loving arms around us until the pain begins to fade.

"And the God of all grace, who called you to his eternal glory in Christ, after you have suffered a little while, will himself restore you and make you strong, firm and steadfast." (1 Peter 5:10)

Painful as it may be... *we must never stop growing.*

Tested Waters

While on vacation to Maui (one of the Hawaiian Islands), our family decided to take the infamous road to Hanna—a winding two lane road that meanders along the Pacific coast and up the side of a mountain. The spectacular views from this vantage point offer travelers one breathtaking sight after another.

Along our journey, we approached a sharp bend in the road and noticed a few local residents standing along the edge of a cliff. Curious to know what was captivating these islanders' attention, we pulled the car off the side of the road to get a closer look. We quickly realized these local residents were not there to look—they were there to jump.

In amazement, we watched as these fearless risk-takers jumped through a narrow passageway between jagged rocks and then plummeted into a miniscule pool of water below. It was a suicide mission as far as I was concerned, but to these local adventurers, it was great fun. It was obvious they had done this many times before and knew exactly how, when, and where to jump. As experienced cliff divers, they would have certainly tested the waters before jumping off the cliff the first time.

Sometimes we look at the faith journey of others and think to ourselves: *There's no way I could do what they are doing. How can they have so much faith?*

We must remember that faith develops over time. If we see someone taking a giant leap of faith, we can be sure that their faith journey has been tested time and time again by taking smaller steps along the way.

"The apostles said to the Lord, 'Increase our faith!'" (Luke 17:5) Even the apostles asked to have their faith increased, and they were with Jesus every day. As Jesus' constant companions, they saw Him perform miracles firsthand, and yet they still had moments of doubt and uncertainty.

Jesus compares our faith to a mustard seed. He says, "I tell you the truth, if you have faith as small as a mustard seed, you can say to this mountain, 'Move from here to there' and it will move. Nothing will be impossible for you." (Matthew 17:20-21)

Mustard seeds are very tiny when they are first planted, yet they develop into sizeable bushes when mature. Like mustard seeds, when we give God even a little bit of our faith, He takes what we have and helps it grow and mature.

God increases our faith through tests and trials. These faith builders help prepare us to fulfill God's plan and purpose throughout our lives.

And like those local cliff divers, the Lord gives us plenty of opportunities to test the waters before He asks us to jump all the way in.

Little by Little

Are you struggling to overcome some obstacle in life? Are you becoming discouraged because things aren't happening as quickly as you hoped? Perhaps the Scripture in Deuteronomy will provide some hope and encouragement:

> Do not be terrified by them, for the LORD your God, who is among you, is a great and awesome God. The LORD your God will drive out those nations before you, little by little. You will not be allowed to eliminate them all at once, or the wild animals will multiply around you. (Deuteronomy 7:21-22)

Our God is an awesome God, and through Him all things are possible. Like a mighty wave crashing against the seashore, the Lord goes before us and drives out our enemies. But when life is at an impasse, it's tempting to become discouraged and start thinking God has forgotten us or He isn't doing anything to help us. When those thoughts and feelings emerge, we must remember that God's timing is perfect. He is often working behind the scenes where we cannot see—although, it is only in hindsight that we recognize this truth.

When it seems as though nothing is moving forward, perhaps God is preparing the field ahead, so when He does act, abundant fruit springs forth. Or perhaps, God is moving on the hearts of those who will be affected once things do move forward. Better yet, is it possible that God is building needed character traits in us while we wait? Character traits like patience, perseverance, humility, diligence, and total abandonment to Him.

In times of discouragement, we must cling to the promises of God. If God directed us this far, He's not going to abandon us. He is closer than we realize. We must cling to what we know is true, and keep seeking God with all of our heart. He promises to guide our every step (Isaiah 30:21). And when patience wears thin, we must call out to Jesus and ask Him to give us the strength, peace, and encouragement needed while we wait.

"God, who has called you into fellowship with his Son Jesus Christ our Lord, is faithful." (1 Corinthians 1:9)

"Know therefore that the LORD your God is God; he is the faithful God, keeping his covenant of love to a thousand generations of those who love him and keep his commands." (Deuteronomy 7:9)

Hope in the LORD

"...but those who hope in the LORD will renew their strength." (Isaiah 40:31a)

We all have days when discouragement takes over and hopelessness settles in. For me discouragement creeps into my life little by little. Minor irritations chip away at my resolve and eventually throw me into a tailspin.

Satan prowls around looking for a break in our wall of defense. This is why we're advised to be self-controlled and alert (1 Peter 5:8a). Once the enemy finds our weak spot, he heads straight for the areas that have proven profitable in past attacks.

Christians are not impervious to Satan's attacks, but we are not helpless victims either. God is with us. He is our strength and shield—our great deliverer. He is the all-powerful, all-knowing, and ever-present God. Circumstances are unpredictable and people are unreliable, but our God is constant. His character remains steadfast and true.

> Do you not know? Have you not heard? The LORD is the everlasting God, the Creator of the ends of the earth. He will not grow tired or weary, and his understanding no one can fathom. He gives strength to the weary and increases the

power of the weak. Even youths grow tired and weary, and young men stumble and fall; but those who hope in the LORD will renew their strength. They will soar on wings like eagles; they will run and not grow weary, they will walk and not be faint. (Isaiah 40:28-31)

When discouragement settles in, put your hope in the LORD. He will fortify your resolve and renew your strength!

The Power of ONE

I t can be tempting to measure success by numbers. After all, isn't that the way of the world? Churches gauge success by attendance. Corporations gauge success by profit margins. Authors gauge success by the number of books sold. Web owners gauge success by the number of visits to their site. I'll be honest with you. I've fallen into the 'success by numbers' trap myself. Whenever I offer a new class, I wonder how many people will attend. If only a few show up, I feel as though I have failed in some way.

Although the world functions in this way, it is not God's way. God does not measure success by quantity—He measures it by our obedience to follow through.

In his Bible study *Gripped by the Greatness of God*, James McDonald shares a personal experience which truly demonstrates the power of one. Following a time when he had been struggling spiritually, James attended a youth conference at the prompting of his pastor. He knew it was time to get his life back on track with God. At the conference a powerful message was preached, leading James to rededicate his life:

> Pastor Maharias challenged us with "Do you want the character of Christ to grow in your mind? Then get the sewage out." He wisely pressed us to make a decision. He challenged us to stand up and make a public decision to put only Christ-honoring messages in our minds. It was one of those times when I knew the Lord was speaking with me, so I stood up. I remember my body felt like lead. Out of several hundred young people, I was the only person to stand that day. *The only one!*

Twenty years later, James had the opportunity to meet Pastor Maharias and asked him if he remembered the conference. The pastor said that he remembered it well because he felt very discouraged afterwards when only one person responded to his message.

James proceeded to share with the pastor how he had been the one who stood up that day. The experience had changed his life.

God has taken this one life (James McDonald) and touched millions of lives around the world. James is the senior pastor at Harvest Bible Chapel (a mega church in Illinois where more than 13,000 people attend worship service weekly). He also started a ministry called A Walk in the Word, which distributes daily podcasts to more than three million people each week. James has written several Bible studies and helped establish more than seventy churches worldwide. These are just a few of the ways

God is working through this "one" man who (through obedience) devoted his life to Christ.

> So the LORD God caused the man to fall into a deep sleep; and while he was sleeping, he took one of the man's ribs and closed up the place with flesh. (Genesis 2:21)

> For this reason a man will leave his father and mother and be united to his wife, and they will become one flesh. (Genesis 2:24)

> Consequently, just as the result of one trespass was condemnation for all men, so also the result of one act of righteousness was justification that brings life for all men. For just as through the disobedience of the one man the many were made sinners, so also through the obedience of the one man the many will be made righteous. (Romans 5:18-19)

> Since that time he waits for his enemies to be made his footstool, because by one sacrifice he has made perfect forever those who are being made holy. (Hebrews 10:13-14)

> I, John, am the one who heard and saw these things. And when I had heard and seen them, I feel down to worship at the feet of the angel who had been showing them to me. (Revelation 22:8)

Do you think that your life is too little to matter? Think again! *In the hands of God, there is great power in one.*

Home Makeover

"And we, who with unveiled faces all reflect the Lord's glory, are being transformed into his likeness with ever-increasing glory, which comes from the Lord, who is the Spirit." (2 Corinthians 3:18)

I enjoy watching home makeover shows on the Home and Garden channel. It's rewarding to see a once cluttered, outdated space transform into a beautiful, tranquil dwelling.

Makeover shows generally start the same way. A homeowner recognizes their plight and seeks help from an interior designer. The designer then assesses the condition of the space and determines how he can best meet the needs of his client. Makeovers are fairly dramatic, leaving the recipients amazed and extremely grateful for the designer's help.

Is your "home" in need of a makeover? Do you struggle to find peace and harmony in the space that was supposed to be a place of refuge? If so, I know a fabulous Designer who can help. And He has a great set of references. I encourage you to go and check out His previous work for yourself. He's designed some great spaces. Heaven, earth, and the universe are just a few of His more famous designs. His amazing makeovers have dramatically changed the homes of many—including my own. And here's the best part. The Designer does everything for free. That's right. A complete transformation for free! There is just one condition. Before the Designer can begin His greatest work, you must first meet with His Son. The Son will connect you to His Father and the two of them will begin work on your "home" right away.

"Do not conform any longer to the pattern of this world, but be transformed by the renewing of your mind. Then you will be able to test and approve what God's will is—his good, pleasing and perfect will." (Romans 12:2)

"You will roll them up like a robe; like a garment they will be changed. But you remain the same, and your years will never end." (Hebrews 1:12)

Entrust your life to the Master Designer and receive the best home makeover faith can buy.

The Delete Button

It seems that I have a little problem hitting the delete button. Perhaps you can relate.

My problem isn't spam emails—those I can easily discard. The problem is all the other transmissions that come to my inbox on a daily basis. As soon as I get ready to hit the delete button, I think to myself. *What if I need to refer to that later?*

Months later, I literally have thousands of emails floating around my inbox, congesting the cyber highway to my computer. Eventually, I must go through the drudgery of weeding these emails out. When I finally take the time to do so, I'm often amazed by the needless information I held on to. How much misery I could have saved myself if I had just hit the delete button the first time around.

We can have a similar mentality when it comes to our brain's inbox. Whether it's the words of others, negative self-talk or lingering memories over past injuries, we just can't seem to hit the delete button in our minds. Before we know it our heart is cluttered with all sorts of negative transmits. The resulting blockage fogs our brain and clogs the outflow of our heart.

"I the Lord search the heart and examine the mind..." (Jeremiah 17:10a)

We need to ask God to help us weed out those negative thoughts floating around our mind's inbox, so we can free up space for something good—truth.

"...the mind controlled by the Spirit is life and peace;" (Romans 8:6b)

When negative thoughts threaten to take up residence in your mind, hit the delete button right away. Take it from someone who knows; you'll save yourself from a whole lot of misery and heartache later on.

"We demolish arguments and every pretension that sets itself up against the knowledge of God, and we take captive every thought to make it obedient to Christ." (2 Corinthians 10:5)

S.O.S

In 1836 Samuel F. B. Morse, along with Joseph Henry and Alfred Vail, developed a method of communication consisting of intermittent electrical pulses sent through the wires of a telegraph system. The language became known as Morse code.

Probably the best-known Morse code signal is the S.O.S, a cyphered gram that has become synonymous with distress calls. The letters associated with the signal have become a popular acronym for phrases such as save our ship or save our soul. I have my own acronym for S.O.S. – *SEEK OUT SUPPORT*.

During an extremely difficult week, Satan was attacking every area of insecurity that I had, and my spirit was sinking fast.

I tried everything to pull myself out of this pit of despair, but nothing worked. I even got up earlier in the morning so I could spend more time than usual in prayer and Bible study, but still, my spirit remained overwhelmed with gloom. I felt weighted down by my wet blanket of despair.

Why, my soul, are you downcast? Why so disturbed within me? (Psalm 42:5a)

I had no idea what caused my gloom and didn't know how to break out of it, but I did recognize my need for help. After a few days of trying to fight my way out of depression alone, I eventually sent out a distress call to my family and friends, asking for prayer.

Shortly after my plea for help, people began calling and sending me messages of hope and encouragement. Slowly, the fog began to lift from my spirit, and within no time, I was back to my old self again.

God recognized our need for human companionship and support from the very beginning. "The Lord God said, "It is not good for the man to be alone. I will make a helper suitable for him." (Genesis 2:18)

The Lord sends us encouragement through scriptures, songs, and sermon messages. But when He hears the desperate cry of a dejected soul in need of support, He goes the extra mile and sends someone with skin.

"You, Lord, hear the desire of the afflicted; you encourage them, and you listen to their cry..." (Psalm 10:17)

Sometimes we just need the extra boost of encouragement through the physical touch or audible voice of a loved one. There is no shame in needing the support of others.

The next time you are burdened with a downcast spirit, send out your own S.O.S—SEEK OUT SUPPORT.

"We urge you, brothers and sisters ... encourage the disheartened, help the weak, be patient with everyone." (1 Thessalonians 5:14)

Left Behind

When my brother and his family came in town for a visit, we decided to all meet up for dinner at a local restaurant. Afterwards, we piled into two vehicles and headed for my parents' condo (two miles away) to spend some additional time visiting.

Shortly after we arrived, someone asked the whereabouts of my nine year old niece. A quick survey of the condo revealed that Sami was nowhere to be found.

It didn't take us long to realize that Sami had been left behind at the restaurant. In a panic, my sister-in-law made a mad dash for the car and took off down the road at lightning speed. With frantic tears streaming down her face, she bolted into the restaurant and began desperately scanning the dining room for her precious daughter. She didn't have to look far. Sami was sitting at the counter with a very nice policeman eating a piece of pie, seemingly unscathed by the incident.

How did this happen?

While we were gathering up to leave the restaurant, my niece went into the restroom without telling anyone. When we got into our cars, I assumed that my niece was with her parents, and her parents assumed that she was with us.

Perhaps you remember another story of a child getting left behind.

Every year Jesus' parents went to Jerusalem for the Festival of the Passover. When he was twelve years old, they went up to the festival, according to the custom. After the festival was over, while his parents were returning home, the boy Jesus stayed behind in Jerusalem, but they were unaware of it. Thinking he was in their company, they traveled on for a day. (Luke 2:41-44a)

We might begin to question Mary and Joseph's parenting abilities. How could they have left their twelve year old son in Jerusalem for an entire day and not realize it? But before we begin to judge the situation, we need to understand a few things.

At the age of twelve, Jesus was teetering between manhood and childhood. Since women and children often traveled in the caravan together, separate from the men, it is believed that because of His age, Jesus could have just as easily traveled with either group. Mary assumed Jesus was with Joseph, and Joseph assumed Jesus was with Mary.

"Then they began looking for him among their relatives and friends. When they did not find him, they went back to Jerusalem to look for him. After three days they found him in the temple courts, sitting among the teachers, listening to them and asking them questions." (Luke 2:44b-46)

Jesus was missing for three days! Can you imagine the panic Mary and Joseph must have felt? My niece was only gone twenty minutes and we were frantic.

"When his parents saw him, they were astonished. His mother said to him, 'Son, why have you treated us like this? Your father and I have been anxiously searching for you. 'Why were you searching for me?' [Jesus] asked.

'Didn't you know I had to be in my Father's house?'"
(Luke 2:48-49)

I find it interesting that neither Jesus nor my niece
were the least bit traumatized by their experience.
According to Jesus, he wasn't lost at all. He was right
where He was supposed to be—with His Father.

I take comfort in knowing that God the Father was
with my niece that day too.

Rest for the Weary

A good night's rest is hard to come by these days.
My restless nights began shortly after I started
having kids and they continue to this day.

When I was pregnant, I didn't sleep well because I
couldn't get comfortable. After the kids were born, I
didn't sleep well because of the baby's crazy sleep
schedule. As the kids got older, I found myself lying
awake with worry and stress. Now that I'm approaching
fifty, I still don't sleep well because back pain and
hormonal hot flashes keep me awake.

What I wouldn't do for a really great night's rest.

God talks about the subject of rest many times
throughout Scripture. From Genesis to Revelation, it is a
subject about which He has a lot to say.

In this day and age, people are constantly on the go.
Taking time to truly rest is a rarity in our culture—
especially in the United States. When we finally do have
an opportunity to slow down, we often feel guilty for
taking time to do so.

God knew that rest would be a stumbling block for us, which is why He instituted a command to rest in His top ten instructions.

> Remember the Sabbath day by keeping it holy. Six days you shall labor and do all your work, but the seventh day is a sabbath to the Lord your God. On it you shall not do any work, neither you, nor your son or daughter, nor your male or female servant, nor your animals, nor any foreigner residing in your towns. For in six days the Lord made the heavens and the earth, the sea, and all that is in them, but he rested on the seventh day. Therefore the Lord blessed the Sabbath day and made it holy. (Exodus 20:8-11)

Even the animals were commanded to rest.
Why?
Because rest is essential for overall health. Lack of sleep causes exhaustion, and exhaustion causes irritability, depression, and even sickness. As we struggle to focus, we become ineffective in all we do. Fatigue impacts us physically, emotionally, and spiritually.

"Come to me, all you who are weary and burdened, and I will give you rest." (Matthew 11:28)

We need to obey God's command to slow down and allow our bodies the adequate time to rejuvenate.

Adequate rest leads to restoration.

Never Forget

"Though they plot evil against you and devise wicked schemes, they cannot succeed; for you will make them turn their backs when you aim at them with drawn bow. Be exalted, O LORD, in your strength; we will sing and praise your might." (Psalm 21:11-13)

September 11, 2001—a day that our country will never forget. Ask anyone who was old enough to remember and they can probably tell you exactly where they were and what they were doing when they heard the tragic news that our country was under attack.

Early that morning the phone rang. It was my husband who was out of town for work.

"Rae Lynn, turn on the television!" From his anxious tone, I knew something was terribly wrong. I was homeschooling our two children at the time, and although we were up and moving, we were clueless about what was taking place. As I rushed to turn on our television, my husband relayed the shocking news.

"Rae Lynn, a plane just crashed into the World Trade Center!"

What? It didn't completely register at first. How does a plane accidentally hit a building? As images appeared on the screen, the kids and I watched in horror as the shocking scene played out. When a second plane flew directly into the south tower, reality sunk in—this was no accident.

Like the rest of the nation, we were paralyzed with shock. Our two children, then nine and fourteen, kept asking me, "Mom, what's going on?" I honestly didn't know.

We were tethered to the television, watching the grave images as they scrolled across the screen, trying to make sense of what we were witnessing. People were jumping out of the smoldering buildings to their death, choosing what must have seemed a better alternative than burning to death in the scorching flames. *I can't even imagine.*

Moments later, the news anchor announced that the Pentagon had also been hit. We were under full throttle attack. I wondered... *will our little town be a target?* While trying to process everything, the thought suddenly occurred to me that my husband who traveled by plane every week could have just as easily been on one of those jets. I trembled at the thought.

During the aftermath, many wondered where God had been on that clear September morning. They questioned why a loving God would allow something so horrific to happen.

In the days, weeks, and months that followed, story after story revealed exactly where God had been. He was right there, providing courage to rescue workers, peace to the fallen victims, and comfort to those who had lost loved ones. "He will cover you with his feathers, and under his wings you will find refuge; his faithfulness will be your shield and rampart." (Psalm 91:4) "I have set the LORD always before me. Because he is at my right hand, I will not be shaken." (Psalm 16:8)

Where was God in the midst of all this?

One little question with enormous implications. Split this sentence in two, and find your answer.

Where was God? *In the midst of all this!*

Walking by Faith

"For I know the plans I have for you," declares the LORD, "plans to prosper you and not to harm you, plans to give you hope and a future." (Jeremiah 29:11)

Sometimes we can wander through life and feel like we're in complete darkness, unable to see the next step before us. Lack of direction can be tiresome, frustrating, and discouraging, especially when we are in the middle of it, but God calls us to walk by faith—not by sight.

So what should we do when discouragement or doubt sets in?

We must cling to Truth!

God provides some wonderful counsel in His Word to usher us from darkness into His wonderful light. "The precepts of the LORD are right, giving joy to the heart. The commands of the LORD are radiant, giving light to the eyes." (Psalm 19:8) "Your word is a lamp to my feet and a light for my path." (Psalm 119:105)

A few years ago, I did a Bible study called *Walking by Faith: Lessons Learned in the Dark* by Jennifer Rothschild. If anyone understands how difficult it is to walk in darkness—it's Jennifer. During her sophomore year of high school, Jennifer noticed that her vision was slowly deteriorating. Upon visiting a specialist, she learned that she was suffering from a degenerative eye disease—one that would eventually cause her complete blindness. *Talk about an uncertain future!*

Jennifer learned first-hand how challenging it can be to walk in darkness, and yet she did not let her physical handicap keep her from living an incredible faith-filled life. Today Jennifer shares her many lessons learned in the darkness and testifies how God is shaping her into the woman He wants her to be.

We must learn to walk by faith through our times of darkness. When we can't see ahead, we must listen for God's direction and entirely rely on His lead. He goes before us and will get us where we need to go. As we move forward, placing one foot in front of the other, God will either shed light on our present path or point us in a different direction.

"Show me your ways, O LORD, teach me your paths; guide me in your truth and teach me, for you are God my Savior, and my hope is in you all day long." (Psalm 25:4-5)

"You are my lamp, O LORD; the LORD turns my darkness into light." (2 Samuel 22:29)

"Send forth your light and your truth, let them guide me; let them bring me to your holy mountain, to the place where you dwell." (Psalm 43:3)

Like Jennifer we must learn to walk by faith—not sight.

Tough or Tender?

"Keep me safe, LORD, from the hands of the wicked; protect me from the violent, who devise ways to trip my feet." (Psalm 140:4)

With a good portion of my childhood spent walking in bare feet, the skin on the bottom of my soles eventually grew thick and calloused, desensitizing me to pain when stepping on sharp objects. I could even run across a gravel driveway and not feel discomfort.

God designed our bodies with the marvelous ability to adapt to our environment. Not only does God give us the ability to adapt physically, He also gives us the ability to adapt emotionally.

As a child I was very sensitive. Even a sad song was enough to get my tears flowing. But like the bottoms of my feet, difficult life experiences caused me to develop a tough exterior. Emotional barriers that I had built up over time kept me from feeling too much pain. For many years I couldn't cry—I just felt numb.

As I grew closer to God, He began breaking down my emotional barriers until I realized I no longer needed them. After a while the tears began to flow again. A quarter century's worth of tears had been bottled up inside, waiting to come out. With my emotional barriers removed, I was able to feel and experience normal pain again.

Pain is good. It keeps us from making the same mistakes over and over and it keeps us out of harm's way. Just as God designed our bodies with the ability to toughen up, He also designed us to be sensitive and feel.

"'Because the poor are plundered and the needy groan, I will now arise,' says the LORD. 'I will protect them from those who malign them.'" (Psalm 12:5)

It's okay to feel pain and cry. God gave us this wonderful form of release as a means to remove toxins from our bodies.

But be encouraged! A day is coming when there will be no more need for earthly tears. "'He will wipe every tear from their eyes. There will be no more death or mourning or crying or pain, for the old order of things has passed away.' He who was seated on the throne said, 'I am making everything new!'" (Revelation 21:4-5)

Until then let the tears flow and remember.

If God sends us on stony paths, He provides strong shoes. ~Corrie Ten Boom

Breath of God

"All Scripture is God-breathed and is useful for teaching, rebuking, correcting and training in righteousness, so that the man of God may be thoroughly equipped for every good work." (2 Timothy 3:16-17)

When I was a Girl Scout, one of the more practical skills that I learned was how to build a campfire. We were taught to blow softly on smoldering coals to get a fire going. A soft and steady flow of carbon dioxide made the embers glow more brightly, causing the hot coals to burst into flames.

Is your walk with God burning bright with intensity, or does it feel more like smoldering coals?

If your passion isn't what it used to be, I have good news for you. The same technique for stoking a campfire can help ignite your passion for God—with one major difference. *We need the breath of God!*

God's Spirit is repeatedly represented through flames and fire in Scripture. The burning bush (Exodus 3), the pillar of fire at night (Exodus 13), fire on the mountain (Exodus 19), the lamp stand in the tabernacle (Exodus 25), and the tongues of fire resting upon the disciples (Acts 2). Each of these represents the manifestation of God's Spirit.

Since all Scripture is God-breathed (2 Timothy 3:16-17), every time you and I study Scripture, God fans the flame of His Spirit in our hearts and ignites His all-consuming fire into our lives.

So, what are you waiting for?

If you want God's Spirit burning with intensity, spend more time with God in His Word.

"The Spirit of God has made me; the breath of the Almighty gives me life." (Job 33:**4)**

Remember

"On my bed I remember you; I think of you through the watches of the night. Because you are my help, I sing in the shadow of your wings. My soul clings to you; your right hand upholds me." (Psalm 63:6-8)

Facts, figures, and dates rarely leave a lasting impression on our minds, but when something traumatic or exciting takes place, it's as if the moment is imprinted in our memories with indelible ink.

Certain memories from my past are so clear that when I reflect upon them, I'm mentally transformed into the moment as if it's happening all over again.

A television program I watched provided some insight concerning this strange phenomenon. A chemical reaction takes place in our brains, causing certain memories to be imprinted with greater intensity. The key factor in this physical response is adrenaline.

When we experience emotions such as fear, panic, pain, love, or excitement, adrenaline is released into our blood stream, sealing the moment into our memory bank. According to science, certain memories become so vivid that we actually relive the physical and emotional sensations originally associated with the event.

For many years, a traumatic incident from my childhood caused me great physical and emotional distress every time the memory was engaged. Thankfully, God has done a great healing work in my life. Today, when the memory is brought to the forefront of my mind, I am less adversely affected.

The word 'remember' appears many times in Scripture, but what might surprise you is the number of times it is used in the context of God remembering. We don't often think in terms of God remembering because He knows everything.

Realizing that God remembers the traumatic event from my childhood somehow gives me comfort. Not only does God remember what happened, He also has great compassion for what I went through. "For he who avenges blood remembers; he does not ignore the cry of the afflicted." (Psalm 9:12)

My healing did not take place overnight. It was a progression that took place over the course of many years. Physical, emotional, and spiritual healing always takes time, but it is possible. I am living proof.

Do certain memories from your past evoke distress when they are engaged? I encourage you to go to the Father for healing. He remembers, He cares, and He is there to turn your troubling past into a distant memory.

"[God] heals the brokenhearted and binds up their wounds." (Psalm 147:3)

Ever Wonder Why?

One of the most difficult concepts for our human minds to grasp is why a loving God would allow so much pain and suffering in the world. We reason that God could stop all the turmoil with one simple command, so why doesn't He?

"'For my thoughts are not your thoughts, neither are your ways my ways,' declares the LORD. 'As the heavens are higher than the earth, so are my ways higher than your ways and my thoughts than your thoughts.'" (Isaiah 55:8-9)

We may not know the mind of God, but we can certainly know the steadfast character of God. Our immutable Father is the same yesterday, today, and tomorrow. He does not change. He is all-knowing, all-powerful, and ever-present.

"I am God, and there is no other; I am God, and there is none like me." (Isaiah 46:9)

God is forgiving, loving, patient, compassionate, and gentle. But let us not forget—God is also sovereign, righteous, and just. If God allows pain and suffering to take place in our lives, we must trust that He has a plan and purpose for it.

"Trust in the LORD with all your heart and lean not on your own understanding; in all your ways acknowledge him, and he will make your paths straight." (Proverbs 3:5-6)

God has this world (and everything in it) in the palm of His hand. He is not surprised by our day to day events. He knows them in advance and has already measured the outcome of each trial against the grand scheme of His design.

"When I consider your heavens, the work of your fingers, the moon and the stars, which you have set in place, what is man that you are mindful of him, the son of man that you care for him?" (Psalms 8:3-4)

It's difficult to see the complete picture of a mosaic up close, but when you step back and view it from a distance you can see how each individual piece plays an intricate part in the picture as a whole.

Life is like a mosaic. Each person's existence is intricately woven into God's beautiful design. Our vision is so limited, but God's perspective is complete. He sees the big picture. He knows how each harmonious piece connects to another.

"And we know that in all things God works for the good of those who love him, who have been called according to his purpose." (Romans 8:28)

"But the plans of the LORD stand firm forever, the purposes of his heart through all generations." (Psalm 33:11)

We must trust the Lord to work out the details of our lives—*even when we don't understand how or why.*

Wait for God's Best

Christian author Beth Moore shared an amusing story about a family of ducks who spent the day contentedly splashing around in a puddle while only a few hundred feet away stood a very large pond.

I wonder how many times in life you and I settle for a "puddle" when just over the horizon God has something so much better waiting for us?

If the Israelites had been a little more patient and had trusted God to provide His very best, they would have seen that their heavenly Father had something so much better waiting for them.

> Then Moses led Israel from the Red Sea and they went into the Desert of Shur. For three days they traveled in the desert without finding water. When they came to Marah, they could not drink its water because it was bitter. (That is why the place is called Marah.) So the people grumbled against Moses, saying, 'What are we to drink?' (Exodus 15:22-24)

Keep in mind that there were hundreds of thousands of men, women, and children in this caravan. It would be difficult to distribute water to every person from a single water supply perhaps no bigger than a well.

This scene from Exodus takes place only three days after the Israelites witnessed God parting the Red Sea. How quick we are to grumble and complain when God doesn't give us what we *think* we need.

I'm afraid human nature hasn't changed much from then until now.

"Then Moses cried out to the LORD, and the LORD showed him a piece of wood. He threw it into the water, and the water became sweet." (Exodus 15:25)

God gave the people what they wanted in that moment. But two verses later we learn something significant. ".... then they came to Elim, where there were twelve springs and seventy palm trees, and they camped there near the water." (Exodus 15:27)

If only they had been patient enough to wait for what God had for them just over the horizon.

The Israelites were willing to settle for Marah (a puddle), when all along God had Elim (a great big pond). With its twelve springs and seventy palms, Elim was more than a watering hole. It was an oasis in the desert. Not only was God prepared to quench His children's thirst, but He was also ready to give them shade and rest—a welcome relief from the hot desert sun.

God is able to do immeasurably more than all we can ask or even imagine. Perhaps we would be wise to wait for God's best.

"Find rest, O my soul, in God alone; my hope comes from him." (Psalm 62:5)

"He who dwells in the shelter of the Most High will rest in the shadow of the Almighty." (Psalm 91:1)

"I wait for the LORD, my soul waits, and in his word I put my hope." (Psalm 130:5)

Don't settle for the puddle—*wait for the pond.*

Beauty from Ashes

"They will rebuild the ancient ruins and restore the places long devastated; they will renew the ruined cities that have been devastated for generations." (Isaiah 61:4)

Forest fires make headline news each year and leave behind a trail of unimaginable destruction. Trained firefighters work day and night to contain the raging monsters, but the wind and extremely dry conditions can make their efforts seem futile.

Seasonal fires may ravage and destroy, but what takes place in the months and years that follow is truly amazing. Over time, new life begins to emerge. Tiny green saplings struggle to the surface, feeding off of the nutrient-filled soil left from the wake of the fire. Ashes from the fire fertilize the ground, making it a catalyst for rich new growth.

Sometimes difficult life experiences can make us feel like we're standing in the middle of a forest fire. The heat and tension can be all consuming. In the midst of the chaos and turmoil, it is difficult to see how anything good could arise from the ashes... and yet that's exactly what God does.

"....to comfort all who mourn, and provide for those who grieve in Zion—to bestow on them a crown of beauty instead of ashes, the oil of gladness instead of mourning, and a garment of praise instead of a spirit of despair. They will be called oaks of righteousness, a planting of the LORD for the display of his splendor." (Isaiah 61:2-3)

In His sovereignty, God uses the very ashes from the torched and torn fragments of our lives to foster rich, new growth. Difficulties strengthen our character, fortify our resolve, and enhance our capacity for compassion.

Nothing is wasted in God's economy. He uses every bit of our ancient ruins to rebuild, restore, and renew that which was once devastated.

"For as the soil makes the sprout come up and a garden causes seeds to grow, so the Sovereign LORD will make righteousness and praise spring up before all nations." (Isaiah 61:11)

A Roaring Lion

"Be self-controlled and alert. Your enemy the devil prowls around like a roaring lion looking for someone to devour." (1 Peter 5:8)

When we look at the behavior of a lion and how it hunts its prey, we gain some insight into the tactics of Satan and his deception.

When a lion hunts, it hides in the tall African grasses and watches its prey from afar. Carefully, it singles out the weak and unsuspecting, scoping out its best opportunity to score an easy meal. Once the lion chooses its victim, it springs forth with great speed, using the element of surprise as its main offense. The herd begins to scatter, but the lion keeps its eyes on the predetermined target. The lion's first tactic is to separate the victim from the rest of the herd, making it an easier mark. The fierce predator wears down its prey with a terrorizing chase until the victim stumbles, falls, and eventually surrenders to the lion's ferocious jaws.

Satan is looking for a victim. He watches from afar, waiting to prey upon the weak and unsuspecting. God tells us to be self-controlled and alert. Our enemy often implements the element of surprise when launching his attacks. In this way, he catches us off guard. Often we don't even realize an attack is taking place until it's too late.

Like a lion separating its victim from the herd, Satan's most profitable tactic of spiritual warfare is to separate Christians from their support system. Isolation is a powerful tool of the enemy. When he can get us alone, we are extremely vulnerable. He can start whispering his lies, putting us at an even greater risk of sinking into a pit of despair. His relentless lies wear us down and we grow weary. Fortunately, Satan's attacks on Christians are limited. Although he cannot tear us away from God, he can certainly keep us from being effective for God's Kingdom.

"Submit yourselves, then, to God. Resist the devil, and he will flee from you." (James 4:7)

God is our deliverer and protector, but we must keep on the full armor of God as a means of daily prevention and protection against Satan's attacks.

"Finally, be strong in the Lord and in his mighty power. Put on the full armor of God so that you can take your stand against the devil's schemes." (Ephesians 6:10-11)

Christians are the top target for the enemy of our souls, but we are not helpless victims. We have the power of God on our side.

"Resist him, standing firm in the faith, because you know that your brothers throughout the world are undergoing the same kind of sufferings." (1 Peter 5:9)

Can You Hear Him?

"Apply your heart to instruction and your ears to words of knowledge." (Proverbs 23:12)

Each year my mom spends a week at a spiritual retreat center in Kentucky. It's a serene and quiet place where she goes to be alone with God. The retreat center has designated areas where talking is permitted, but for the most part speaking aloud is discouraged. The silence allows visitors to be completely focused on God. Eliminating distractions from outside influences provides visitors with the best opportunity to hear God speak to their heart.

At times I've wondered how anyone could go an entire week without speaking aloud, yet at other times I'm envious. My mom has invested much time into building intimacy with God—time that's void of interruptions. I wouldn't mind having an entire week alone with God myself. My mom always comes away from her retreats feeling refreshed and renewed.

What about you?

Do you take time to be quiet before the Lord?

"I will give you the treasures of darkness, riches stored in secret places, so that you may know that I am the LORD, the God of Israel, who summons you by name." (Isaiah 45:3)

Our time alone with God will never be wasted. In fact, it will make us better parents, spouses, co-workers, and friends. I have come to realize that we don't need to hear the words of another human being nearly as much as we need to hear the Words of God.

"I have treasured the words of his mouth more than my daily bread." (Job 23:12b)

May we all see the importance of taking time to be alone with God.

Lukewarm—Yuck!

Have you noticed that some things taste better depending on temperature? Coffee tastes better when it's hot, and milk tastes better when it's cold. Take a swig of either of these beverages at room temperature and you're likely to gag. That in-between temperature just won't do.

Apparently, God feels the same way. "I know your deeds, that you are neither cold nor hot. I wish you were either one or the other! So, because you are lukewarm—neither hot nor cold—I am about to spit you out of my mouth." (Revelation 3:15-16)

According to God's Word, lukewarm Christians just won't do. God would rather us be hot or cold—one or the other. Lukewarm faith is kind of like lukewarm milk—yuck.

We know that deeds cannot save us because we are saved by faith in Jesus Christ. However, God tells us in His Word that our deeds are a good indicator of the degree of our faith.

"What good is it, my brothers, if a man claims to have faith but has no deeds?" (James 2:14)

"As the body without the spirit is dead, so faith without deeds is dead." (James 2:26)

"You foolish man, do you want evidence that faith without deeds is useless?" (James 2:20)

Scripture tells us that faith without action is dead. (James 2:17)

We must put our faith into action by doing the Lord's work here on earth. What good is it for us to be saved if all we do is sit around *believing* in God?

"You believe that there is one God. Good! Even the demons believe that—and shudder." (James 2:19)

According to the book of Revelation, we are better off cold than lukewarm. Do you know why? Lukewarm Christians might as well be dead in Christ.

How are others going to learn about Jesus if we never get out there and introduce Him through our actions?

Remember how you felt when you first gave your life to Christ. Try to keep that same zeal and passion throughout your entire faith journey.

Keep your passion searing hot as you put your faith into action.

Full of Compassion

Throughout the Gospels, we find Jesus administering compassion to those around Him. A man with leprosy is made clean. One who was paralyzed gets up from his mat and walks home. A bleeding woman is healed by just a touch of Jesus' garment. And one of my personal favorites, Jesus raises his dear friend Lazarus from the grave. These accounts and others speak volumes about Christ's compassion towards the needy. Yet, there is one act of compassion that is greater than them all.

"For God so loved the world that he gave his one and only Son, that whoever believes in him shall not perish but have eternal life." (John 3:16)

Jesus (God in the flesh) taking on the form of man and dying on the cross for our sins was Christ's greatest act of compassion yet.

When Jesus felt compassion, He didn't just feel sorry for those who were afflicted, He took action and helped them.

There is much we can learn through our Lord's example of compassion—principles we can apply towards our interactions with others.

"Each one should use whatever gift he has received to serve others, faithfully administering God's grace in its various forms." (1 Peter 4:10)

Compassion requires caring for one another's needs as best we can. I've found that we are often more sympathetic towards others when we can relate on some level. Let me show you what I mean.

After a hard landing on the metal bar surrounding our trampoline, I found myself lying flat on my back with extreme pain surging through my right ankle. Looking down, I noticed blood seeping through my sock. One minute things were fine and dandy, and the next I was headed to the hospital for a lengthy stay. My compound fracture required three surgeries, two months in a cast, and several months of physical therapy.

During my recovery, even the simplest of tasks like making a bed became difficult. I felt so helpless. Thankfully, many wonderful people came to my family's aid and started caring for our needs. They cooked meals, watched our kids, and helped out with some housework. It was definitely a humbling experience for me.

Hard as it was for me to accept help, I did consent to everyone's assistance. I had no choice. Because of what I went through, I now feel more empathy towards others facing similar circumstances. This is one of the reasons God allows suffering into our lives. Through the memory of our own torment, we are able to empathize with the pain of others.

"Be imitators of God, therefore, as dearly loved children and live a life of love, just as Christ loved us and gave himself up for us as a fragrant offering and sacrifice to God." (Ephesians 5:1-2)

Like Jesus, our compassion should become a catalyst for taking action, helping others in need.

New Growth

Winter can be a dreary time—drab and grey. But when spring bursts forth, bright green grass covers the landscape, and flowers emerge from their hibernation. Song birds announce the arrival of each sunrise, while bees ready themselves to gather nectar and pollinate the budding plants and flowers.

The transformation of spring appears to take place overnight; however, new life works its way to the surface long before we see it emerge. Unseen growth takes place all winter long while nature prepares for yet another season.

Perhaps we should reflect upon and assess the spiritual growth taking place in you and me. Are we growing in our relationship with God or are we stagnant? Let's compare where we are today with where we were a year ago. Can we see new growth in our spiritual lives? Has worship grown more meaningful? Do we have more Scriptures tucked into our memory than we did a year ago? Do we see less sin in our life? Do we trust God more?

Each of these indicators can be a visible gauge to measure spiritual growth. Since some changes appear slowly, we must take inventory of our lives periodically to truly perceive the transformations taking place.

"See, I am doing a new thing! Now it springs up; do you not perceive it? I am making a way in the desert and streams in the wasteland." (Isaiah 43:19)

Each spring, my husband and I spruce up our yard by clearing away the dead leaves and plants that threaten to smother our lawn and landscape. Once decaying undergrowth is removed, new plants and grass have adequate space to grow and flourish.

Sometimes it's necessary to incorporate a similar practice into our faith journey. Could your spiritual life use some sprucing up? Begin by clearing away any stagnant areas which are no longer producing good fruit.

Perhaps you have been serving in the same area of ministry for years, but your passion has lost its zing. Maybe it would be wise to look for other service opportunities. Not only would this benefit you personally, but it also might open up a door for someone else. Another's contribution just might bring the fresh perspective needed to aid the ministry's ability to produce a greater harvest of fruit.

Once we clear away the dead foliage of seasons past, we can flourish among the new opportunities God brings our way. God ordains different seasons for our spiritual life, and with each new season, He provides rich new growth.

"See, the former things have taken place, and new things I declare; before they spring into being I announce them to you." (Isaiah 42:9)

I pray that each new season pours forth an abundant harvest of luscious, spiritual fruit.

"This is to my Father's glory, that you bear much fruit, showing yourselves to be my disciples." (John 15:8)

Lessons Learned

"When pride comes, then comes disgrace, but with humility comes wisdom." (Proverbs 11:2)

Take it from someone who knows—humility can be a painstaking teacher. With more than my fair share of humbling moments, I remember one incident in particular. The lesson was painful but lasting.

I was probably about eleven or so when my friends and I decided to give smoking a try. In hindsight… *it was a bad idea.* But at the time, we thought we were cool. Until we got caught by our dads, that is.

Our first mistake was approving my friends' suggestion to borrow a few cigarettes from her dad's pack. *Did I mention the pack was full?* We figured with all those cigarettes, surely her dad wouldn't miss a few. As you can probably guess, this little hypothesis led to our downfall.

We grabbed the stogies and headed for the woods. Far away from the watchful eyes of others, we lit up and began puffing away. We were feeling quite grown up until we heard muffled voices in the distance. We promptly disposed of the evidence but only moments before our dads appeared in the clearing. The smoke didn't even have time to clear the air.

I'm sure guilt was written all over our faces. My heart was pounding so hard in my chest that I began feeling dizzy, a combination of fear and nicotine. One by one, our dads walked up and asked if we had been smoking. My friends denied it vehemently, but lying was never my strong suit. I knew that if my dad was asking the question—*he already knew the answer.*

"When anyone is guilty in any of these ways, he must confess in what way he has sinned..." (Leviticus 5:5)

Tears burst forth as I spilled the ugly truth, incriminating myself and my friends. They shot evil looks my way for betraying them, but what could I do? Our dads were on to us. Denying our folly would only make matters worse.

There was a heavy price to pay for each one of us, but because I told the truth, I wasn't punished as severely as my friends.

I learned an important lesson that day. When you mess up—fess up. I also learned that mercy results from a humble and contrite spirit. I'm very grateful that my parents recognized the opportunity to teach me these important, life-altering lessons.

"He who conceals his sins does not prosper, but whoever confesses and renounces them finds mercy." (Proverbs 28:13)

"Then I acknowledged my sin to you and did not cover up my iniquity. I said, 'I will confess my transgressions to the LORD'—and you forgave the guilt of my sin." (Psalm 32:5)

In His Image

"So God created man in his own image, in the image of God he created him; male and female he created them." (Genesis 1:27)

Our daughter and son-in-law love to capture life's moments through the lens of a camera, so I wasn't surprised when they began to purchase professional photography equipment, turning their hobby into a part-time business. They have a gift for taking amazing pictures and an exceptional way of capturing the image of God through each of their subjects, whether it be man, creature, or nature.

From the very beginning, they recognized their talent was a gift from God and understood the importance of using it for God's Kingdom. Heather and David gave their venture a truly fitting name—*His Image Photography*.

I love their mission statement: *We believe that every human being is created in the image of God, and that each person is a beautifully unique reflection of Him. We use photography to capture this matchless beauty, to share and remember life's greatest moments that have been given to us by Him.*

You and I have been created in the image of God, but sin leaves its dirty residue on our hearts, marring our ability to reflect God's image as He originally intended. When Jesus went to the cross, He paid the penalty for our sins, but we must still go through the refining process before Christ's image becomes visible to those around us.

"For God's vision to be impressed on our hearts, we must sit in stillness at His feet for quite a long time." *~Streams in the Desert*

God's ultimate purpose for each and every one of us is that we would reflect the image of our Creator. The more time we spend in God's presence, the more we begin to resemble our Creator and reflect His image.

"Our hearts are like a photographer's film—the longer exposed, the deeper the impression. *~Streams in the Desert*

"And we, who with unveiled faces all reflect the Lord's glory, are being transformed into his likeness with ever-increasing glory, which comes from the Lord, who is the Spirit." (2 Corinthians 3:18)

"Now we see but a poor reflection as in a mirror; then we shall see face to face. Now I know in part; then I shall know fully, even as I am fully known." (1 Corinthians 13:12)

How well are you reflecting God's image?

Like images from a camera, *the longer exposed the deeper the impression.*

Don't Get Too Comfortable

If there is one thing I have learned as a Christian, it's that my comfort days are over. Just when I begin settling into a season of life or an area of ministry, God picks me up and plunks me down into something new and unfamiliar. Since I'm a creature of habit who thrives on routine, this constant shaking-up can be a bit unsettling. Although change is disconcerting, it has helped me grow a lot as a Christian.

> Sometimes we can settle into a spiritual comfort zone, unaware that our spiritual health may be slowly but surely deteriorating. But trying new spiritual activities can help our spirits remain whole and strong and keep us in touch with God's will. When we move beyond our comfort zone, we grow. ~ *Upper Room*

Over the years I've learned to trust God more. As a result, I continually learn new things about myself.

Although I am quiet by nature, I can now go into a group of strangers and strike up a conversation without a lot of anxiety.

I've always thought of myself as a follower, and yet God continually places me in positions of leadership.

I've always enjoyed reading and learning, but now I have opportunities to write and teach.

If I had rejected God's invitation to step out of my comfort zone each time things grew uncomfortable, I would have missed out on some pretty amazing experiences and wouldn't be doing many of the things I do today.

"In a desert land he found him, in a barren and howling waste. He shielded him and cared for him; he guarded him as the apple of his eye, like an eagle that stirs up its nest and hovers over its young, that spreads its wings to catch them and carries them on its pinions." (Deuteronomy 32:10-11)

Like a baby eagle that is learning to fly, sometimes we just need a little push to get out of the nest. "Even youths grow tired and weary, and young men stumble and fall; but those who hope in the LORD will renew their strength. They will soar on wings like eagles; they will run and not grow weary, they will walk and not be faint." (Isaiah 40:30-31)

Embrace the challenges God brings your way. Be bold for Christ and never fear—*God is there to catch you if you fall.*

No Pain – No Gain

I go through spurts of being physically active, but after a while, I usually give up on the whole exercise thing. There are always plenty of excuses to keep me from engaging in physical activity, but more often than not, I give up on exercise because of pain or discomfort.

Whether I have sore muscles, a pulled tendon, or a plantar fasciitis flare up, as soon as pain enters the picture, I grow discouraged and give up. I want to be physically fit, but I am unwilling to do the work it takes to achieve the desired result.

When it comes to one's spiritual health, it's easy to adopt a similar attitude. We start out really motivated in our pursuit of God, but then something happens and we drift away from where we need to be.

And what is the reason for this change? Pain or discomfort gets in the way. Perhaps a schedule change makes it more difficult to spend time with God. Sometimes the only way to get devotion time in is to get up forty-five minutes earlier in the morning. It's easy to be committed those first few mornings, but exhaustion quickly sets in, and the snooze button gets hit again and again. Eventually, morning devotions stop altogether. Promises to do it later in the day are proffered but "later" comes and goes with none of the promises fulfilled.

Can you relate?

Although I used to be this way, I now go to great lengths to protect my morning time with the Lord. Spending time with God is like receiving daily bread. I can't live without it!

"I have not departed from the commands of his lips; I have treasured the words of his mouth more than my daily bread." (Job 23:12)

I admit that it has taken me some time to get to the place of spending every morning with God. When I first tried to implement a time of devotions, I allowed little things to get in the way and made excuses. But now I will even get up at 4:00 a.m. to pray and read my Bible before I do anything else. It's that important to me.

How did I get here?

Probably the same way a person makes exercise part of their daily routine—I pushed through the pain. Over time, I began seeing results. I noticed a difference in my attitude and had more patience, peace, and joy in my life. Not only did I notice a difference, but my others noticed a difference in me too. Bottom line—I saw results when I made my spiritual health a priority.

What about you? Would you like to be more spiritually fit? Make time alone with God a priority in your life. Push through the discomfort, discouragement, and exhaustion and you too will see great results. You know what they say…. *no pain—no gain!*

"As the deer pants for streams of water, so my soul pants for you, O God. My soul thirsts for God, for the living God. When can I go and meet with God?" (Psalm 42:1-2)

Now, if I can just apply this same principle to my physical health, I'll be doing great!

Of Great Worth

My husband and I love to watch the *Antique Roadshow*—a television program where guests are invited to bring their antiques to have them appraised by experts who determine their value. The show is interesting because you never know what treasures will be discovered during each episode.

Sometimes a guest has no idea what their item is—let alone its worth. It's intriguing to watch a person's reaction once they realize the value of their possession. Interestingly enough, some items are highly valued not because of what they are or what they can do, but because they were created by a specific designer.

During one episode in particular, an odd looking vase was brought in for evaluation. The expert began sharing factual information about the item, when it was made, what it was intended for, etc. At the end of his assessment, the appraiser revealed the identity of the one who designed the vase—*Tiffany*. That little piece of information helped to explain what came next—the vase's value. I gasped to learn that the urn was worth tens of thousands of dollars!

> For you created my inmost being; you knit
> me together in my mother's womb. I praise
> you because I am fearfully and

wonderfully made; your works are wonderful, I know that full well. My frame was not hidden from you when I was made in the secret place. When I was woven together in the depths of the earth, your eyes saw my unformed body. All the days ordained for me were written in your book before one of them came to be. (Psalm 139:13-16)

You and I are highly valued indeed, but our worth does not come from how we look or what we can do. Our value comes from the One who made us.

"And the LORD has declared this day that you are his people, his treasured possession as he promised, and that you are to keep all his commands." (Deuteronomy 26:18)

Like hidden treasure brought to the *Antique Roadshow*, once we realize that our great worth comes from our Designer, we will have a better appreciation of our true value in this world.

Chipping Away

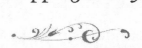

Before Jesus started His public ministry, He was a carpenter. Since most structures in biblical times were hewn from rock, many scholars believe our Lord's carpentry skills included stone masonry.

While our home was being built several years ago, I watched a stonemason working diligently on what was to become the front of our house. The stonemason separated each rock, piece by piece, and evaluated each stone's potential in the formation of our home. If a stone wasn't quite right, he took his tools and carefully chipped away, bit by bit, until the fragment remaining was the perfect size and shape for the predetermined space. The broken pieces were not discarded; but rather they were incorporated elsewhere in the design of our home.

Like the stonemason, God carefully chips away at our lives, smoothing and shaping us for His plan and purpose. Sometimes, in the sculpting process, sections of our lives must be broken away in order for us to be used according to God's design. Yet, like the broken fragments in the building of our home, these severed portions are never wasted. God incorporates them elsewhere in His majestic formation.

"The carpenter measures with a line and makes an outline with a marker; he roughs it out with chisels and marks it with compasses. He shapes it in the form of man, of man in all his glory, that it may dwell in a shrine." (Isaiah 44:13)

"'For my thoughts are not your thoughts, neither are your ways my ways,' declares the LORD. 'As the heavens are higher than the earth, so are my ways higher than your ways and my thoughts than your thoughts.'" (Isaiah 55:8-9)

We may not fully understand God's plan right now, but one day it will be clear. Until then, we must continually surrender our lives into the hands of the skilled Artisan. He knows His craft extremely well.

Let the broken pieces fall where they may. God's masterpiece will soon be realized. Only then will we finally understand how each intricate piece has played an important part in God's magnificent design.

"As you come to him, the living Stone—rejected by men but chosen by God and precious to him—you also, like living stones, are being built into a spiritual house to be a holy priesthood, offering spiritual sacrifices acceptable to God through Jesus Christ." (1 Peter 2:4-5)

As God chips away at the jagged fragments, may we continually surrender our lives to the Master's vision and design.

Getting Through to God

"If a man cannot get through to God it is because there is a secret thing he does not intend to give up." ~Oswald Chambers

When I first surrendered my life to Christ, I was on fire for God. I was at church every time the doors opened and was in no less than two Bible studies at any given time. I had a voracious hunger for learning and a hearty passion to serve.

After some time, however, I came to a place in my faith journey where I seemed to hit a plateau. It felt as though I had stopped growing. I wanted more from my relationship with God, but for some reason, I couldn't get there. I didn't understand what had happened. It felt like God had distanced Himself from me.

The truth was that I had distanced myself from God. My eating disorder secret was creating a barrier between me and my Lord, and it became very clear—I needed to come clean. I couldn't go deeper in my relationship with God until I dealt with my sin-filled stronghold. God is holy—He cannot tolerate sin.

"'Do not come any closer,' God said. 'Take off your sandals, for the place where you are standing is holy ground.'" (Exodus 3:5)

Deliberate sin becomes a wedge that keeps us from drawing as close to our Heavenly Father as He would like. Only through the precious blood of Jesus can we come before God unblemished, but in order to receive the forgiveness that Jesus offers, we must first acknowledge our sin and repent. When we have unrepentant sin, sin that we knowingly continue to commit without regard for God and others, it creates a barrier in our relationship with God.

"Then I acknowledged my sin to you and did not cover up my iniquity. I said, 'I will confess my transgressions to the LORD'—and you forgave the guilt of my sin." (Psalm 32:5)

Once I acknowledged to God and others that my eating disorder was in fact sin, my faith journey began to soar. I was able to experience deep, spiritual intimacy that satisfied the longing in my heart.

Are you struggling to grow closer to God?

Perhaps a prayerful inventory of your life will reveal some areas needing change or redirection. As He does with me, God will help you identify the areas of your life that need attention. Through the process of sanctification, God will help clear the path towards a closer walk with Him.

"If we confess our sins, he is faithful and just and will forgive us our sins and purify us from all unrighteousness." (1 John 1:9)

Marco – Polo

In the game Marco—Polo, the seeker is at a definite disadvantage because he cannot see where he is going. Blindfolded, his only sense of direction comes from carefully listening to the voices of those around him.

In our faith journey with God, we may not know the way to go, but we can call out to the Lord and listen for His voice and direction.

> Before they call I will answer; while they are still speaking I will hear. (Psalm 65:24)

> Call to me and I will answer you and tell you great and unsearchable things you do not know. (Jeremiah 33:3)

> But if from there you seek the LORD your God, you will find him if you look for him with all your heart and with all your soul. (Deuteronomy 4:29)

> For everyone who asks receives; he who seeks finds; and to him who knocks, the door will be opened. (Matthew 7:8)

I was going through something very difficult and needed clear and specific direction from God. A friend that I cared about was about to engage in something that was ethically and morally wrong. Since I was unsure of the manner in which I should approach the situation, I did the only thing I knew to do. I cried out to God in prayer. Thankfully, He heard my plea for help and wasted no time in directing me through His Word. "Send forth your light and your truth, let them guide me; let them bring me to your holy mountain, to the place where you dwell." (Psalm43:3)

Sometimes God whispers His directions, and sometimes He shouts them. This time God shouted His direction! His voice was unmistakable. I love how God is faithful and eager to reveal Himself to us.

In this particular case, God was asking me to take a tough stand and speak truth to my friend about the situation. I have to tell you, I really didn't want to say anything because I knew there was a very real risk that I would lose the friendship altogether.

God doesn't promise a challenge free life, but He does promise to be by our side each time we step out and face life's challenges—especially when we are obedient to what He has called us to do. "I have told you these things, so that in me you may have peace. In this world you will have trouble. But take heart! I have overcome the world." (John 16:33) "For our light and momentary troubles are achieving for us an eternal glory that far outweighs them all. So we fix our eyes not on what is seen, but on what is unseen. For what is seen is temporary, but what is unseen is eternal." (2 Corinthians 4:17-18)

I took the tough stand with my friend, and although our friendship suffered for a time, in the end, God redeemed the relationship and taught us both valuable lessons through the experience.

God brings peace when we seek His guidance and trust His higher ways.

Streak Free

"Cleanse me with hyssop, and I will be clean; wash me, and I will be whiter than snow." (Psalm 51:7)

Cleaning the outside windows of our home is quite a chore, especially since the front glass panes extend to the second story. The only way to reach these mammoth windows is with a special pole that extends like a telescope. Twice a year, my husband and I wash, scrub, rinse, and wipe dry our colossal panels to remove the dirty residue that's built up over time.

To ensure the glass is thoroughly clean, we walk into the house and examine the windows from a different perspective. Once we are confident the job is complete, we put away our cleaning tools and admire our crystal clear view.

The windows might appear flawless at first glance, but the next morning reveals a different story. As the bright morning sun pours through the clear glass panes, streaks and spots that were once invisible to the naked eye make their presence known. Strangely, we couldn't perceive these imperfections until they were highlighted against the backdrop of the sun.

As Christians, we can talk the talk and walk the walk, but God's light will eventually illuminate our flaws.

"...let us draw near to God with a sincere heart in full assurance of faith, having our hearts sprinkled to cleanse us from a guilty conscience and having our bodies washed with pure water." (Hebrews 10:22)

Deep-rooted sin is more visible against the backdrop of the One True Light—Jesus Christ. We must continually allow God's Son to illuminate our flaws, so we can become pure and holy children of God.

Here on earth, there will always be flaws on the transparent window of our lives, but when we reach our eternal home in heaven, we will truly enjoy a spot-free, unobstructed view.

Until then, *God still has some cleaning to do.*

Restless Nights

"Come to me, all you who are weary and burdened, and I will give you rest." (Matthew 11:28)

Sometimes, when I wake up in the morning, I'm more tired than when I went to sleep the night before. This especially happens when I wake up in the middle of the night and can't stop my mind long enough to relax and fall back to sleep. I often lie awake for hours, tossing and turning.

God designed our bodies to rest, so when we aren't getting enough sleep, it shows up in our temperament the next day. We become grumpy, emotional, and unfocused. That's not good.

I've tried many different relaxation methods when sleep eludes me, but so far, the only thing I've found to help me fall back to sleep is to say my prayers. I used to feel bad for engaging in prayer to help me sleep because I often drift off mid-sentence, leaving God hanging. *Surely God wouldn't approve of this tactic for falling asleep.*

Then a friend shared that she does the same thing, only she doesn't feel bad about it. As she puts it, what better way to fall asleep than in the arms of Jesus?

She is absolutely right. It's not as if those restless nights are my only prayer time. As a matter of fact, I pray several times a day. This is just another prayer time that comes with an added benefit—sleep!

This method works because we feel God's presence with us in the dark. God's presence brings peace. Our minds are focused on Him and not everything else going on in our lives.

"The LORD replied, 'My Presence will go with you, and I will give you rest.'" (Exodus 33:14)

"Peace I leave with you; my peace I give you." (John 14:27)

The next time you have a restless night, give it a try. Snuggle up with God, start praying, and fall asleep in the arms of Jesus.

Fighting Squirrels

"If you keep on biting and devouring each other, watch out or you will be destroyed by each other." (Galatians 5:15)

O ur home is nestled in the woods among towering trees. Because of the slope in our backyard, the deck is practically eye level with many of our tree tops. It is not unusual to see squirrels scampering up and down the trees, skipping from one branch to another.

One particular afternoon, while sitting on the back deck, I watched two squirrels playing a game of chase. What appeared to be fun and games quickly turned ugly. The rodents began a rowdy scuffle, apparently fighting for the territory rights of a particular tree.

As the chase ensued, they bounded from one tree limb to the next until the fight commenced on the edge of a branch no thicker than my thumb. With shrieks and squeals, the two wrestled high above the wooded floor. All at once, the branch gave way, sending both varmints plummeting towards the ground sixty feet below. I watched in horror, certain that the squirrels had met their demise.

Sometimes, in life, we can find ourselves in a similar predicament. Relationships that were once thriving and strong grow cold and distant over time. Miscommunication and misunderstanding are often the offenders behind conflict and heartache.

"What causes fights and quarrels among you? Don't they come from your desires that battle within you? You want something but don't get it." (James 4:1-2)

God provides instructions for settling conflict in our lives, and it always involves face-to-face communication.

"If your brother sins against you, go and show him his fault, just between the two of you." (Matthew 18:15a)

Sadly, in this technological age, many choose less confrontational methods for resolving conflict, such as sending an email or text message. These superficial forms of communication can be a problem when they are interpreted by the reader in ways the writer never intended. As a result, the reader's misinterpretation often causes more damage than good.

> Likewise the tongue is a small part of the body, but it makes great boasts. Consider what a great forest is set on fire by a small spark. The tongue also is a fire, a world of evil among the parts of the body. It corrupts the whole person, sets the whole course of his life on fire, and is itself set on fire by hell. (James 3:5-6)

We need to settle matters in a God honoring manner. We must learn to share what's on our mind in a truthful, loving way—face-to-face and heart-to-heart.

"[Paul and Barnabas] had such a sharp disagreement that they parted company. Barnabas took Mark and sailed for Cyprus, but Paul chose Silas and left, commended by the believers to the grace of the Lord." (Acts 15:39-40)

Like it was with Paul and Barnabas, the end result may be a parting of ways, but don't assume this is God's will every time. God's specialty is restoration. He can work miracles through individuals who are truly committed to honoring Him in all they do.

"Bear with each other and forgive whatever grievances you may have against one another. Forgive as the Lord forgave you." (Colossians 3:13)

Perhaps you're wondering what happened to the fighting squirrels in my back yard. At first, they lay still on the ground and didn't move a muscle. I assumed they were dead. But after several moments, the squirrels jumped up and took off running as if nothing had ever happened.

Maybe there's hope for our conflicts yet.

Are You Listening?

"I will instruct you and teach you in the way you should go; I will counsel you and watch over you." (Psalm 32:8)

Most of the time God speaks to us through His Word, but there are times when He takes a more intimate approach and speaks in unique and personal ways known only to us. God knows us so well. He knows exactly how to get our attention.

"God's voice thunders in marvelous ways; he does great things beyond our understanding." (Job 37:5)

Several years ago, our son finally entered the public school system after being home schooled for many years. Entering high school can be a scary enterprise for anyone, but for someone who hadn't been to traditional school since first grade, it was an even more daunting prospect.

During registration week, the students have an opportunity to get their books, practice their locker combinations, and locate their classrooms before the first day of school. This particular year, however, the school was undergoing construction. For safety reasons, no student was permitted to explore the building prior to the first day of school. Talk about a stressful situation. The thought that our youngest was heading into an unfamiliar environment and I couldn't be there to help him navigate through it brought me to the verge of tears.

As we stood in line to get his schedule and pay for his books, I don't remember praying, but God evidently heard the unspoken prayer in my heart and was compassionate to my plight. When we received my son's class schedule, his locker combination was typed in the top right hand corner of the page... 27-37-47 (777). God's perfect number.

As I stared at the numbers on the schedule, God spoke to my heart and reassured me. *Rae Lynn, you have diligently watched over your son for the last 14 years.... I'm taking it from here. Don't worry. I will be with him, walking by his side every step of the way. He will be just fine.*

"The voice of the LORD is powerful; the voice of the LORD is majestic." (Psalm 29:4)

I felt a rush of God's peace and confidence, knowing full well that God would follow through with His promise. God spoke in a manner which He knew would get my attention. It was undeniably Him.

God is speaking. The question is... *are we listening?*

"Speak, LORD, for your servant is listening." (1 Samuel 3:9)

Hedge of Protection

"But let all who take refuge in you be glad; let them ever sing for joy. Spread your protection over them, that those who love your name may rejoice in you." (Psalm 5:11)

Right after I graduated from high school, I landed a job working the early shift at a daycare center near my home. Early one morning, I was heading to work in my newly purchased car—a 1979 MG Midget Convertible. It was a sporty and fun two-seater—perfect for a girl of nineteen. My job was only ten minutes from our house, but as soon as I began driving, the cool temperatures outside caused my windows to fog over. I reached for the dash to find the defrost control, but because the car was still new to me, I had trouble finding the correct knob. Instead of pulling off the road to assess the situation, I continued driving—a big mistake!

I only took my eyes off the road for a brief second, but that was all it took. A sharp bend in the road caused my tires to veer off the side of the road. As I jerked my steering wheel to regain control, I overcompensated, sending my car into an out of control spin. Before I knew what was happening, the vehicle started flipping.

After what seemed like forever, the car finally grew still. I was conscious but in shock. Don't ask me how this happened, but my little convertible was upside down, while I was right side up. This was before the era of mandatory seatbelts. As reality set in, the first thing I noticed was my radio blaring out a song by the Pointer Sisters—*"I'm So Excited"*. How ironic!

Recognizing my need to get out of the car, I tried to open the door, but it was jammed. Unfortunately, I had seen too many movies where cars blew up after a crash, so I did the only thing I knew to do—scream!

Hearing my cries, a man asked if I was okay and assured me that help was on the way. After a few moments, I noticed that the soft top of my convertible was torn so I wriggled my way towards the opening and found an escape route.

Free from the wreckage, the nice man helped me over to his vehicle. As we sat waiting for the ambulance, I felt a throbbing sensation in my left arm. Looking down, I was shocked to find my limb hanging at an unnatural angle. It was definitely broken.

Later the EMT affirmed, "Honey, God must have been holding you by the seat of your pants. You're very lucky to be alive."

I was taken to the hospital, but other than a broken arm and a few cuts and bruises, I was no worse for wear. My car was totaled—but I was not.

The man who witnessed the accident later told me that when he saw my car roll, he thought there was no way anyone could have lived through it. Then, when he heard me screaming, he prepared himself for a bloody mess. He said the next thing he knew, I had emerged from the mangled car with barely a scratch on me. His assessment: "Someone was definitely looking out for you."

Someone was looking out for me—God. His angels surrounded me and kept me safe. God placed a hedge of protection around my body, and as a result, I was not seriously hurt. For whatever reason, God decided it was not my time to go. And for that, I am very grateful.

"For he will command his angels concerning you to guard you in all your ways; they will lift you up in their hands, so that you will not strike your foot against a stone." (Psalm 91:11-12)

"You are my hiding place; you will protect me from trouble and surround me with songs of deliverance." (Psalm 32:7)

Miracles still happen—*I'm living proof!*

Wiped Clean

"Then I acknowledged my sin to you and did not cover up my iniquity. I said, "I will confess my transgressions to the LORD"—and you forgave the guilt of my sin." (Psalm 32:5)

"Blessed is he whose transgressions are forgiven, whose sins are covered." (Psalm 32:1)

It was time to have our carpets cleaned. Initially, I decided we would clean only the first and second floors, since that is where most of the traffic occurs, but once the cleaning representative was on the scene, he convinced me to have our downstairs carpets cleaned, as well. Adding the basement wasn't going to cost much more, so I decided it was a good idea.

After the carpets were sanitized, they looked and smelled great, but after a couple of weeks, my husband noticed some bluish stains beginning to surface on the basement carpet. Since we rarely use that room, we were a little perplexed as to how the stains got there.

I called the cleaning company right away and explained the situation. They informed me that sometimes the flooring people write on the backing of the carpet so they know where the carpet is to be installed. She explained that if the carpet had never been cleaned (which it hadn't) it was possible that the marker had risen to the surface when the rug began to dry. She offered to send out a technician to determine what could be done.

When he arrived, the tech sprayed a clear liquid on the surface of the carpet and then blotted the area with a white towel. Like magic, the stains disappeared.

"Wash away all my iniquity and cleanse me from my sin." (Psalm 51:2)

This situation reminded me that when we receive Jesus as our Lord and Savior, our sins are wiped clean by the blood of Christ. Our transgressions are forgiven, but we still have a sinful nature. Sin continues to surface in our lives.

On this side of heaven, we can never be completely sinless. Just like the stains on my basement carpet, when we confess our transgressions to Jesus, He wipes our sin stains clean.

"I, even I, am he who blots out your transgressions, for my own sake, and remembers your sins no more." (Isaiah 43:25)

"...let us draw near to God with a sincere heart in full assurance of faith, having our hearts sprinkled to cleanse us from a guilty conscience and having our bodies washed with pure water." (Hebrews 10:22)

The Secret Places

"Listen to my prayer, O God, do not ignore my plea; hear me and answer me. My thoughts trouble me and I am distraught at the voice of the enemy..." (Psalm 55:1-3)

"God is the only one who can tend to the secret places where pain calls to bondage." ~Beth Moore

There is a place in each of our souls where no human can possibly go. And yet, this is the one place we must allow God to enter so He can minister to our deepest needs.

"God is the only one who is never intimidated by the depth and length of our needs." ~Beth Moore

I was having one of those days where I was feeling extremely discouraged. I had shared my dejected heart with my sister and a few close friends, and although they offered some wonderful encouragement and helped me see to things from a better perspective, it wasn't until I allowed God all the way into my heart that my spirit truly begin to lift.

Later that evening, I had a good long cry. Sometimes a girl just needs to do that. Then I prayed, read some Scriptures, and went to bed. I didn't sleep very well, but the next morning God spoke the words that I needed to hear through the following devotion:

"Never fear the fierce storms that even now may be blowing through your life. Storms bring blessings, and rich fruit will be harvested later." ~*Streams in the Desert*

I cried again, but this time they were tears of joy. God hadn't forgotten me after all. All at once my spirit was lifted, and I felt a wash of God's love.

"....Call upon me in the day of trouble; I will deliver you, and you will honor me..." (Psalm 50:15)

Very Last Nerve

Several years ago, we had a robin terrorizing our home every morning. At the first sign of daylight, the bird threw himself into our window...*smack*... *smack*... *smack!* This became our wakeup call every morning at 6:00 am. I began to wonder if the bird was possessed or something. Either that or the collisions into our windowpane had caused the poor fowl to develop some brain damage. One thing was for sure; the crazy bird was getting on my very last nerve!

My husband and I grew extremely annoyed and tried everything we could to get the aggressor to stop his maddening assault. We pounded on the window pane, trying to scare it away, but it was only a temporary fix. We even tried putting a rubber snake on the windowsill outside, but the bird wasn't the least bit intimidated. Like clockwork, the relentless flying creature continued his attack on our home.

We eventually grew so crazy with frustration that one morning, before the sun came up, my husband hid in our kid's playhouse to see if he could catch the winged demon in action. Armed with our son's BB gun, my husband waited and waited, oblivious to the questioning neighbors peering out their windows at him. After a full two hours—you guessed it—the bird never showed.

Later that same day, I was in my bedroom changing clothes and noticed the beady-eyed little villain staring at me through the glass. I screamed and shut the blinds. How could one little bird wreak so much havoc!

Things aren't always as they seem. After reading an article in a magazine, I learned that robins are territorial birds. Apparently, our little pest was guarding his domain. He must have seen his own reflection in our window pane and thought the image was another bird. The bird wasn't possessed at all; he was just doing what his instincts told him to.

"The fear of the LORD is the beginning of wisdom; all who follow his precepts have good understanding." (Psalm 111:10a)

We often misinterpret the actions of others when it comes to things that greatly annoy or frustrate us. Convinced that the person is purposely trying to irritate us, we fail to see that in reality they are simply responding in ways that come most naturally to them. These 'instincts' are often learned behaviors that develop over many years and become gut reactions that are provoked by negative emotions. Like that little bird, the person is probably clueless that their behavior is bothersome to others.

"But it is the spirit in a man, the breath of the Almighty, that gives him understanding." (Job 32:8)

Is there someone who is getting on your very last nerve? Perhaps you should share your distress. Open communication just might lead to better understanding. Who knows, a little thoughtful consideration coming from each side just might lead to changed hearts for everyone.

"My heart is changed within me; all my compassion is aroused." (Hosea 11:8e)

What happened to our little winged assailant? The bird continued its assault until fall. Then we finally had some peace and quiet... at least for a little while. The following spring the robin was back!

Picture Perfect

"Then the trees of the forest will sing, they will sing for joy before the LORD..." (1 Chronicles 16:33)

One summer afternoon, a dear friend invited me to her home for a visit. Because this friend has the gift of hospitality and a unique way of making others feel extra special, I was excited about spending the day with her.

Her two-story house was nestled in the woods and situated on a secluded two acre lot. When I got out of my vehicle, I could hear enchanting classical music in the distance. My friend greeted me with a hug and immediately ushered me to her lovely garden.

Words cannot adequately describe the beauty and serenity surrounding her home. With more plants and flowers than you could imagine, the landscape beds were decorated with tasteful ornaments, bird baths, stepping stones, and water features. The in-ground pool and water fountain completed the picture-perfect outdoor haven. It was too much to take in. Absolutely gorgeous.

The clear sunny day with seventy degree temperatures provided a perfect backdrop for lunch by the pool. When I asked my friend about the beautiful music playing in the background, she told me it was a CD from a band called the Secret Garden. *How fitting, I thought to myself.*

"My heart is steadfast, O God; I will sing and make music with all my soul." (Psalm 108:1)

I enjoyed the afternoon so much that it felt as though I were experiencing a little piece of heaven. Every one of my senses was awakened that day. My eyes feasted upon the rich mosaic of vibrant colors, while my nose drew in the fragrant aromas of the plants and flowers. The melodious tunes floating in the air calmed my spirit, while the sun warmed my body. When my friend served lunch, even my taste buds were overjoyed.

"… you will fill me with joy in your presence, with eternal pleasures at your right hand." (Psalm 16:11)

Moments such as these cause me to long for heaven. Although this afternoon with my friend was spectacular by mortal standards, it does not compare with what we will experience in paradise. According to Scripture we cannot image the splendor awaiting us. Although my friend's beautiful garden certainly whets my appetite for what is to come. "No eye has seen, no ear has heard, no mind has conceived what God has prepared for those who love him." (1 Corinthians 2:9)

Thank you Lord for delightful days, treasured friends, and special memories that keep us yearning for eternity with You.

Breaking Free

While I was growing up, our family had many pets. We had the usual companions: dogs, cats, hamsters, and fish. But we also had a few less traditional animals: a turtle, bunny, squirrel, and raccoon.

As far back as I can remember, my dad was a hunter. The sport took him all over, even to Africa a couple of times. Most of his excursions, however, involved hunting for wild game on our farm in Indiana.

Every once in a while, my dad found orphaned baby creatures on his hunting expeditions. I didn't question why the critters were parentless. I suppose naivety has its benefits. Since Dad didn't want to leave the helpless orphans in the woods without their mother, he brought them home and cared for them until they were old enough to return to the wild.

One such animal was a raccoon that we appropriately named Rascal. The domesticated rodent became our family pet and drew lots of attention from curious neighbors. Rascal grew to be quite large—more than thirty pounds. It was amusing to see people's reactions to seeing a raccoon on the end of a leash walking through the subdivision.

Rascal seemed to enjoy his stay with us at first, but he eventually grew restless. A recurring screech from his barred enclosure indicated that he yearned for freedom. During one of his routine feedings, Rascal jumped out of his cage and scampered off into the woods. I never saw him again.

Raccoons are meant to be free and so are we.

Jesus said, "I have come that they may have life, and have it to the full." (John 10:10b)

Jesus died on the cross to give us abundant new life and freedom, yet many of us remain ensnared like prisoners, trapped inside sin and circumstance.

"So if the Son sets you free, you will be free indeed." (John 8:36)

"It is for freedom that Christ has set us free. Stand firm, then, and do not let yourselves be burdened again by a yoke of slavery." (Galatians 5:1)

Jesus has set us free. Perhaps it's time to start living like it.

Daddy's Home

Since our children are five years apart, our daughter had a fair amount of time as an only child before Ben came along. Heather was the apple of our eye and daddy's little girl. Every night when Gerry came home from work, Heather ran to greet him, squealing with delight. Daddy was finally home! Gerry would reach down, scoop up his little girl into his arms, and dance around the living room singing their special song, "Daddy's Home" by Cliff Richards.

For years, our sweet little girl thought this song was just for her—that daddy made it up. Imagine her surprise when she heard the song playing on the radio many years later.

"Daddy" she scolded "I thought that was our special song!"

It was.

Imagine Daddy's surprise when many years later Heather had this song playing during their father/daughter dance at her wedding. I stood on the side of the dance floor bawling my eyes out, picturing the two of them twirling around our living room those many years ago.

Where did the time go? "What is your life? You are a mist that appears for a little while and then vanishes." (James 4:14b)

My heart aches when I think of how quickly those precious years flew by. I remember being anxious to see our children reach new milestones in life, but now I realize, looking back, it would have been better for me to slow down and thoughtfully live out each moment.

The Bible tells us that our days are all numbered. Time, once it has passed, is something we can never get back. For this reason, we need to make the most of each and every day and hour, savoring each moment we have left.

It is said that with age comes wisdom. As I rapidly approach the years that bring understanding, allow me to share some advice that I've gleaned over the years.

Don't wish your life away. And don't place so much focus on tomorrow that you forget to enjoy today.

"...encourage one another daily, as long as it is called today..." (Hebrews 3:13a)

Deliver Me from Temptation

"No temptation has seized you except what is common to man. And God is faithful; he will not let you be tempted beyond what you can bear. But when you are tempted, he will also provide a way out so that you can stand up under it." (1 Corinthians 10:13)

When I was a little girl, I had a major sweet tooth. Combine my weakness for sweets with the stockpiles of candy in my grandparent's home, and the stage was set for my fall into temptation.

While mom was busy visiting with my grandparents in another room, I seized the opportunity to restock my candy supply, stuffing handfuls of sugary treats into my purse.

I thought I was being sneaky, but in all likelihood, my grandmother noticed the significant gouge to her candy supply after each one of my visits. She never said anything, but then again, she didn't have to. I felt horribly guilty afterwards. Remorse gnawed away at my innards like a vulture feasting on road kill. I had to eat the candy in secret because if anyone saw me, they would surely ask where it came from.

Oh what a tangled web we weave when first we practice to deceive.

Unbeknownst to me at the time, my eating disorder behavior was developing. My actions may have seemed harmless, but in reality, I was stealing food, eating in secret, hiding it from others, and feeling guilty about it—a familiar pattern that followed me later in life.

Children learn to deceive very young. Deceptive kids become deceptive teenagers, and deceptive teenagers become deceptive adults, a ruse that becomes more dangerous and complex with the progression of age.

"'Can anyone hide in secret places so that I cannot see him?' declares the LORD. 'Do not I fill heaven and earth?' declares the LORD." (Jeremiah 23:24)

God taught me that it is always best to be honest and own up to shortcomings. I'm not perfect by any stretch of the imagination, but now I try hard to live according to God's ways. Temptation will always find us because we live in a fallen world. Satan is on the prowl, looking for someone to devour (1 Peter 5:8).

So how can we stay strong and keep from falling during times of temptation?

First, identify your areas of weakness. (Satan already knows them and pursues ways to place you into positions of temptation, so be on guard.) Next, minimize your risks. (If you know it is a dangerous road to travel—don't walk down it.) Finally, continuously tap into God's strength through prayer.

"Submit yourselves, then, to God. Resist the devil, and he will flee from you." (James 4:7)

Temptations will surely come, but we needn't give in to them. The Lord is our strength.

"Therefore, since through God's mercy we have this ministry, we do not lose heart. Rather, we have renounced secret and shameful ways; we do not use deception, nor do we distort the word of God. On the contrary, by setting forth the truth plainly we commend ourselves to every man's conscience in the sight of God." (2 Corinthians 4:1-2)

Know His Voice

Family and friends, with whom we spend a lot of time, become so familiar that even when we can't physically see them, we can identify who they are by their voice.

My husband has a very distinct voice, deep and raspy. As soon as I pick up the phone, I know it's him. On the other hand, if I answer the phone and it's someone I haven't spoken to in a while, I might not recognize them by voice alone. The more familiar we are with someone, the more readily we recognize their voice.

"My sheep listen to my voice; I know them, and they follow me." (John 10:27)

Jesus often paralleled nature with spiritual principles. I don't know about you, but I am able to grasp spiritual concepts more readily when I can draw parallels to everyday things. The Bible often references the parallel of sheep and shepherd to our relationship with God.

"As a shepherd looks after his scattered flock when he is with them, so will I look after my sheep. (Ezekiel 34:12a)

"When Jesus landed and saw a large crowd, he had compassion on them, because they were like sheep without a shepherd." (Mark 6:34)

Sheep know the voice of the shepherd because they spend so much time in his presence. Every day, the shepherd leads his flock and the sheep listen for his voice and direction. He leads them to green pastures, calm streams, and safe places of rest.

There are many voices in this world competing for our attention. It's easy to become so overwhelmed that we struggle to hear God's voice above the clamor.

The Lord is our Shepherd. We must spend time in His presence daily so that we can get to know His voice. Then we can we distinguish the Lord's voice above all the others.

Jesus says, "I am the good shepherd; I know my sheep and my sheep know me...." (John 10:14)

"Listen and hear my voice; pay attention and hear what I say." (Isaiah 28:23)

A Little Elbow Grease

"Now we ask you, brothers, to respect those who work hard among you, who are over you in the Lord and who admonish you." (1 Thessalonians 5:12)

My parents made sure that my siblings and I shared in the household chores. It was a way to instill good work ethic into our character at a young age. Although I didn't understand the value of doing chores back then, I can now see how even small responsibilities taught me to work hard and take pride in a job well done.

Every night, we took turns setting the table for dinner and washing dishes. I'm not sure whether non-stick cooking spray was around back then, but if it was, my mom didn't use it. Pots and pans became so soiled with baked-on food it was like cement. If you happened to be the unlucky one on dish duty, you had major scrubbing to do.

Sometimes (if mom was feeling generous), she would allow us to soak the pot overnight, but most of the time she insisted that we put a little 'elbow grease' into our scrubbing—just one of her many creative expressions Apparently, elbow grease helped you get the job done right. It represented perseverance, resolve, and determination.

Now that I'm an adult, cleaning dirty dishes seems like a welcome chore compared to some of the responsibilities I face. My daily duties may have changed over the years, but the same principles for tackling tough projects apply today.

Is there an overwhelming project that's threatening your resolve? Don't give up. God will provide strength and encouragement when you need it most.

"All hard work brings a profit, but mere talk leads only to poverty." (Proverbs 14:23)

Take one day at a time, do each job to the best of your ability, and when the job gets really tough, *apply a little elbow grease.*

Wind Knocked Out

The wooden staircase leading to the second story of our one hundred year old farmhouse in Indiana was extremely slippery. I learned the hard way why NOT to wear socks when going down the stairs, but sometimes I grew careless and forgot. Not only did it hurt to fall down the stairs, but it knocked my wind out, and I felt like I couldn't breathe.

On more than one occasion, my dad came to my rescue. Seeing the panic in my eyes, he would wrap his arms around me, reassuring me that I was going to be okay. He rubbed my back until I settled down and could breathe easy again. Once he knew I was doing better, he sent me on my way—but not before a gentle reminder to be more careful on the stairs the next time around.

Sometimes life can throw us a curve ball and we feel as though the wind has been knocked out of us. A pink slip from a job, a diagnosis from a doctor, a late night phone call, or a legal notice from a mail carrier are reasons enough to make anyone gasp for breath.

After receiving a hateful email from someone who I thought was a friend, it felt as though I had been punched in the gut. I was beyond hurt. I sat staring at the computer screen in disbelief. Hot tears streamed down my cheeks as I tried to process the words I was reading. I didn't know what to think. I was in complete shock.

Thankfully, God came to my rescue. He pulled me close and gently wrapped His arms around me. I felt His presence so powerfully that day. Even though I was hurting, I felt a sense of peace. Eventually, I settled down and could breathe easy again. The pain was still fresh, but I knew God was with me.

Over the next several days, God reassured me that everything was going to be okay. He encouraged me to get back out there and fight the good fight but not before giving me a gentle reminder to be more careful in the future.

"Though they plot evil against you and devise wicked schemes, they cannot succeed." (Psalm 21:11)

"Be very careful, then, how you live—not as unwise but as wise, making the most of every opportunity, because the days are evil." (Ephesians 5:15-16)

Satan can knock us down, but as long as we cling to our heavenly Father, he can't knock us out. God is strengthening His mighty warriors for battle. He must ensure we are coated with tough armor for what lies ahead.

"To inoculate me from the praise of man, He baptized me in the criticism of man, until I died to the control of man." ~Francis Frangipane

> Finally, be strong in the Lord and in his mighty power. Put on the full armor of God so that you can take your stand against the devil's schemes. For our struggle is not against flesh and blood, but against the rulers, against the authorities, against the powers of this dark world and against the spiritual forces of evil in the heavenly realms. (Ephesians 6:10-12)

Be self-controlled and alert, and recognize your true opponent in battle is Satan—not man.

Lost and Found

It seems that every camping adventure with our good friends involved some kind of excitement. The trip I'm about to describe was no exception.

It was Father's Day weekend, and with temperatures rising, our families decided to spend the afternoon by the pool. Since pets are not permitted in the pool area, our friends had to leave their dog behind, in the tent. When Victor was securely tucked away, we were ready for some fun in the sun.

After a long swim in the cool refreshing water, the adults spent a few minutes lounging by the poolside while the kids continued to swim and play. Sometime later, a park ranger came into the pool area and held up a small black and brown dog, asking if it belonged to anyone.

Someone from our group said, "I think that's Victor."

Victor's owner adamantly replied, "No, no... that's not Victor."

Then someone else chimed in, "I don't know... that really looks like Victor."

Still not convinced, the owner walked over to get a closer look. With wide eyes she looked back at us and gasped, "Oh my goodness... that is Victor!"

The little escape artist broke out of the tent, grew frightened, and began terrorizing the campground. The park ranger was alerted, and after realizing the little dog was lost, he decided to try and reunite the pup with his owners.

Have you ever been lost?

Unlike Victor's owners, our heavenly Father knows the exact whereabouts of each and every one of His children—physically and spiritually. Like the father of the prodigal son, God anxiously awaits our homecoming and rushes to greet us with open arms.

> But while he was still a long way off, his father saw him and was filled with compassion for him; he ran to his son, threw his arms around him and kissed him... the father said to his servants,

"Quick! Bring the best robe and put it on him. Put a ring on his finger and sandals on his feet. Bring the fattened calf and kill it. Let's have a feast and celebrate. For this son of mine was dead and is alive again; he was lost and is found." So they began to celebrate. (Luke 15:20, 22-24)

That park ranger could have decided it was too much of a bother to connect a little dog with his owners. He could have left the job for someone else—but he didn't. He took his responsibility seriously and did what he could.

As Christians, our greatest privilege is to help another find his way to the Father. May we use every opportunity that we're given to help point the lost in the right direction—Jesus.

"Jesus answered, 'I am the way and the truth and the life. No one comes to the Father except through me.'" (John 14:6)

Facebook—Friend or Foe?

In this electronic age, we can know the intimate details of another's life whether they are family, friends or acquaintances on the other side of the world. Social networking sites, such as Facebook, provide ample opportunities for staying connected.

Christians are wise to harness this means of communication to spread the love of Jesus. Social networking sites can be used as a tool to help us accomplish that end, but we should also combine it with personal interaction.

As the Son of God, Jesus didn't actually have to be on the scene to perform a miracle: "The centurion replied, 'Lord, I do not deserve to have you come under my roof. But just say the word, and my servant will be healed....' Then Jesus said to the centurion, 'Go! It will be done just as you believed it would.' And his servant was healed at that very hour." (Matthew 8:8, 13)

Although Jesus didn't have to be on the scene to perform a miracle, most of the time, He healed in person, through physical touch.

"Jesus reached out his hand and touched the man. 'I am willing,' he said. 'Be clean!' Immediately he was cured of his leprosy." (Matthew 8:3)

"But Jesus came and touched them. 'Get up,' he said. 'Don't be afraid.'" (Matthew 17:7)

Expressing kind loving words through Facebook has its benefits, but let's face it—a cyber-hug doesn't always cut it.

One of the most effective ways that we have to express love and compassion is through face-to-face interaction.

"A new command I give you: Love one another. As I have loved you, so you must love one another." (John 13:34)

We all have busy lives, but we can't afford to lose physical interaction with others. There are some things that just can't be conveyed through written words no matter how hard we try. Tools like Facebook are great supplements for witnessing and building relationships, but let us not forget the example of Jesus.

"Filled with compassion, Jesus reached out his hand and touched the man." (Mark 1:41a)

Mankind still needs face to face interaction and physical touch.

Life Isn't Fair

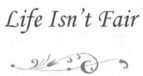

"I have told you these things, so that in me you may have peace. In this world you will have trouble. But take heart! I have overcome the world." (John 16:33)

Have you noticed how some people's lives have heartache after heartache, while others seem practically carefree?

My aunt is a remarkable woman who knows all about the hard knocks of life, yet she is one of the most joyful people I know. Her laugh is contagious, her attitude infectious, and her ability to overcome adversity is beyond comprehension.

Tragically, my aunt lost three of her four children to a genetic brain disease discovered by the age of two. This disorder progressively deteriorated brain function until each of their small bodies fell victim to its attack. One by one, my precious cousins went home to be with the Lord when they were only four years old.

Losing one child is unimaginable—losing three is incomprehensible.

Unfortunately, this would not be my aunt's only loss. My uncle died suddenly from a heart attack after twenty-five years of marriage. He was forty-six years old.

How much loss and suffering can one person take?

My aunt finally remarried, but after eleven years of marriage, her second husband died from esophageal cancer. It was a slow and agonizing death. I asked permission to share my aunt's heart-wrenching story and she responded, "If it can help somebody, then by all means you can share my story."

My aunt recalled that it was only through the strength of God that she was able to get through those tragic seasons of life. God placed loving people along her journey to pick up the pieces and help her carry on.

"The LORD, the LORD, the compassionate and gracious God..." (Exodus 34:6)

Did my aunt come through all of this without scars? Of course not—deep wounds always leave scars. But like any flesh wound, my aunt's scars serve as gentle reminders of God's love and compassion when life just isn't fair.

Like the tempered skin of wounds healed over, the scars of life make us stronger than before.

Built to Last

After a year of apartment living, my husband and I finally purchased our first home. Money was tight back then, so when it came time to buying appliances—we purchased used—not new. We searched newspaper ads until we found a great deal on a washer, dryer, and refrigerator. The washer/dryer set was over ten years old when we purchased them, and the refrigerator was even older than that. They were crazy '70s colors, but we didn't care. We were just happy to have something that worked. Amazingly, these same appliances continued working after fourteen years of marriage. When we finally did replace these relics, the newly purchased appliances began having problems within a few short years.

It seems that things are no longer built to last. Manufacturers are more concerned about making money by getting a product onto the market in record time than putting out a product that lasts.

A similar mentality can be applied to Christianity. Many today do not put forth the time and effort needed to build a strong, lasting relationship with God. As a result, when tragedy or hard times strike, their faith falters.

"But since they have no root, they last only a short time. When trouble or persecution comes because of the word, they quickly fall away." (Mark 4:17)

Is your relationship with God built to last?

Today, we have better technology than ever before, yet consumer products last only a fraction of the time. In the same way, we have more Christian books, movies, stores, churches, and resources than ever before, yet many feel spiritually empty inside.

The problem isn't available resources or know-how. The problem is where we place our priorities.

Make a commitment today to prioritize your relationship with God.

"I long to dwell in your tent forever and take refuge in the shelter of your wings." (Psalm 61:4)

After all... forever is a very long time.

Life Is Short

"Even though I walk through the valley of the shadow of death, I will fear no evil, for you are with me; your rod and your staff, they comfort me." (Psalm 23:4)

Just three days into my seventh grade year, I received some tragic news during morning announcements. One of my closest friends had been diagnosed with leukemia.

Two days prior, my friend mentioned that she had a doctor's appointment after school because she hadn't been feeling well all summer. Her energy level had been so depleted that even walking up the stairs was exhausting. I remember thinking she looked very pale—not at all like the Diane I knew and loved.

For the first time in my life, I suddenly became very aware of my own mortality. I had experienced bereavement before, but this was my friend—someone my own age. I understood just enough about leukemia to realize that it often ended in death. Tragically, my friend lost her battle with the disease less than three years later.

"What man can live and not see death, or save himself from the power of the grave?" (Psalm 89:48)

As we grow older, death becomes a glaring reality. We may feel no different in our spirit than we did twenty years ago, but our bodies speak a different story. Aches, pains, and inevitable weight gain become incessant reminders that we're not as young as we used to be.

We are told that our time on earth is merely a blink of an eye compared to eternity. As I approach the fifty year mark, in all likelihood, my life is more than half over. It's a sobering thought to say the least. So, what am I going to do with the remainder of my days here on earth?

I am going to spend each of my waking moments becoming a vessel that God can pour His love and blessings through. I am going to live each day sharing the message of hope that comes from knowing Jesus Christ, and I am going to be a light in this dark world. *Why?* Because when my time on earth is finished and I gaze into the eyes of Jesus, I want to hear Him say…"Well done, good and faithful servant! You have been faithful with a few things; I will put you in charge of many things. Come and share your master's happiness!" (Matthew 25:21)

Like my friend Diane, we will one day face our own mortality. And when we do, if we have put our hope and faith in Jesus, the end is just the beginning.

Rubik's Cube Life

Have you ever tried to navigate your way through a Rubik's cube? The goal of this brainteaser is to line-up coordinating colors on each side of the block. Back in the '80s this challenging puzzle was all-the-rave. Nearly every child had one, and if you didn't have one, you knew someone who did. The cube was packaged with all the colors properly aligned (proving the puzzle was indeed solvable), but as soon as you began twisting and turning the blocks this way and that, all the colors became jumbled. The challenge of the piece was to realign the cube back to its original form, but as far as I could tell—the task was impossible.

I remember spending hours trying to figure out how to achieve the proper alignment, but no matter how hard I tried, I was only able to solve one side of the puzzle. Whenever I began working on another side, the previously aligned colors got mixed-up again.

Sometimes my life is like that Rubik's cube. Just about the time I get one aspect of my life in order, it seems that other areas suffer from lack of attention. When I spend time working on the ministry, I have less time to devote to housework or family. When organizing our home, my job and family show signs of neglect. I'm even perplexed when it comes to relationships. When I focus on one, another suffers. I just can't seem to keep everything working at the same time.

Can you relate?

"I know, O Lord, that a man's life is not his own; it is not for man to direct his steps." (Jeremiah 10:23)

I recently watched a YouTube video with step by step instructions for how to solve a Rubik's cube. It was fascinating. Ironically, the first step for solving a Rubik's cube is to line-up one of the sides into the formation of a cross.

How interesting.

With the cross in place, solving the rest of the puzzle is just a matter of following an algorithm (sequence of steps) to realign the colors in their proper place.

Keeping our lives in balance requires a similar mentality. Christ must be at the center of all we do, and we must ask God to help us prioritize our steps along the way. God is first... then family, job, and everything else.

"Blessed are those who have learned to acclaim you, who walk in the light of your presence, O Lord." (Psalm 89:15)

Life is a challenge for sure. But as long as we keep the proper algorithm in place, solving life's challenges and maintaining balance is just a few twists and turns away.

"I guide you in the way of wisdom and lead you along straight paths. When you walk, your steps will not be hampered; when you run, you will not stumble." (Proverbs 4:11-12)

A Bonus Gift

Not long ago, a friend of mine had surgery and needed to spend some additional recovery time in a rehabilitation center. I wondered how she was handling being away from her family so long, so I decided on a visit to help lift her spirits.

I considered bringing her a gift. Perhaps a book with a captivating story and positive message would help keep her mind off her troubles.

The smile on my friend's face when I walked into the room warmed my heart. We spent a few minutes chatting about the progress of her recovery. She mentioned that it was hard to be confined to bed, but she was making the best of it.

After some small talk, I handed her the colorful gift bag. Peering inquisitively into the sack, she reached inside and pulled out her gift.

"Thank you so much, Rae Lynn! This will really help pass the time."

Mission accomplished! I was positively beaming to know that she liked her gift.

She then took a second look inside the bag and to my surprise pulled out another item. Oops! (Note to self: If you are going to recycle a bag, make sure the bag is empty.)

My friend offered more thanks, although I must say she looked a bit confused by her little bonus gift. Neatly enclosed in Saran wrap was a chocolaty covered treat about two inches square.

Allow me to explain. The gift bag was taken from a Christmas party that I had attended the day before. Because I was too full to eat my dessert at the actual party, I brought my tasty treat home to save for later. Apparently, I stuck the treat in the gift bag and forgot about it.

I could feel my face turning red with embarrassment but secretly hoped my friend wouldn't notice.

I should have apologized to my friend and explained what had happened, but instead, I tried to pass it off as though the whole thing was intentional. I said something about how institution food can be really awful and thought this would a little something she could enjoy.

As soon as the words left my mouth, I felt a stab of conviction in my heart. I just spoke a bold face lie!

"You know my folly, O God; my guilt is not hidden from you." (Psalm 69:5)

Accidentally leaving something in a gift bag was not a sin; so why did I feel the need to cover it up? In a word— pride. I didn't want my friend to realize the bag had been recycled.

Let me offer a lesson that I'm still in the process of learning myself. It's okay to admit that we are not perfect. It is okay to make mistakes and let others know about it. What's not okay is to make a mistake and then lie about it. Making mistakes doesn't make us weak; it makes us human. The only one who is perfect is God. That's why we desperately need Him each and every day.

"As for God, his way is perfect: The Lord's word is flawless; he shields all who take refuge in him. For who is God besides the Lord? And who is the Rock except our God? It is God who arms me with strength and keeps my way secure." (2 Samuel 22:31-33)

I'm not perfect and never will be—but that's okay. I have a perfect Father, who loves me despite my flaws, and that's good enough for me.

"But he said to me, 'My grace is sufficient for you, for my power is made perfect in weakness.' Therefore I will boast all the more gladly about my weaknesses, so that Christ's power may rest on me. That is why, for Christ's sake, I delight in weaknesses, in insults, in hardships, in persecutions, in difficulties. For when I am weak, then I am strong. (2 Corinthians 12:9-10)

Spirit of Receiving

Perhaps you have heard the saying: It is better to give than receive. I believe a more accurate rendering of that statement would be: *it is easier to give than receive.* God has been working on me in the area of learning how to be a good "receiver". I love to pour myself out to others, but receiving (accepting from others) has always been a struggle for me. When someone does something nice for me, I feel guilty and think to myself: Surely I don't deserve such kindness. When someone gives me a compliment, I smile and say thank you, but in my heart, I don't believe the accolade is true. When someone offers help, I gracefully decline and resolve to do it on my own.

Why is it so hard for me to receive—to accept?

Sometimes this mindset spills over into my spiritual life, too. I go to God in prayer and present my requests, but then I continue charging forward, as if I need to solve each dilemma on my own. I know that God is more than capable of answering my prayers without assistance, so why don't I just accept His help and let go?

Insecurity definitely plays a part in my personal failure to receive. But ultimately, my reluctance can be attributed to a far deeper issue—P-R-I-D-E. That five letter word that's been driving sin and rebellion since the beginning of time.

"Pride brings a person low, but the lowly in spirit gain honor." (Proverbs 29:23)

My husband and I are part of a small group through our church. Once a week, we meet with these Christian friends to study God's Word and fellowship. One evening, our group practiced a humbling exercise aimed at nurturing our spirits to receive. Each person took a turn in the "hot seat" while others went around the room expressing appreciation and love for that person. Wow, what a powerful exercise in receiving. We went through two boxes of tissues by the end of the evening.

"If you, then, though you are evil, know how to give good gifts to your children, how much more will your Father in heaven give good gifts to those who ask him!" (Matthew 7:11)

Since our Heavenly Father loves to give, we need to learn how to receive.

This precept seems like a fairly elementary teaching of Christianity. Yet, after this exercise, each person in our small group recognized that this lesson was one that we hadn't fully (pardon the pun) received.

I learned through this experience that having a spirit of receiving requires humility. It is not based on merit—we don't deserve it. It is not based on success—we can do nothing to earn it. It is a gift, plain and simple, a gift that can only be fully appreciated when we open ourselves up to receive.

"Ask and it will be given to you; seek and you will find; knock and the door will be opened to you. For everyone who asks receives; he who seeks finds; and to him who knocks, the door will be opened." (Matthew 7:7-8)

Unmerited Grace

I was chewing on a tootsie roll when I bit into something crunchy. Cautiously, I worked the hard matter towards the front of my mouth. After peering closely at the object between my fingers, I determined that it was part of my tooth. A quick survey of my mouth revealed that half of one of my molars was gone. Yikes! I immediately contacted my dentist to have the tooth fixed and thankfully (I use that term loosely), an appointment was open the following week.

As I sat down in the chair, my dentist welcomed me with a warm smile. Looking at my chart he said, "Hmmm, it looks like you haven't been to see us in a while, Rae Lynn." (Okay, he was being very nice. It had been two full years since my last visit.)

My fear of the dentist began as a child. Every six month cleaning came with an added bonus—a return trip to get a tooth filled. It seems that I was cursed with soft enamel that gravitated towards decay. Now, as an adult, I avoid going to the dentist like the plague.

"Well, Rae Lynn, while you're here, we should go ahead and do a cleaning and examination to rule out any other potential problems." (That sly dog! He was taking advantage of this opportunity. Who knew when I would be back?)

He cleaned my teeth, thoroughly examined my mouth, and took some x-rays. With fear and trepidation, I sat waiting—certain of my fate. To my surprise (and his) the dentist looked at me and said, "Looks like your chipped tooth is the only one in need of repair."

Cue the orchestra. *Hallelujah! Hallelujah!*

I hadn't been to the dentist in two full years, and I had no other cavities? I got the exact opposite of what I deserved in wake of my obvious dental negligence. I was beyond grateful.

"And if by grace, then it is no longer by works; if it were, grace would no longer be grace." (Romans 11:6)

When you and I accept God's gift of salvation through Jesus Christ, we receive unmerited grace every day of our lives. Sinners that we are, we still get to go to heaven. How awesome is that? We don't deserve it. We can do nothing to earn it. It is a free gift—plain and simple.

Unmerited grace. *Now that's better than a clean dental check up!*

> But because of his great love for us, God, who is rich in mercy, made us alive with Christ even when we were dead in transgressions—it is by grace you have been saved. And God raised us up with Christ and seated us with him in the heavenly realms in Christ Jesus, in order that in the coming ages he might show the incomparable riches of his grace, expressed in his kindness to us in Christ Jesus. (Ephesians 2:4-7)

Outstretched Arm

O n the television program *The Voice*, contestants participate in blind auditions before a panel of judges, who are veterans in the music industry. Since they are unable to see the contestants, the judges must evaluate each performance solely on vocal talent. I appreciate this aspect of the program because the entertainment business is oftentimes prejudiced when it comes to physical appearance. There is a great deal of pressure to look a certain way.

Even before her winning title in 2012, Cassadee Pope's performances were ranking number one on the iTunes's chart. I enjoyed watching the budding star perform because each time she hit a high note, she stretched her arm high above her head as if gathering an extra burst of power from thin air.

In Scripture, God's outstretched arm is often depicted as being the avenue through which His amazing power is unleashed.

> With my great power and <u>outstretched arm</u> I made the earth and its people and the animals that are on it… (Jeremiah 27:5)
> Therefore, say to the Israelites: 'I am the Lord, and I will bring you out from under the yoke of the Egyptians. I will free you from being slaves to them, and I will redeem

you with an <u>outstretched arm</u> and with mighty acts of judgment.' (Exodus 6:6)

Has any god ever tried to take for himself one nation out of another nation… by a mighty hand and an <u>outstretched arm</u>, or by great and awesome deeds, like all the things the Lord your God did for you in Egypt before your very eyes? (Deuteronomy 4:34)

In the Old Testament, God's outstretched arm released several terrible plagues on the Egyptians, revealing the LORD's mighty power over the created world. Each plague was a direct attack against the false Egyptian gods. The LORD needed to establish His authority in the eyes of both the Egyptians and the Israelites because the Hebrew nation had become indoctrinated into the Egyptian culture that worshiped literally thousands of gods.

My favorite display of God's awesome power is found in the New Testament—Christ's outstretched arms on the cross. "For God was pleased to have all his fullness dwell in him, and through him to reconcile to himself all things, whether things on earth or things in heaven, by making peace through his blood, shed on the cross." (Colossians 1:19-20)

"Greater love has no one than, this that he lay down his life for his friends." (John 15:13

There is no greater love than what was displayed through Christ's outstretched arms on the cross. And we get to reap the rewards of that powerful love to this day!

Special Reunion

S ome friends are so special that no matter how much time passes between visits, you get right back into the groove of where your friendship left off.

When our treasured neighbors moved back home to care for their aging parents, I was very sad. Although we are a two hour drive from one another, our hearts have remained closely knit. Our relationship with this couple is fortified through Christian fellowship. God is the third cord of the strand that braids our lives closely together. "...A cord of three strands is not quickly broken." (Ecclesiastes 4:12b)

We recently had the opportunity to meet with our dear friends over dinner and catch up on one another's lives. It was a special time of laughter and fun as we reminisced over days gone by. It felt as though no time had passed since our last get-together.

Reunions on earth are wonderful, but think how amazing it will be to reconnect with loved ones in heaven. Perhaps, like connecting with old friends, we will feel as though no time has passed between us.

If your heart is heavy over the physical or emotional separation of a loved one, allow me to offer you some words of encouragement.

"The Lord is close to the brokenhearted and saves those who are crushed in spirit." (Psalm 34:18)

Time on earth is a mere blip compared to eternity's timeline. Rest assured, we will be with our loved ones again. When we join them for our eternal gathering in heaven, God's presence will make each reunion special indeed.

"Shout for joy, O heavens; rejoice, O earth; burst into song, O mountains! For the Lord comforts his people and will have compassion on his afflicted ones." (Isaiah 49:13)

"I will turn their mourning into gladness; I will give them comfort and joy instead of sorrow." (Jeremiah 31:13b)

Some Things Never Change

My sister and I love spending time together, but this wasn't always the case. During childhood, we shared a bedroom. As you can probably imagine, our living situation caused a fair amount of tension in the home. More than a few sibling rivalries erupted over our close quarters. Although I looked up to my sister and wanted to be like her, she and I couldn't have been more different.

My sister loves change. As a matter of fact, she thrives on it. Me—I'm a creature of habit. Sharing a bedroom with this fundamental difference in our personalities caused friction in our relationship more times than I can count.

It was a common occurrence for me to come home and find our bedroom completely rearranged. Beds, dressers, nightstands—everything would be in a different place. It drove me crazy!

At first, I would hate the changes made to our room, but as time went by, I slowly began to embrace the new arrangement—sometimes I even came to like it better. Unfortunately, just about the time I got used to the new configuration (you guessed it), she changed the room again.

We often hear the expression that change is good, and depending on the circumstance, it can be. However, change is not always good. In fact, I can think of one way in particular that I'm extremely thankful for rock solid stability. "I the LORD do not change." (Malachi 3:6a)

What a comforting thought. "Jesus Christ is the same yesterday and today and forever." (Hebrews 13:8)

God is perfect—therefore He does not need to change.

We, on the other hand, need modification. Since God's ultimate purpose is that we become a reflection of Him, we must allow God to mold and shape us as necessary.

"And we, who with unveiled faces all reflect the Lord's glory, are being transformed into his likeness with ever-increasing glory, which comes from the Lord, who is the Spirit." (2 Corinthians 3:18)

How ironic. The One who never changes is the only One who can evoke true and lasting change in you and me.

Rejection Hurts

I'm not someone who deals with rejection well. I take it far too personally. God's definitely tried to toughen me up in this area, but even after many rounds of practice, my tempered exterior remains paper thin.

Thankfully, God hasn't given up on me. He continues to teach me in spite of my mortal weakness. I've heard it said that God will continue teaching us painful lessons until we pass the test with flying colors. Unlike a harsh taskmaster, our Teacher sympathizes with our weakness and understands our worldly troubles. He is patient and gentle, even when we fail.

"For we do not have a high priest who is unable to sympathize with our weaknesses, but we have one who has been tempted in every way, just as we are—yet was without sin." (Hebrews 4:14-15)

God came physically to this earth through Jesus, and because of this truth, our Lord really does understand what we are going through. If anyone can relate to our times of hurt and rejection, it is Jesus.

"He was despised and rejected by men, a man of sorrows, and familiar with suffering. Like one from whom men hide their faces he was despised, and we esteemed him not." (Isaiah 53:3)

"[Jesus] is 'the stone you builders rejected, which has become the capstone.'" (Acts 4:11)

Christ provided us with ample warning that we will be rejected from time to time. "If the world hates you, keep in mind that it hated me first." (John 15:18)

Jesus goes on to explain why we must suffer these difficulties. "If you belonged to the world, it would love you as its own. As it is, you do not belong to the world, but I have chosen you out of the world. That is why the world hates you." (John 15:19)

We live in the world, but we are not of the world. We belong to God, and because of this fact, we will suffer rejection, disdain, and yes—even hatred. I'm not going to lie—rejection hurts; but I take comfort in knowing I'm in good company. Christians around the world are experiencing the same thing.

Shifting Blame

"My lord, let the blame be on me alone." (1 Samuel 25:24a)

Several years ago, there was a popular situation comedy on television called *Family Matters*. One of the show's main characters was Steve Urkel. His plaid shirt, high water pants, black rimmed glasses and spiffy suspenders said it all. Steve was an A+ nerd! Because Steve was very clumsy, nearly every episode included his infamous line, *"Did I do that!"*

At least the quirky character made an attempt to accept responsibility for his actions, especially when his mistakes caused others grief.

Accepting blame is not a popular notion among mankind. No one really likes to admit when they are in the wrong—including me. And yet, I have to believe that if every one of us accepted responsibility for our own mistakes or short comings, without making excuses or blaming others, it would definitely bring about positive change in the world.

Instead of blaming people or circumstances for making us late, why not accept responsibility, apologize, and allow for extra travel time in the future?

Instead of blaming parents, children, or siblings for our problems today, let's recognize that we have a choice as to how we are going to handle things from this day forward. Positive change in our actions today will impact generations tomorrow.

Instead of being bitter, let's find ways to make it better.

Rather than blaming others because we are struggling with our job, marriage, family, church, or finances, perhaps we should reflect inward and acknowledge where our own deficiencies have contributed to these problems. We just might impart lasting change to others by re-adjusting our own attitude.

Shifting blame is not a new concept. In fact, it's been taking place since the very beginning of time. The first humans did the very same thing.

> And [God] said… 'Have you eaten from the tree that I commanded you not to eat from?' The man said, 'The woman you put here with me—she gave me some fruit from the tree, and I ate it.' Then the LORD God said to the woman, 'What is this you have done?' The woman said, 'The serpent deceived me, and I ate.' (Genesis 3:11-13)

Adam blamed Eve—Eve blamed the serpent—and round and round it went.

God gives us free will, and with that free will, we are given the freedom to choose how we will handle each moment.

"He will keep you strong to the end, so that you will be blameless on the day of our Lord Jesus Christ." (1 Corinthians 1:8)

When we make a conscious effort to accept responsibility for our own blunders and offer grace when others do the same, we gain inner peace, freedom from the burden of guilt, and become truly blameless in the eyes of God.

"To the faithful you show yourself faithful to the blameless you show yourself blameless..." (2 Samuel 22:26)

> And this is my prayer: that [our] love may abound more and more in knowledge and depth of insight, so that [we] may be able to discern what is best and may be pure and blameless until the day of Christ, filled with the fruit of righteousness that comes through Jesus Christ—to the glory and praise of God. (Philippians 1:9-11)

Making the Best of It

"Set your minds on things above, not on earthly things."
(Colossians 3:2-3)

Torrential downpours prevailed the day of our
daughter's wedding, creating less than desirable
conditions for outdoor photos. But thankfully
every once in a while, when we needed it most, the rain
stopped and the sun came out.

After the wedding ceremony, the sun peaked through
the clouds long enough for the photographer to get some
great outdoor pictures of the bride and groom on the
grounds of the golf club where the reception was being
held. All the while, anxious wedding guests awaited the
couple's arrival into the reception hall. It seemed to be
taking an awfully long time, and I soon discovered why.

While I was mingling with the guests at the reception,
the photographer's assistant tapped me on the shoulder,
pulled me aside, and informed me that our daughter
needed me.

As I approached the scene, our daughter and new son-
in-law had concerned looks on their faces. During their
photo session, David accidentally stepped on his bride's
dress, tearing the bustle ties that were attached to her long
train. Since Heather and David had a choreographed
ballroom dance that they had been working on for
months, this was a problem. Their dance would be
impossible without her dress tied up.

We were ill-equipped for such a mishap. We didn't have needle and thread to sew the bustle strings back together, so I was a bit perplexed as to how we were going to fix the problem.

The reception coordinator pulled me aside and said that she had an idea. Desperate for a solution, I was all ears. Lo and behold, her little remedy involved rubber bands. She suggested that we gather sections of the dress underneath with tightly wound rubber bands. This would help hold the bustle in place.

Guess what? It worked! Ten minutes later, the train was up and out of the way and no one was the wiser. (*The rubber bands were our little secret.*)

"...call upon me in the day of trouble; I will deliver you..." (Psalm 50:15)

There's no sense getting all upset and frustrated over circumstances we cannot control. Stressing out only causes us greater anxiety. When things don't go as planned, we need to step back, take a deep breath, and remember, we have a great big God who can help us through anything life throws our way.

"Ah, Sovereign LORD, you have made the heavens and the earth by your great power and outstretched arm. Nothing is too hard for you." (Jeremiah 32:17)

Bedrock of Faith

New York City is home to one the largest collections of skyscrapers in the world. Would you like to know how the city is able to support the weight of so many hefty buildings? It has to do with the foundation on which the city is built—bedrock.

Bedrock refers to massive rock formations that are deeply embedded deep into the earth's crust. This naturally occurring matter is strong enough to hold enormous pressure and weight.

"Therefore everyone who hears these words of mine and puts them into practice is like a wise man who built his house on the rock." (Matthew 7:24)

"But everyone who hears these words of mine and does not put them into practice is like a foolish man who built his house on sand." (Matthew 7:26)

Let me ask you a question. Upon which foundation are you building your life?

"The LORD is my rock, my fortress and my deliverer; my God is my rock, in whom I take refuge, my shield and the horn of my salvation." (2 Samuel 22:2-3a)

If we want our foundation to be rock solid, we need to build upon the bedrock of faith—Jesus Christ. "See, I lay in Zion a stone that causes men to stumble and a rock that makes them fall, and the one who trusts in him will never be put to shame." (Romans 9:33)

When we build upon the Rock, our lives will be able to withstand enormous pressure because Jesus bears the weight for us. "The rain came down, the streams rose, and the winds blew and beat against that house; yet it did not fall, because it had its foundation on the rock." (Matthew 7:25)

Are you going through difficult times? Is the weight too heavy to bear?

"Come to me, all you who are weary and burdened, and I will give you rest. Take my yoke upon you and learn from me, for I am gentle and humble in heart, and you will find rest for your souls. For my yoke is easy and my burden is light." (Matthew 11:28-30)

Jesus (the bedrock of our faith) is able to carry the weight of the entire world on His shoulders.

His Plan – My Purpose

"But the plans of the LORD stand firm forever, the purposes of his heart through all generations." (Psalm 33:11)

At the core of every human being lies an intense desire to matter, to know that our lives have meaning and purpose. This longing is not sin. God created us with this intense desire so that we would one day seek Him. Our ultimate purpose here on earth is fulfilled through our knowing Jesus Christ as our personal Lord and Savior.

In His infinite wisdom, God has set forth a perfect plan and purpose for our lives. An interesting thing happens when we trust God's higher ways. *His plan becomes our purpose.*

As Christians, we have a universal purpose in this world to love, serve, and worship our King. In addition, we are called to love one another and share the Gospel throughout the world. But what about our individual purpose in this world? Does God have something specific for each one of us?

The answer is yes. But in order to know and understand our specific purpose, we must first know and understand our Father. He holds the key to our purpose-filled future. "I cry out to God Most High, to God, who fulfills his purpose for me." (Psalm 57:2)

I have learned that in order to fulfill God's purpose, we must trade our personal goals, aspirations, and ways for His. Easier said than done. It takes a whole lot of surrender on our part. That's because we greatly struggle to let go of what we hold so tightly—our dreams. Our dreams become such a part of us that we fear by letting them go we will lose a part ourselves.

"Then Jesus said to his disciples, 'Whoever wants to be my disciple must deny themselves and take up their cross and follow me. For whoever wants to save their life will lose it, but whoever loses their life for me will find it.'" (Matthew 16:24-25)

Our dreams are so limited. God has something so much better waiting for us. He can fill us with His greater plan and purpose, but we must first unclench our fists and empty our hands of our self-appointed agendas. As long as we have our own plan in place – God's plan will never fully flourish.

"The LORD will fulfill his purpose for me; your love, O LORD, endures forever— do not abandon the works of your hands." (Psalm 138:8)

I don't know about you... but I want God's plan to be my purpose. "Many are the plans in a man's heart, but it is the LORD's purpose that prevails." (Proverbs 19:21)

Active Duty

M en and women around the world serve in the armed forces, protecting our freedoms and making our country safe. I've always held a great deal of respect for these individuals because they live so sacrificially, giving up many of the creature comforts you and I take for granted. They sacrifice precious time with family and friends, hot meals, daily showers, and peaceful rest. Some even make the ultimate sacrifice by giving their lives to protect you and me.

"The LORD Almighty is mustering an army for war." (Isaiah 13:4)

You and I may not be part of the armed forces but as Christians, we are part of God's army. In order to serve our Commander in Chief, we too must make sacrifices in the interests of others. God calls us to serve, defend, and protect those in our care. Depending on where we serve, we may experience different obstacles on the battlefield. Our obstacles may differ, but our enemy is the same.

"For our struggle is not against flesh and blood, but against the rulers, against the authorities, against the powers of this dark world and against the spiritual forces of evil in the heavenly realms." (Ephesians 6:12)

If we're serving on the home front, the battle is up close and personal. The risks to our loved ones are immediate. We must protect the interests of our children and spouse at all costs. It can be a daily struggle to fight against the enemy who is trying to destroy our family unit, but remember, "The one who is in you is greater than the one who is in the world." (1 John 4:4)

If we're serving outside the home, our battlefield has different challenges. Reputation, honor, and respect are at stake as we accept God's higher standard of conduct in the work place and beyond. Satan is always on the prowl, waiting for his opportunity to destroy our honor and means of financial support. "Be self-controlled and alert. Your enemy the devil prowls around like a roaring lion looking for someone to devour." (1 Peter 5:8)

If you're serving on the mission field, you will likely face harsh conditions, rejection, and even persecution. The sacrifices will be many, but the rewards in heaven are great. "Blessed are you when people insult you, persecute you and falsely say all kinds of evil against you because of me. Rejoice and be glad, because great is your reward in heaven, for in the same way they persecuted the prophets who were before you." (Matthew 5:11-12)

We must defend, preserve, and protect that which God has placed in our care. As long as we have breath, we are on active duty.

Serving in the Lord's army is a lifetime commitment. We must give it our all and be ready to make sacrifices when necessary. After all… *eternal lives are at stake!*

Removing Your Mask

As autumn approaches each year, stores gear up for the season by stocking every kind of costume and masquerade imaginable. Some masks seem inconsequential, while others offer a pretty convincing disguise.

It seems that some do not wait until Halloween to cloak their true identity. For years I disguised the real me by wearing a mask. My disguise was so convincing that even close family members didn't know my true identity. I wanted people to believe I had it all together, but in reality—I was a mess.

Pretending to be someone you are not is exhausting. My fear of rejection was so intense that I did everything I could to keep my true identity a secret. I reasoned that if others knew the real me they would abandon me. Keeping up this façade became a necessary evil to ensure love and acceptance from others.

That was then. This is now.

God has taught me a very valuable lesson, and I want to share it with you. *Satan has power when things are kept a secret.* However, the minute we take off our masks and reveal our true identity, Satan loses a whole lot of power over our lives. Not only does he lose power, but the most amazing thing happens. We give others permission to remove their masks as well. That's when real healing begins.

Be true to yourself and save the mask for Halloween.

"Rather, we have renounced secret and shameful ways; we do not use deception, nor do we distort the word of God. On the contrary, by setting forth the truth plainly we commend ourselves to every man's conscience in the sight of God." (2 Corinthians 4:2)

It Could Be Worse

One evening, the cable and Internet went out at the same time. I'm embarrassed to admit that I became quite annoyed because I couldn't engage in my normal evening routine. In my selfish frustration, I wondered: Did someone cut the lines? How long will the service be out? Will I be able to get online tomorrow?

After some time went by, a service truck pulled up to the end of our driveway, so my husband went out to investigate. When Gerry came back in, he informed me that every third house on our street had not only lost cable and Internet service, but their electricity had gone out too. Here I was grumbling about no television, and half my street was without electricity. Things could have been much worse.

I realize this is a minor example, but isn't this how we often react when things aren't going our way? We have a pity party for ourselves and fail to realize that there are far greater struggles are going on around us.

"Do nothing out of selfish ambition or vain conceit, but in humility consider others better than yourselves. Each of you should look not only to your own interests, but also to the interests of others." (Philippians 2:3-4)

We need to adopt the example left by Jesus, who always focused on others. Jesus commonly gave up creature comforts for Himself, so He could minister to others.

"Jesus replied, 'Foxes have holes and birds of the air have nests, but the Son of Man has no place to lay his head.'" (Matthew 8:20)

Jesus didn't even have a place to call home during His three years of ministry. He went from city to town to village, healing the sick, raising the dead, rescuing the lost, and feeding the hungry. Jesus always looked to the needs of those around Him. "Your attitude should be the same as that of Christ Jesus: Who, being in very nature God, did not consider equality with God something to be grasped, but made himself nothing, taking the very nature of a servant, being made in human likeness." (Philippians 2:5-7)

Having our cable go out was a good thing. It helped me realize my selfish attitude and caused me to reflect on the fact that I need to be more focused on others and less focused on me.

"So then, just as you received Christ Jesus as Lord, continue to live in him, rooted and built up in him, strengthened in the faith as you were taught, and overflowing with thankfulness." (Colossians 2:6-7)

Follow the Leader

In the game Follow the Leader, one person performs different actions for the others to mimic. If the leader crawls on all fours, the followers crawl on all fours. If the leader skips around the room, the followers skip around the room. This is a simple childhood game, but following the leader in real life is serious business, especially when the leader is Jesus. "'Come, follow me,' Jesus said, 'and I will make you fishers of men.'" (Matthew 4:19)

Sometimes what Jesus asked His followers to do was extremely difficult. "Jesus looked at him and loved him. 'One thing you lack,' he said. 'Go, sell everything you have and give to the poor, and you will have treasure in heaven. Then come, follow me.' (Mark 10:21)

In order to be a true disciple of Jesus, we must walk as He walked. Jesus didn't ask His followers to do anything that He hadn't already done. Even in our childhood game, the leader performed the action first. Not only did the leader's example prove the task was indeed possible to accomplish, but it also demonstrated the manner in which it should be practiced. In much the same way, the example Jesus left for us shows us what to do and how to do it.

"Then Jesus said to his disciples, 'If anyone would come after me, he must deny himself and take up his cross and follow me.'" (Matthew 16:24)

Jesus came to this earth to show us the way to live. He also came to provide us with the only way to eternal life. Ironically, New Testament Christians were referred to as *followers of The Way*. Notice it was called *the way*, not one of many ways.

"Jesus answered, 'I am the way and the truth and the life. No one comes to the Father except through me.'" (John 14:6)

Not only did Jesus' death on the cross provide us with the way to eternal life, but Jesus also showed us the way to live abundant and fulfilling lives here on earth. Two thousand years ago, Jesus walked this planet Himself, so He completely understands and can empathize with what we face in this world on a daily basis. "For we do not have a high priest who is unable to sympathize with our weaknesses, but we have one who has been tempted in every way, just as we are—yet was without sin." (Hebrews 4:15)

Let's follow the Leader and walk as Jesus walked.

More than Conquerors

My husband Gerry travels a lot for his job, and although I have adjusted to this way of life to a degree, it is never easy. I miss him a lot when he is gone. He usually travels during the week, but every once in a while, the company plans a mandatory trip over the weekend.

When he's gone during the week, I keep busy with the ministry and housework, but the weekends are another story. Weekends have always been family time in our home.

Gerry and I are in a season of life where our kids are grown and have their own lives. We cherish our time together because we are better able to focus on one another—something that was difficult to do when our kids were young. When he travels over the weekend now, I get very lonely.

Realizing that one of his weekend trips was fast approaching, I asked God to help me get through it. As the time drew near for him to leave, I could feel myself slipping into depression. I have learned through personal experience that depression can cause a person to withdraw from others. Unfortunately, isolation only feeds depression. Realizing this fact, I knew it was in my best interest to stay busy and surround myself with friends and family.

As Friday approached, I called a friend and asked if she would like go to dinner and a movie. She accepted the invitation and we were able to catch up with one another's lives and see a great 'chick flick' at the same time. I was partway through the weekend and had avoided slipping into a pit of despair.

On Saturday, I cleaned the house and tackled some laundry before heading out to a wedding celebration with my daughter and son-in-law. When I arrived back home, it was late and I went straight to bed. I was halfway there.

Sunday morning, my son went to church with his girlfriend. Since I didn't want to go to my church alone, a friend invited me to attend church with her family. I was nearly through the weekend now—almost there!

Upon coming home from church, I went to my computer and spent some time writing. Later that evening I attended a friend's cookout. After a full day of activities, I was tired and called it a night. The weekend was over and I had survived without experiencing any depression.

Do you not know? Have you not heard? The Lord is the everlasting God, the Creator of the ends of the earth. He will not grow tired or weary, and his understanding no one can fathom. He gives strength to the weary and increases the power of the weak. Even youths grow tired and weary, and young men stumble and fall; but those who hope in the Lord will renew their strength. They will soar on wings like eagles; they will run and not grow weary, they will walk and not be faint. (Isaiah 40:28-31)

God's hand helped me through the weekend. He made sure I was with others and blessed me in so many ways. This experience reminded me that through Christ we are more than conquerors. He is ready and willing to come to our aid—all we need to do is ask.

"No, in all these things we are more than conquerors through him who loved us." (Romans 8:37)

Take the First Step

Could you use a little encouragement concerning a looming obstacle? Is fear immobilizing you? Does your barrier seem so menacing that you can't imagine crossing over without experiencing life-altering consequences?

"Joshua told the people, 'Consecrate yourselves, for tomorrow the LORD will do amazing things among you.'" (Joshua 3:5)

The Israelites would be able to relate to your dilemma. They, too, faced a seemingly impossible situation, a barrier that stood between them and the land God had promised. The children of God needed to cross the Jordan, but this wasn't just any river. It was a river at flood stage. Needless to say, the action God was asking them to take required a whole lot of faith and courage. Crossing this waterway during this particular time of year could have tragic consequences, if they were crossing the Jordan alone. But they weren't alone. God was with them and gave very specific instructions on how they should proceed:

> When you reach the edge of the of the Jordan's waters, go and stand in the river. Now the Jordan is at flood stage all during harvest. Yet as soon as the priests who carried the ark reached the Jordan and their feet touched the water's edge, the water from upstream stopped flowing. It piled up in a heap a great distance away, at a town called Adam in the vicinity of Zarethan, while the water flowing down to the Sea of the Arabah (the Salt Sea) was completely cut off. So the people crossed over opposite Jericho. The priests who carried the ark of the covenant of the LORD stood firm on dry ground in the middle of the Jordan, while all Israel passed by until the whole nation had completed the crossing on dry ground. (Joshua 3:8,15-17)

God cleared the pathway but only *after* His people acted in accordance to His direction.

The Levite priests stood in the middle of the dry riverbed, holding up the Ark of the Covenant, while the Israelites crossed over. It was a tangible illustration of God's faithfulness. God was with them every step of the way.

Is it possible that God is waiting for you to take the first step of faith in obedience *before* He parts your Jordan?

Like the Israelites, we are never alone. Pray fervently, and then listen closely for God's direction through the counsel of His Word. When you are confident that He is leading you in a particular direction, step out in faith and watch God part the waters.

"Ah, Sovereign Lord, you have made the heavens and the earth by your great power and outstretched arm. Nothing is too hard for you." (Jeremiah 32:17)

Lust for More

"No one can serve two masters. Either you will hate the one and love the other, or you will be devoted to the one and despise the other." (Matthew 6:24)

In our futile thinking and flawed human nature, we assume that if a little is good then a lot must be better. *Why is that?*

Satan camps out in the pleasure center of our brains. He dangles the bait; you want

more! We bite. The hook paralyzes us because our brain's pleasure center is all about 'more'. In all areas of our lives, we've come to believe the lie that 'more is better'.
~*Torn Between Two Masters*, Kimberly Davidson

Satan uses discontentment as a powerful tool to keep our hearts far from God. He hopes that our never-ending search to be filled by the things of this world will direct us away from what can truly satisfy. *And he's right.*

In our lust for more of the world, we drift further and further from God. Unfortunately, indulging in pleasures of the flesh is like pouring water into a broken cistern.

"My people have committed two sins: They have forsaken me, the spring of living water, and have dug their own cisterns, broken cisterns that cannot hold water." (Jeremiah 2:13)

By convincing us that God is holding out on us, Satan keeps us from experiencing true contentment. It's the same tactic he used in the very beginning. God gave Adam and Eve a garden filled with a vast variety of fruits and vegetables to eat. There was just one fruit they were commanded not to eat—the fruit from the tree of the knowledge of good and evil. Isn't it just like man to want the one thing we shouldn't have?

"When I want to do good, evil is right there with me. For in my inner being I delight in God's law; but I see another law at work in the members of my body, waging war against the law of my mind and making me a prisoner of the law of sin at work within my members." (Romans 7:21-23)

Enlightenment is the key to change. When we begin to understand the root of our discontentment and realize Satan's tactics of deception are the same today as they were in the Garden of Eden, we can move towards finding true satisfaction through God.

Satisfaction and complete contentment are only possible when we seek God with all of our heart and allow His Spirit to reign in our lives. "But seek first his kingdom and his righteousness, and all these things will be given to you as well." (Matthew 6:33)

Reaching New Heights

"It is God who arms me with strength and makes my way perfect. He makes my feet like the feet of a deer; he enables me to stand on the heights." (Psalm 18:32-33)

Veteran mountaineers pave the way for those coming behind by securing hand and footholds and mapping out a safe route to the top of a mountain. They tether their team to a safety rope, which is fastened to special gear securely locked in place along the route. If someone loses their footing and begins to fall, the safety gear keeps the climbers from plummeting too far.

"Cast your cares on the LORD and he will sustain you; he will never let the righteous fall." (Psalm 55:22)

Tandem mountain climbing has some similarities to the Christian journey. Those who go before us, map out the best route to the top, while those who come behind need our example to spur them on to greater heights. "Therefore encourage one another and build each other up, just as in fact you are doing." (1 Thessalonians 5:10)

I've heard it said that the healthiest Christians have individuals in their lives that are traveling *before, beside, and behind*. Those who travel before, pave the way for others, discipling and inspiring them to keep moving forward. Those who travel beside, share each other's life experiences with love and support. And those who travel behind, spur us towards discipling others. As we pave the way for others, we have a responsibility to model genuine faith and reflect the radiance of Christ in our lives.

We are on this journey together, so why not watch out for one another? When we see someone stumble, let's offer our hand to help them back up. If we see someone veering off the clearly marked path, we can walk beside them and lovingly guide them back on track. We are all working to reach the summit. The journey is much more enjoyable when we scale the mountain together.

"Two are better than one, because they have a good return for their work: If one falls down, his friend can help him up." (Ecclesiastes 4:9-10)

"If the LORD delights in a man's way, he makes his steps firm; though he stumble, he will not fall, for the LORD upholds him with his hand." (Psalm 37:23-25)

With each step up, we are reaching new heights.

Therefore I Will Boast

"Then I heard the voice of the Lord saying, 'Whom shall I send? And who will go for us?' And I said, 'Here am I. Send me!'" (Isaiah 6:8)

Although I have shared my testimony of being set free from bulimia many times, each and every occasion holds special significance for me, because I have the opportunity to boast about my weakness.

Perhaps you are wondering why anyone would want to boast about his weakness.

The reason is simple. My weakness is the avenue through which God's power is made perfect.

"But he said to me, 'My grace is sufficient for you, for my power is made perfect in weakness.' Therefore I will boast all the more gladly about my weaknesses, so that Christ's power may rest on me." (2 Corinthians 12:9)

When we are real with people and remove our mask, no longer pretending that we have it all together, we give others permission to do the same.

"Do your best to present yourself to God as one approved, a workman who does not need to be ashamed and who correctly handles the word of truth." (2 Timothy 2:15)

I definitely want to be approved by God as someone who unashamedly does God's work and correctly handles truth. Whenever I speak at conferences, retreats, youth groups, church events, and schools about how God set me free from bulimia through the truth of His Word, I'm completely amazed that God would allow me to be used in this way.

It's just like God to take the very thing that once held a person in bondage and turn it into their life's mission. I'm absolutely blown away by that concept.

God will use your humble heart to prick the hearts of those listening. Through your example they too will learn how to get real with God. So go ahead—boast!

"If I must boast, I will boast of the things that show my weakness." (2 Corinthians 11:30)

Defining Moments

Insecurity has always been a major weakness of mine, and Satan knows it. He plays ruthlessly upon this flaw in my character, and I often find myself at the mercy of his cunning campaigns. A particular experience from my childhood became a defining moment in my life.

Our next door neighbors' niece and nephew from England came to stay with them over the summer, and the girl and I became fast friends. Despite our three year age difference we spent a lot of time together. My new friend's brother was really cute and I had a major crush on him. He had a great sense of humor and his English accent was irresistible. Whenever he was around I tried my best to get his attention. But who was I kidding? I was twelve and he was seventeen.

Like many older brothers, he was in the habit of teasing his sister. She seemed to be such a good sport about it, so I joined in with his heckling, thinking I was being cool.

Then one day, without warning, my new friend quit hanging out with me. Every time I called to see if she wanted to hang out she was busy. It became obvious that she didn't want to be my friend anymore, but I honestly had no idea why.

After several days of trying to figure out what went wrong, I finally decided to go over and ask my friend if I had done something to upset her. She eventually opened up and shared with me how my teasing had hurt her.

> Likewise the tongue is a small part of the body, but it makes great boasts. Consider what a great forest is set on fire by a small spark. The tongue also is a fire, a world of evil among the parts of the body. It corrupts the whole person, sets the whole course of his life on fire, and is itself set on fire by hell. (James 3:5-6)

I was devastated to realize how my actions had hurt my new friend but grateful that she was honest with me. I learned that day that we can be oblivious to the fact that we have hurt someone until they point it out. After I apologized for my thoughtless behavior, we spent the remainder of the summer together, having fun.

"Set a guard over my mouth, O LORD; keep watch over the door of my lips." (Psalm 141:3)

This was a defining moment in my life, and the experience continues to taint my outlook in relationships to this day. Whenever someone grows distant, I automatically assume that I've done something wrong. Thankfully, I've learned this about myself and come right out and ask a person if I did something to upset them. I would rather know the truth than live completely oblivious to the fact that I've caused someone else pain.

Life experiences can definitely play a big role in shaping our immediate response to given situations.

Perhaps you can identify your own defining moments in life. We need to ask God to illuminate the tangled roots from our past that are distorting our perceptions of the here and now. Understanding the root causes of our character deficiencies today, can help us change for the better tomorrow.

"Send forth your light and your truth, let them guide me;" (Psalm 43:3)

The Cup of Hope

D o you have a particular cup in your home that is more than just a cup? Perhaps you received a coffee mug as a gift from a loved one, or maybe you have a cup with a colorful motif from a favorite vacation spot. Some cups hold special significance because they remind us of cherished memories from days gone by.

The night before His betrayal, Jesus and His disciples shared a special meal together for Passover. During this special meal, four cups were shared, each representing a particular promise made by God. Passover was celebrated by the Jewish nation every year to remember the deliverance of the children of Israel from slavery in Egypt. Many Jews celebrate the traditional Passover meal to this day. The pastor from my church preached a sermon near Easter on the four cups shared during the Passover feast. The four cups represent the promises of God found in Exodus 6:6-7.

The Cup of Salvation – "I will bring you out."
The Cup of Deliverance – "I will deliver you."
The Cup of Redemption – "I will redeem you."
The Cup of Hope (or Praise) – "I will take you."

As Jesus shared the Passover meal with His disciples, He did so in the traditional Seder (order of sequence) manner. When it came time to drink from the last cup— *The Cup of Hope*—Jesus offered it to His disciples but did not drink from it Himself.

"Then [Jesus] took the cup, gave thanks and offered it to them, saying, 'Drink from it, all of you. This is my blood of the covenant, which is poured out for many for the forgiveness of sins. I tell you, I will not drink of this fruit of the vine from now on until that day when I drink it anew with you in my Father's kingdom.'" (Matthew 26:27-29)

Through this final Passover feast with His disciples, Jesus revealed that He is the fulfillment of all God's promises. (He is our Cup of Hope.) Jesus paid the penalty for our sins through His death and resurrection, and because of this, we now have hope for eternal salvation.

'Do not let your hearts be troubled. Trust in God; trust also in me. In my Father's house are many rooms; if it were not so, I would have told you. I am going there to prepare a place for you. And if I go and prepare a place for you, I will come back and take you to be with me that you also may be where I am. You know the way to the place where I am going.' Thomas said to him, 'Lord, we don't know where you

are going, so how can we know the way?'
Jesus answered, 'I am the way and the
truth and the life. No one comes to the
Father except through me. If you really
knew me, you would know my Father as
well. From now on, you do know him and
have seen him.' (John 14:1-7)

God's promise was fulfilled through His Son. Jesus
died to give us new life—He is our Cup of Hope! *Now
that's a cup with a whole lot of significance.*

Getting to the Bottom of It

"...call upon me in the day of trouble; I will deliver you."
(Psalm 50:15)

After suffering several days with severe headache
pain and pressure behind his left eye, my husband
finally gave in and went to a nearby urgent care
center. Gerry had gone to the eye doctor two days earlier,
but the examination revealed the problem was not in his
eye. Something else had to be causing his pain. The eye
doctor suggested a warm compress and Advil (both of
which my husband tried), but the throbbing continued.
With no relief in sight, we began to wonder if this could
be something serious. What if he was on the verge of a
brain aneurism?

At the urgent care center, the physician asked several
questions, trying to determine what might be going on. It

seems the science of medicine is a process of elimination. Questions, tests, and symptoms must be examined to rule out what an ailment is not, before determining a probable diagnosis. Based on his symptoms and the examination, the urgent care physician told us my husband was likely experiencing cluster migraines.

An hour after taking the prescribed pain medication and receiving an injection for some immediate pain relief, my husband's headache was finally gone.

Sometimes in life, we experience an emotional or spiritual ache that requires some investigating. Understanding the root of our pain is the first step to finding lasting relief. We need to quit treating our symptoms with temporary fixes from the world and look for lasting relief—the kind that can only come through the Great Physician, Jesus Christ.

Pray for God to show you where your life might be out of balance. Then request His prescription to help you get back on track. Do some investigating, and eventually, God will help you get to the bottom of your pain and provide you with lasting relief.

"Search me, God, and know my heart; test me and know my anxious thoughts. See if there is any offensive way in me, and lead me in the way everlasting." (Psalm 139:23-24)

Small World After All

*I*t's a *Small World After All*, written by the Sherman brothers, fittingly encapsulates the childlike wonderment of this planet we call home. The well-known entrepreneur, Walt Disney, popularized the song and connected its lyrics to his theme parks around the globe.

When I was a child, I had no concept of the real size of the world. I assumed the lyrics of the song to be true—the world was small and everything in it revolved around me.

As I got older, learning about other countries and cultures through geography and social studies classes helped me realize the vast magnitude of our planet. Apparently, the world did not revolve around me after all.

When I became a Christian, the world became small again. I no longer viewed creation against the backdrop of my own meager existence but learned to perceive the world against the backdrop of my GREAT BIG GOD.

"I am God, and there is no other; I am God, and there is none like me." (Isaiah 46:9) "I am the Alpha and the Omega, the First and the Last, the Beginning and the End." (Revelation 22:13)

As I continue to serve my Lord, I'm blown away by the sheer magnitude of God's infinite wisdom, power, and presence. His ways are so much higher and better than my own. God is more than able to break down the earthly barriers threatening to overwhelm my mortal existence.

After sharing my testimony through an online conference, I received a message from a young woman who lived halfway around the world, in Australia. She learned about Living in Truth Ministries through the online webcast. Later, she contacted me to share her personal struggles. It became a bold reminder that God's Kingdom has no boundaries.

"Jesus looked at them and said, 'With man this is impossible, but not with God; all things are possible with God.'" (Mark 10:27)

Are you overwhelmed by some big obstacle in life? Stop viewing the situation from the world's perspective, and start seeing it against the backdrop of your great big God. *Compared to Him, it truly is a small world after all.*

"Who among the gods is like you, O LORD? Who is like you— majestic in holiness, awesome in glory, working wonders?" (Exodus 15:11)

"You are awesome, O God, in your sanctuary; the God of Israel gives power and strength to his people. Praise be to God" (Psalm 68:35)

Quiet Strength

"Again the one who looked like a man touched me and gave me strength. 'Do not be afraid, O man highly esteemed,' he said. 'Peace! Be strong now; be strong.' When he spoke to me, I was strengthened and said, 'Speak, my lord, since you have given me strength.'"
(Daniel 10:18-19)

As Jesus and His disciples made their way toward the Garden of Gethsemane, the weight that Jesus was about to endure was unimaginable. I cannot comprehend the dread of knowing the full extent of one's future suffering.

Jesus' physical suffering was horrific to be sure, but His spiritual suffering was even worse. The Son of God would have to bear the weight of every sin on that cross—a fate even worse than death. The weight was more than man alone could bear, but of course, Jesus was not an ordinary man. Only God could bear the weight of the sins of the world. Jesus (God in the flesh) not only carried our sins, but He also carried the strength and comfort of His Father.

One morning during my devotion time, the Lord led me to Scripture after Scripture, revealing the place where our strength can be found.

"O LORD, be gracious to us; we long for you. Be our strength every morning, our salvation in time of distress." (Isaiah 33:2)

"...In repentance and rest is your salvation, in quietness and trust is your strength..." (Isaiah 30:15b)

"I know what it is to be in need, and I know what it is to have plenty. I have learned the secret of being content in any and every situation, whether well fed or hungry, whether living in plenty or in want. I can do everything through him who gives me strength." (Philippians 4:12-13)

Jesus understood the importance of gaining strength through daily prayer and quiet time with God. Throughout His life, Jesus made a practice of spending time away from the watchful eyes of others to be alone with His Father.

The night before His crucifixion, Jesus needed the strength of His Father more than ever. Deep in the garden of despair, on bended knees and in humble submission, the strength of Jesus was renewed.

If God in the flesh needed the strength of His Father, how much more do we?

Is there something weighing heavy on your heart, exhausting all of your strength? Go to a quiet place, and spend time alone with the Father. Take your concerns to the Lord, and you, too, will find inner peace to face whatever tomorrow brings.

"I pray that out of his glorious riches he may strengthen you with power through his Spirit in your inner being...." (Ephesians 3:16)

"That power is like the working of his mighty strength, which he exerted in Christ when he raised him from the dead and seated him at his right hand in the heavenly realms." (Ephesians 1:19-20)

His Crown Jewels

David's son, Solomon, was instructed to build a magnificent temple—a dwelling place for the LORD. He took his job very seriously, making sure that only the finest materials were used in the Temple's construction. Materials such as pure gold, precious gems, and fine linen were carefully chosen to represent God's holy dwelling.

Today, God dwells in a different temple—you and me. As sons and daughters of His Majesty, we are the crowning jewels of our King. Precious in His sight, we are shining forth His brilliance.

"Do you not know that your body is a temple of the Holy Spirit, who is in you, whom you have received from God? You are not your own; you were bought at a price. Therefore honor God with your body." (1 Corinthians 6:19-20)

"I delight greatly in the LORD; my soul rejoices in my God. For he has clothed me with garments of salvation and arrayed me in a robe of righteousness, as a bridegroom adorns his head like a priest, and as a bride adorns herself with her jewels." (Isaiah 61:10)

Precious stones such as emeralds, rubies, and sapphires do not simply appear overnight. They are the result of a geological phenomenon that takes place over many years. Amazingly, ordinary rocks become gems when they are exposed to intense heat and pressure.

Are you weighted down by the pressures of life? Does it seem as though heartache and adversity follow you wherever you go?

Take heart! Like ordinary rocks beneath the earth's crust, you are slowly being transformed into precious gems—jewels that are fit for a KING.

"The LORD their God will save them on that day as the flock of his people. They will sparkle in his land like jewels in a crown." (Zechariah 9:16)

Royal Family

While walking through the royal palace in London, I began to recognize the great obligation that accompanies the Queen's position of honor. I never realized how much work and responsibility came with such a position. Our visit to the English palace shed new light on my once lofty perception of the royal family.

As we departed the tour, my husband purchased a souvenir book to remember our visit. The book chronicled Queen Elizabeth's calendar year, highlighting her various duties as head of the state and nation. It's very interesting to view Queen Elizabeth's life in such detail. She has quite the reputation to uphold.

It turns out that you and I do not need to travel across an ocean to encounter members of the royal family. In 1 Peter 2:9 we're told that we "are a chosen people, a royal priesthood, a holy nation, a people belonging to God, that

[we] may declare the praises of him who called [us] out of darkness into his wonderful light."

We are sons and daughters of the KING—adopted into the Royal Family through the precious blood of Jesus. As Christians, we bear the name of our Lord—Christ. Through Him we are representatives of the Royal Family.

> Jesus said, 'My kingdom is not of this world. If it were, my servants would fight to prevent my arrest by the Jews. But now my kingdom is from another place.' 'You are a king, then!' said Pilate. Jesus answered, 'You are right in saying I am a king. In fact, for this reason I was born, and for this I came into the world, to testify to the truth. Everyone on the side of truth listens to me.' (John 18:36-37)

Like Queen Elizabeth, our position of honor bears immense responsibility. As representatives for His Majesty, we are called to conduct our affairs in ways that honor Him.

> As a prisoner for the Lord, then, I urge you to live a life worthy of the calling you have received. Be completely humble and gentle; be patient, bearing with one another in love. Make every effort to keep the unity of the Spirit through the bond of peace. There is one body and one Spirit— just as you were called to one hope when you were called— one Lord, one faith, one baptism; one God and Father of all, who is over all and through all and in all. (Ephesians 4:1-6)

We must never take for granted the great responsibility that comes from being sons and daughters of the KING.

"Therefore, my brothers, be all the more eager to make your calling and election sure. For if you do these things, you will never fall, and you will receive a rich welcome into the eternal kingdom of our Lord and Savior Jesus Christ." (2 Peter 1:10-11)

Generations to Come

"I will establish my covenant as an everlasting covenant between me and you and your descendants after you for the generations to come, to be your God and the God of your descendants after you." (Genesis 17:7)

My husband took on the large task of transferring our home videos to DVD. After the job was complete, we sat down to view these treasured memories and reminisce over days gone by. It's one thing to view still-life photos. It's quite another to watch your children in motion—running, laughing, playing, and talking. What a blessing to have these treasured memories for generations to come.

Reminiscing about days gone by has caused me some deep reflection. I've come to realize just how much each and every decision we make affects future generations. When we're young, we don't often concern ourselves with such things. We tend to live in the moment, not thinking terribly much about the past or future. Growing older has its advantages. Reflecting on the past can be a good thing, especially if we allow it to change us for the better.

"Remember the days of old; consider the generations long past." (Deuteronomy 32:7a)

Like it or not, our today is directly linked to our past. And how we approach tomorrow is directly linked to our actions in the here and now. Reflection can be a great teacher when it helps us ward off future mistakes. What we do today does matter, and it will impact generations to come, whether we like it or not. I don't believe God wants us to become obsessed by this realization, just more aware.

"But the plans of the LORD stand firm forever, the purposes of his heart through all generations." (Psalm 33:11)

Ideally, we should be more conscious of the things we say and do, considering the eternal ramifications of our actions and how they will affect future generations. What we say and how we say it is important. What we do and how we do it is important. Our lives interconnect from generation to generation in ways that we don't even realize.

We should never take for granted the great responsibility we have been given to be representatives of Jesus Christ. Our actions today will impact the generations to come.

May even our thoughts be taken captive and made obedient to Christ.

Filling Your Void

There is a place in the center of our being that is so deep no man, woman, or object could ever reach it. It is a place that God designed solely for Himself. In this space the Lord ministers to our spirit and brings healing, restoration, and fulfillment into our lives. This void is the very life-source that causes man to seek, know, and love our Heavenly Father.

So strong is the desire within us to have this space occupied that we often spend an incredible amount of time, energy, and money looking for a willing tenant. Relationships, substances, money, careers, and material possessions compete for residency. Unfortunately, Satan is all too willing to assist us in our search.

Long ago, Jesus saw a desperate need in the heart of a Samaritan woman who was coming to find water at the well. *What she found filled more than her water jar.*

Jesus, knowing her greatest need, offered the woman at the well the same thing He offers you and me today—Living Water.

"Jesus answered, 'Everyone who drinks this water will be thirsty again, but whoever drinks the water I give him will never thirst. Indeed the water I give him will become in him a spring of water welling up to eternal life.'" (John 4:13-14)

Are you feeling vacant after an endless search for fulfillment? Continually fill your spirit with the living water that Jesus has to offer and you will never be empty again.

"And my God will meet all your needs according to his glorious riches in Christ Jesus." (Philippians 4:19)

Bones and Hearts that Ache

I've had my share of misfortunes in life and a few broken bones to prove it. My tail bone, left wrist, right ankle, pinky finger, three toes, and ribs have all been broken. Believe it or not, each of these injuries occurred during separate accidents.

Although my mishaps took place years ago, I have painful reminders of my injuries to this day. When drastic weather change occurs, my frame racks with pain. Arthritis has settled into my joints, causing my bones to ache. This constant reminder of past hurts helps me remember that I need to be more careful in the future.

"Have mercy on me, Lord, for I am faint; heal me, Lord, for my bones are in agony." (Psalm 6:2)

Bones are not the only part of me that aches. My heart winces when I recall emotional grievances—those inflicted on me as well as pain I've caused others. I'm saddened to learn when I've hurt someone.

Recently, I discovered that my actions had caused a dear friend some heartache. The moment that I became aware of my fault in the matter, my heart was distressed. Seeking forgiveness and trying to make amends, I called my friend and asked if we could meet over lunch. Thankfully, she agreed. We were finally able to talk openly about the festering wounds that were leftover from a misunderstanding and we both agreed to forgive and forget. Life is simply too short to fixate on past grievances. We decided to erase the past and embrace the future.

"Bear with each other and forgive one another if any of you has a grievance against someone. Forgive as the Lord forgave you." (Colossians 3:13)

My conscience still stings when I recall this incident, but like broken bones that have mended and continue to ache, my pain serves as a good reminder that I need to be more careful in the future.

I'm with Him

My husband is a savvy traveler. Because his job requires him to travel over 200 days a year, Delta Airlines has bestowed upon him platinum flying status. His elite standing provides him with various perks and travel conveniences that the average traveler does not receive. After many years of sacrifice, hard work, and plenty of headaches, my husband's premier ranking has become a blessing to our family.

Whenever Gerry and I fly together, I get to benefit from those perks. For instance, I don't have to pay extra for checked luggage, I get to go through a special security-check line without waiting, and I'm able to sit in the Crown Room while waiting for a flight. Sometimes I even get upgraded to first class seating. My husband made all the sacrifices, yet I get to benefit. *How cool is that?* I did absolutely nothing to earn or deserve these advantages, but I get to profit simply because I'm with him.

You and I get to benefit from something else that we did nothing to deserve—eternal life in heaven. Jesus paid our way to get there. It cost us nothing—but it cost Him plenty.

"When the soldiers crucified Jesus, they took his clothes, dividing them into four shares, one for each of them, with the undergarment remaining. This garment was seamless, woven in one piece from top to bottom." (John 19:23)

On the cross Jesus gave everything. All was stripped away—even His clothes. Jesus was betrayed, humiliated, beaten, and abandoned. Although He was completely innocent, He never once tried to defend Himself. He willingly went to the cross so that you and I wouldn't have to face the penalty we deserve. "...Jesus said, 'It is finished.' With that, he bowed his head and gave up his spirit." (John 19:30)

Jesus sacrificed His life and so much more, all to ensure that we could be in heaven with Him. Believe and receive. It's really that simple.

"Consequently, just as the result of one trespass was condemnation for all men, so also the result of one act of righteousness was justification that brings life for all men. For just as through the disobedience of the one man the many were made sinners, so also through the obedience of the one man the many will be made righteous."(Romans 5:18-19)

When we get to heaven we need only to say, *"Please excuse me—I'm with Him."*

"Salvation is found in no one else, for there is no other name under heaven given to men by which we must be saved." (Acts 4:12)

"For it is by grace you have been saved, through faith—and this not from yourselves, it is the gift of God…" (Ephesians 2:8)

Clearing a New Path

"Do not follow where the path may lead. Go instead where there is no path and leave a trail." ~George Bernard Shaw

Our weekend getaways to the farm in Indiana provided a welcome escape from the hustle and bustle of suburbia. We had a big field next to the farmhouse with a trail for our little Honda 90 motorcycle. It was great fun. The path was well-worn and easy to travel, but every once in a while, we would veer off the beaten path and explore other parts of the field.

The grass and weeds outside of the path were so tall that they often obstructed our view from obstacles before us. Sometimes we would hit a big bump and practically fall off the motorcycle. It was definitely safer to stay on the beaten path but not nearly as interesting.

"He guides me in paths of righteousness for his name's sake." (Psalm 23:3)

When I first started Living in Truth Ministries, I had absolutely no idea what I was doing. This ministry was (and still is) unchartered territory—a path I've never before traveled. Because everything is new to me, I've made some mistakes along the way.

Sometimes it feels like those times when I strayed off the main motorcycle trail as a child—exciting yet scary. I can't always see what's up ahead, and the unexpected bumps can nearly knock me down, but still, I continue to press on.

Think about it. Somebody had to clear the original motorcycle path when I was a kid. Doing so would have taken great amounts of time and effort. They would have had to bore through the weeds, rocks, and bumps in order to create a safe path for others to travel.

I may not always know what's up ahead on this ministry journey, but I need to remember that I'm not clearing this path alone. The bumps will keep coming, but that's okay. Jesus is walking ahead of me, leading the way and minimizing my risks. He also goes behind me and is ready to catch me when I fall. "You broaden the path beneath me, so that my ankles do not turn." (Psalm 18:36)

In reality, I don't need to know where I'm going because Jesus knows the way.

He knows your way too.

Whether you're clearing a new trail or traveling a well-worn path, keep your eyes on Jesus and trust his higher ways.

"When my spirit grows faint within me, it is you who knows my way." (Psalm 142:3)

"...in all your ways acknowledge him, and he will make your paths straight." (Proverbs 3:6)

Standing in the Gap

I had been struggling with feelings of depression and loneliness. The kids are grown, my husband travels a lot for his job, and, although there is plenty of ministry work to keep me busy, I spend much time alone. To make matters worse, menopause is fast approaching—so hot flashes, mood swings, and lack of sleep magnify my emotions to the tenth degree. My attitude was growing more and more negative, and I started feeling sorry for myself. I'm usually a positive person, so this downward spiral was out of character. I hated how I was feeling and eventually cried out... *Lord, please help me!*

"In my distress I called to the LORD; I cried to my God for help. From his temple he heard my voice; my cry came before him, into his ears." (Psalm 18:6)

Shortly after my cry for help, God showed me the way out of my depression and loneliness. Allow me to share with you what God has taught me. Perhaps you are in a similar season of life and could use some encouragement.

A lovely woman from our church gave an inspiring talk about the importance of prayer in our daily lives. Early in her message she spoke about the fact that many women are in a season of life where their time is not their own. Therefore, time spent in prayer can be a challenge. Because they have young children and homes to keep up, or maybe even jobs outside the home, their prayer lives might consist of short little prayers being lifted up to God throughout the day. I remember those days.

In that moment, God spoke to my heart and reminded me that I am in a different season of life—a season that has fewer distractions. I am able to devote much more time and focus to prayer. I felt the Lord saying to my heart. *Rae Lynn, every time you feel lonely, stand in the gap for some of these women who don't have as much time for prayer.*

It was such a revelation. God has really changed my perspective on being alone. It is so encouraging for me to think that God can use me to stand in the gap for others who don't have as much time to pray.

"May my prayer be set before you like incense; may the lifting up of my hands be like the evening sacrifice." (Psalm 141:2)

The spirit of depression finally lifted and I have peace to face a new season of life... *even when I am alone.*

"With this in mind, be alert and always keep on praying for all the Lord's people." (Ephesians 6:18b)

Life and Laundry

"Commit to the LORD whatever you do, and your plans will succeed." (Proverbs 16:3)

While sorting through clothes to go into the washing machine, I started to think about the commonalities between life and laundry.

When I tackle laundry, I gather all the dirty clothes and sort them into piles. The largest pile determines where I'm going to begin. If the white pile is biggest, I start there. If the color pile is biggest, I start there. (You get the idea.) Once I have the biggest load of laundry out of the way, I feel a sense of accomplishment, and the pressure from my work load lessens.

Prioritizing my life can be somewhat similar. I often seize the day by taking on the biggest projects, first. Once the big tasks are out of the way, my stress level decreases, and I can move on to other tasks. Unfortunately, I sometimes become a little too relaxed with the seemingly smaller projects, and just as my last load of laundry might sit in the dryer for days until I finally get around to folding and putting it away, my seemingly smaller projects sometimes get neglected because I procrastinate in getting them done.

In both life and laundry, neglecting our duties can lead to unsightly wrinkles that will need to be ironed out, eventually. Those seemingly smaller projects are just as important as the big ones. When we don't complete them in a timely manner, there is often negative consequences—even added work later on.

What about you? Are there areas of your life that are not receiving the full attention they deserve? Sometimes the smallest things in our eyes are the biggest things in God's. I don't know about you, but I'm feeling convicted to treat all areas of my life with equal care and attention.

Oops... I just remembered. I left a load of laundry in the dryer.

What can I say? I'm a work in progress.

Just the Facts, Ma'am

Years ago, there was a popular television program called *Dragnet*. The show's detective (Joe Friday) became famous for coining the phrase, "Just the facts, ma'am." It was his way of keeping the witness focused on the facts rather than any circumstantial evidence surrounding the case.

Emotions can take me down a path of chasing after feelings rather than the cold hard facts. My husband frequently reminds me that I need to get my feelings off my shoulders. When emotions are clouding my judgment, he is quick to point me back to the reality of a situation.

I believe one of the reasons God designed marriage between a man and a woman is to help us become more objective. Men and women are different in many ways. Women can benefit from the balance of a man's straightforward (no nonsense) approach to life, and men can benefit from a woman's keen ability to read between the lines and determine the deeper issues at hand.

"Do not conform any longer to the pattern of this world, but be transformed by the renewing of your mind. Then you will be able to test and approve what God's will is - his good, pleasing and perfect will." (Romans 12:2)

I definitely need to focus more on the facts rather than feelings. My feelings are often deceptive and lead me astray. When I am unsure of how to handle a situation, I need to first review all the facts. I must ask myself, what do I know to be true in this situation, and what am I projecting with my emotions? Focusing on the facts (those things which we know to be true) can help us sort through any emotions that may be muddying the waters. We can then discard any assumptions based on emotions alone. This helps us view the situation more clearly.

Paul has some great advice for keeping our focus where it needs to be: "Finally, brothers, whatever is true, whatever is noble, whatever is right, whatever is pure, whatever is lovely, whatever is admirable—if anything is excellent or praiseworthy—think about such things." (Philippians 4:8)

Careful meditation on the facts is an effective tool for keeping our hearts and minds focused on truth. We're not alone. The Holy Spirit is our guide and He will lead us into all truth (John 16:13).

"Send forth your light and your truth, let them guide me." (Psalm 43:3)

Keep the focus where it needs to be—on truth. *Just the facts, ma'am!*

Greatest Harvest

"I am the true vine, and my Father is the gardener. He cuts off every branch in me that bears no fruit, while every branch that does bear fruit he prunes so that it will be even more fruitful. You are already clean because of the word I have spoken to you. Remain in me, and I will remain in you." (John 15:1-4)

The lesson of the vine and branches was taught during some final moments that Jesus shared with His disciples following the last supper. It is evident, through Scripture, that Jesus knew the time was drawing near for His death.

If you knew you were about to die and had only a short time left with your closest family and friends, what would you say?

Jesus used His time to do what He had done so many times before—*teach.*

Like every good teacher, Jesus used relatable objects and situations to best communicate His message.

"No branch can bear fruit by itself; it must remain in the vine. Neither can you bear fruit unless you remain in me. I am the vine; and you are the branches. If a man remains in me and I in him, he will bear much fruit; apart from me you can do nothing." (John 15:4b-5)

The ultimate goal, when tending a vineyard, is to cultivate and foster the greatest possible harvest of fruit. Jesus isn't just talking about grapes in this passage. He is talking about spiritual fruit. Our Master Gardener desires to cultivate in us the greatest possible harvest of spiritual fruit. But what is spiritual fruit?

> The fruit of the righteous is a tree of life, and he who wins souls is wise. (Proverbs 11:30)

> But the fruit of the Spirit is love, joy, peace, patience, kindness, goodness, faithfulness, gentleness, and self-control. (Galatians 5:22)

> All over the world this gospel is bearing fruit and growing, just as it has been doing among you since the day you heard it and understood God's grace in all its truth. (Colossians 1:6)

Bruce Wilkinson, author of *Secrets of the Vine,* explains that spiritual fruit represents good works, a thought, attitude, or action that God values because it glorifies Him. He goes on to say that bearing fruit is not some unique phenomenon reserved for certain Christians but is the destiny of every believer.

"And we pray this in order that you may live a life worthy of the Lord and may please him in every way: bearing fruit in every good work, growing in the knowledge of God..." (Colossians 1:10)

If we want our lives to bring forth an abundant harvest of fruit, we must follow Jesus' instructions: *Surrender to the Gardener and remain in the Vine.*

Heart Transplant

Each time I get my driver's license renewed, I'm asked if I would like to be an organ donor. The question always seems to catch me off guard, and I need to pause and think about it.

Some organs (like kidneys) can be shared without harm to the donor. But others, such as the liver or heart, can only be transplanted after the donor has died. *One must die so that another can live.* It is a challenging concept for our mortal minds to comprehend, yet that's exactly what Jesus did for you and me.

"He himself bore our sins in his body on the tree, so that we might die to sins and live for righteousness; by his wounds you have been healed." (1 Peter 2:24)

"This is how God showed his love among us: He sent his one and only Son into the world that we might live through him." (1 John 4:9)

We have the greatest example of sacrificial giving through Jesus Christ.

My dilemma over becoming an organ donor is fairly simple. I worry that someone might deem my life unimportant and, therefore, allow me to die so someone else might live. I suppose it's a good thing Jesus didn't think that way.

Jesus is the exact representation of His Father, perfect in every way, and yet He willingly gave up His life so that you and I would have eternal life with Him.

Your attitude should be the same as that of Christ Jesus: Who, being in very nature God, did not consider equality with God something to be grasped, but made himself nothing, taking the very nature of a servant, being made in human likeness. And being found in appearance as a man, He humbled himself and became obedient to death—even death on a cross! Therefore God exalted him to the highest place and gave him the name that is above every name, that at the name of Jesus every knee should bow, in heaven and on earth and under the earth, and every tongue confess that Jesus Christ is Lord, to the glory of God the Father. (Philippians 2:5-11)

Sin is a contaminant that causes decay in our spirit. This decay left untreated will lead to spiritual death. Thankfully, God offers a heart transplant to anyone willing to acknowledge that he is a sinner, believes Jesus paid the price for our sins, and confesses Jesus as our Lord and Savior. It's that easy! The very One who performs our surgery will also provide us with a clean and perfect heart. "For God so loved the world that he gave his one and only Son, that whoever believes in him shall not perish but have eternal life." (John 3:16) "But God demonstrates his own love for us in this: While we were still sinners, Christ died for us." (Romans 5:8)

Jesus not only embraced humility in esteeming Himself to be nothing, but he also made the sacrifice for those who did not yet know Him and would even reject Him. Now that's some seriously sacrificial love.

"Greater love has no one than this, that he lay down his life for his friends." (John 15:13)

Fatal Attraction

While playing softball outside with the kids, our fun in the sun was cut short when a dark cloud started moving directly towards us. As the cloud got closer, it made a strange buzzing sound, almost like a weed eater. We quickly realized the cloud was a swarm of bees.

I gathered the kids to my side, scrambling as fast as I could towards the house. From the kitchen window, we watched the bees settle into one of the trees out front. My husband and I didn't want these unwelcome guests to establish a nest in our yard, so we began making some phone calls to see what could be done.

Within hours a local bee keeper arrived on the scene and escorted the bees to their new home. He explained that sometimes a hive becomes over populated, leaving the queen with inadequate space for laying her eggs. She abandons the nest, and since the bees are attracted to the queen, many will either follow her or establish a new home.

Sometimes a similar scenario takes place in a large church.

Some time ago, we were part of a congregation that was blessed with a talented and dynamic preacher. It was not uncommon to laugh, cry, and suffer painful conviction all in one sermon message. The church grew rapidly, tripling in size over a few short years. The preacher was adored by everyone.

Then, without warning, the pastor abruptly left our congregation. Everyone was in shock. Many began to wander aimlessly, wondering whether they should try and follow this beloved leader or simply look for a new church home. The church lost many of its members during this shake up.

So, what happened?

No one can say for sure, but I have my personal theory. Because the preacher was dynamic, he received a lot of attention. (I don't believe he encouraged this celebrity-like interest, but sometimes the one receiving the devotion has little control over these things.) The attraction became fatal when this man was placed on a pedestal above everyone else. "They worshiped their idols, which became a snare to them." (Psalm 106:36)

This is a common tactic of the enemy. He deceives us into thinking that something other than God can satisfy. (Satan used this very same tactic in the Garden of Eden). Idol worship manifests itself in many different ways— including the worship of man. Anytime we take our focus away from God and place it elsewhere, we set ourselves up for a hard fall. Like Adam and Eve, it doesn't take long to realize we've been duped by the enemy.

God will not share His throne with anyone—not even a preacher man. When we allow other things in the world to take the place of God, it often results in some kind of fatality. We need to keep our focus on God and God alone.

"But if serving the LORD seems undesirable to you, then choose for yourselves this day whom you will serve, whether the gods your forefathers served beyond the River, or the gods of the Amorites, in whose land you are living. But as for me and my household, we will serve the LORD." (Joshua 24:15)

Measuring Up

"...until we all reach unity in the faith and in the knowledge of the Son of God and become mature, attaining to the whole measure of the fullness of Christ."
(Ephesians 4:13)

When my siblings and I were young, our mom kept growth charts for each of us. Every year, she entered her collection of data into a journal to track our progress. Gathering the information involved a tape measure, straight wall, flat floor, and trustworthy scale.

I didn't mind her growth measuring process when I was young, but as I got older (about seven or so), I began to hate the whole experience. I distinctly remember the day it became humiliating for me. It was the year that I began understanding the information my mom was collecting. (Or more accurately, the moment I began comparing my measurements to my sister.)

Although my sister was five years older than me, I weighed only a couple of pounds less than her. Her body type was naturally tiny and petite. Mine was not. Compared to her, I felt like a big, fat elephant. Although I didn't let my mom know it, I was mortified by the whole thing, especially when I realized that I was bigger than my sister. Words cannot describe how relieved I became the year that my mom finally stopped recording our height and weight.

As an adult, I realize that comparing ourselves to others is never a healthy practice. We either come away feeling deflated (loathing ourselves), or we come away feeling prideful, believing we are better than those around us. Critical thought patterns can lead to destructive behavior patterns, especially when they're not dealt with in a godly manner.

There was nothing wrong with my mom wanting to journal our measurements. She was doing what many mothers do, recording the developmental milestones of her children. Satan, however, used this opportunity to twist my perception, turning my thought patterns into an all-consuming, self-loathing mindset that eventually became a harmful weapon of self-destruction.

By age fifteen, I was in bondage to my eating disorder. I hated who I was on the inside and detested how I looked outside. My self-esteem was defaced in the wake of Satan's deception. And all because the enemy recognized my weakness and used it to his advantage.

"Jesus said, 'If you hold to my teaching, you are really my disciples. Then you will know the truth, and the truth will set you free.'" (John 8:31-32)

In order to truly overcome self-destructive thought patterns, we must renew our minds with God's truth. "We demolish arguments and every pretension that sets itself up against the knowledge of God, and we take captive every thought to make it obedient to Christ." (2 Corinthians 10:5)

When Satan tempts us to compare ourselves with others, we need to remember the true standard by which all things are measured—God's incomparable love.

"The LORD does not look at the things man looks at. Man looks at the outward appearance, but the LORD looks at the heart." (1 Samuel 16:7b-c)

May our hearts and minds be renewed by accepting this truth: *We are loved by God, and it has absolutely nothing to do with our outward appearance.*

"The Lord does not look at the things people look at. People look at the outward appearance, but the Lord looks at the heart." (1 Samuel 16:7)

When we play the comparison game, what we're really doing is comparing the inside of ourselves with the outside of someone else. I can tell you from personal experience—the exchange always comes up short.

> I pray that out of his glorious riches he may strengthen you with power through his Spirit in your inner being, so that Christ may dwell in your hearts through faith. And I pray that you, being rooted and established in love, may have power, together with all the saints, to grasp how wide and long and high and deep is the love of Christ, and to know this love that surpasses knowledge—that you may be filled to the measure of all the fullness of God. (Ephesians 3:17-19)

Lord, help us to stop comparing ourselves with others so that we can learn to be content with who You created us to be. Your Word tells us that we were created in Your image and You knit us together in our mother's womb. We are fearfully and wonderfully made. Help us to remember how much we are loved by You— the only One who truly matters. Fill us to the fullest "measure" of Your incomparable love. Amen

Making Sense of It

"But the LORD provided a great fish to swallow Jonah, and Jonah was inside the fish three days and three nights." (Jonah 1:17)

So much is packed into this Scripture for us to glean. In this verse, we're told that the LORD provided a great fish to swallow Jonah. But at first glance, this doesn't seem to be a manner of provision at all.

If you're familiar with the story, you know that Jonah spent three days and nights in the belly of the great fish—not very pleasant accommodations to be sure. Scientists explain that the acid from the fish's stomach would have likely disintegrated all the hair from Jonah's body and stripped away the pigment from his skin. When the fish finally spewed Jonah out onto dry land, the poor fella looked and smelled pretty bad.

And this was God's provision for Jonah?

"'For my thoughts are not your thoughts, neither are your ways my ways,' declares the LORD. 'As the heavens are higher than the earth, so are my ways higher than your ways and my thoughts than your thoughts.'" (Isaiah 55:8-9)

Perhaps you can relate to Jonah's undesirable provisions from the LORD. The loss of a job, loved one, home, health or some other type of hardship might cause us to experience feelings of abandonment, confusion, uncertainty, and fear. I am not suggesting that God causes our calamities. (We live in a fallen world, and because of this reality, we experience hard times in life.) I do believe, however, that God uses adversity, difficulty, and tragedy to bring about His intended purpose for our lives.

A lost job teaches us to be more dependent on God. "But seek first his kingdom and his righteousness, and all these things will be given to you as well. Therefore do not worry about tomorrow, for tomorrow will worry about itself. Each day has enough trouble of its own." (Matthew 6:33-34)

Losing someone we thought we could never live without teaches us that God is the only one who merits that responsibility in our lives. He will never leave or forsake us. "Though my father and mother forsake me, the LORD will receive me." (Psalm 27:10)

The loss of a home or other earthly possession teaches us to put less emphasis on the things of this world.

> Do not store up for yourselves treasures on earth, where moth and rust destroy, and where thieves break in and steal. But store up for yourselves treasures in heaven, where moth and rust do not destroy, and where thieves do not break in and steal. For where your treasure is, there your heart will be also. (Matthew 6:19-21)

Declining health forces us to rest and trust God more. "Come to me, all you who are weary and burdened, and I will give you rest." (Matthew 11:28)

Strained relationships better equip us to live in harmony with others. "If it is possible, as far as it depends on you, live at peace with everyone." (Romans 12:18)

Challenging circumstances make us more compassionate towards others in similar situations. "Therefore if you have any encouragement from being united with Christ, if any comfort from his love, if any common sharing in the Spirit, if any tenderness and compassion, then make my joy complete by being like-minded, having the same love, being one in spirit and of one mind." (Philippians 2:1-2)

Like Jonah, no matter what difficulties we face in life, if we keep God at the center, we will one day see how God really did provide during those dark and difficult days.

"Jesus replied, 'You do not realize now what I am doing, but later you will understand.'" (John 13:7) "Trust in the LORD with all your heart and lean not on your own understanding." (Proverbs 3:5)

Change of Direction

"Show me your ways, O LORD, teach me your paths."
(Psalm 25:4)

One time when we were traveling to Florida, I took the wheel for a while so my husband could get some rest. Gerry had been driving for several hours straight, so by the time he settled into the passenger seat, he was ready for a little nap. In a matter of moments, he was fast asleep.

Ninety minutes later, he awoke and checked the map to see how far we had gone. Unfortunately, the roadway signs were not connecting with what the map indicated. It didn't take long for us to realize that I had accidentally merged onto a different highway while he was asleep. We had been traveling in the wrong direction for at least an hour. With two kids in the back seat, anxious to reach our destination, this little detour wasn't the best start to our vacation. I felt bad for making such a careless mistake.

We can encounter similar circumstances when traveling the highway of life. The sudden realization that we are heading in the wrong direction can be painful. We might feel as though we've wasted too much time and grow disheartened, discouraged, or even depressed because of our error. We need not feel this way because God can use every one of our misdirected moves and bring good from them... *if we let Him that is.*

"Whether you turn to the right or to the left, your ears will hear a voice behind you, saying, 'This is the way; walk in it.'" (Isaiah 30:21)

At some point, God jolts us back into reality (sometimes painfully so) to redirect us down the path He desires. "Trust in the LORD with all your heart and lean not on your own understanding; in all your ways acknowledge him, and he will make your paths straight." (Proverbs 3:5-6)

I wish I could say our little vacation mishap was the only time I've found myself heading in the wrong direction, but I've found myself needing God's course correction many times throughout life. Sometimes I'm misdirected in a relationship, other times, by a poor decision. No matter what the circumstance, if we surrender the situation over to God, He will get us back on track and teach us valuable lessons along the way.

"Although the Lord gives you the bread of adversity and the water of affliction, your teachers will be hidden no more; with your own eyes you will see them." (Isaiah 30:20)

The straight and narrow path may be rough at times, but a sense of peace will accompany our journey once we realize God is traveling with us. He watches over our journey and redirects our steps along the way. He is completely trustworthy and always has our best interests at heart.

Keep connected to Jesus, and He will make your path straight.

"'For I know the plans I have for you,' declares the LORD, 'plans to prosper you and not to harm you, plans to give you hope and a future.'" (Jeremiah 29:11)

"You have made known to me the paths of life; you will fill me with joy in your presence." (Acts 2:28)

Spoiler Alert!

When I was about five years old, my brother, sister, and I combined our allowances to purchase a gift for my Dad's birthday celebration. Giving presents to my dad was a lot of fun because he always tried to guess his gift before opening it. It became a game that we all enjoyed.

"What do you think it is, Daddy?" I giggled with delight.

He looked at the package closely, turning it over in his hands this way and that. Then, he held the bundle up to his ear and gave it a gentle shake, careful to not damage the contents inside. After a thorough evaluation, he was ready to make his prediction.

"Hmmm," he said confidently, "It feels like… socks!"

"No, Daddy," I gestured towards the package in his hands, "It doesn't feel like socks. It feels like gloves!"

Laughter erupted from everyone in the room, but I had no idea why.

Have you ever had someone spoil the surprise for you? Perhaps they told you the ending of a movie, or maybe someone let a comment slip about the upcoming surprise party in your honor. Or worse yet, maybe the sonogram technician forgot to ask you and your wife to look away when trying to determine the sex of your baby.

Sometimes we like surprises. One of the greatest joys of my relationship with God is discovering the little surprises He has for me. Treasures in His Word, amazing opportunities that I never dreamed were possible, and miracles taking place in the lives of those around me are just a few of the ways that God astonishes me. But there are some elements of my faith journey that I'm glad are not a surprise.

"Do not be surprised, my brothers and sisters, if the world hates you." (1 John 3:13) "Dear friends, do not be surprised at the fiery ordeal that has come on you to test you, as though something strange were happening to you." (1 Peter 4:12) "I have told you these things, so that in me you may have peace. In this world you will have trouble. But take heart! I have overcome the world." (John 16:33)

I'm not surprised when difficulties come because God has clearly warned me about them. God's warnings are reassuring. Knowing ahead of time that we will face trials on earth helps us endure and persevere. Trials and tests will come, but they will not last forever. Our King is coming for us, and Scripture tells us to be ready. We may not know when or where, but one thing is for sure… *Jesus is coming back!*

> …the sun will be darkened, and the moon will not give its light; the stars will fall from the sky, and the heavenly bodies will

be shaken. Then will appear the sign of the Son of Man in heaven. And then all the peoples of the earth will mourn when they see the Son of Man coming on the clouds of heaven, with power and great glory. And he will send his angels with a loud trumpet call, and they will gather his elect from the four winds, from one end of the heavens to the other. (Matthew 24:29-31)

It is truly the best spoiler alert ever!

True Love Awaits

"How beautiful you are, my darling! Oh, how beautiful! Your eyes behind your veil are doves." (Song of Songs 4:1)

A bride anxiously awaits her walk down the aisle, reminded that months of preparing and years of courting have led up to this day. Peering through stained glass doors of the chapel, she catches a glimpse of her fetching groom standing poised and ready to receive his new bride. Her heart quickens when uneasy thoughts begin to surface in her mind. *Will he think I'm beautiful? Will I measure up to his expectations?*

As if reading her thoughts, the father pulls his daughter to his side and whispers, "You are stunning!"

At that very moment, the music crescendos, the chapel doors swing open, and the honored guests rise to their feet. The beautiful bride sweeps through the regal doorway with elegance and grace. The expectant groom gazes upon his beloved, as if seeing her for the first time. The adoration in his eyes, and the smile on his face, calms her spirit and melts her fears.

Scripture provides many parallels, analogies, and metaphors comparing our relationship with Christ to a marriage. What beautiful imagery for us to ponder.

In biblical times, once a couple became betrothed (engaged), the groom would go back to his father's house and begin building a section of the home where the couple would live. The bride would use that time to prepare herself for the life they would share together. Ironically, the bride never knew when her groom would come for her. She just knew to be ready at any moment's notice.

Like the bride described in my introduction, we must ready ourselves to meet our Groom—Jesus. "You also must be ready, because the Son of Man will come at an hour when you do not expect him." (Luke 12:40)

Jesus is preparing a place for us in heaven, a place where we will live with Him forever.

> Do not let your hearts be troubled. Trust in God; trust also in me. In my Father's house are many rooms; if it were not so, I would have told you. I am going there to prepare a place for you. And if I go and prepare a place for you, I will come back and take you to be with me that you also may be where I am. (John 14:3)

Our minds cannot conceive the splendor awaiting us in heaven, but Scripture assures us it is truly amazing! "No eye has seen, no ear has heard, no mind has conceived what God has prepared for those who love him…" (1 Corinthians 2:9)

Betrothed to Christ, we do not need to fear death for it is merely a doorway leading to eternal life with Jesus.

"Come, you who are blessed by my Father; take your inheritance, the kingdom prepared for you since the creation of the world." (Matthew 25:34b)

Like a bride on her wedding day, when we look into the eyes of our beloved Jesus, we will finally understand the full measure of His incomparable love.

Figure Eights

When I was a kid, I loved to watch figure skating during the winter Olympic games. The skaters would effortlessly glide across the ice, elegantly performing twists, turns, jumps, and figure eights.

Once in a while, it was cold enough for the lake to freeze, providing the perfect opportunity for my friends and me to practice our own maneuvers on the ice. Unfortunately, the only skill that we somewhat mastered was the infamous figure eight.

"I wish the only direction existing for a Christian was onward to maturity, but unfortunately some of our footprints in the sand look a lot like figure eights." ~Beth Moore

As I look back over my life, impressions of a few figure eight patterns remain on the surface of my spiritual journey. I try hard to move steadily forward, but sometimes, I find myself circling back towards old patterns of behavior or attitudes that I thought were put to rest long ago. It is during these times that I suddenly realize I'm not as far along on this spiritual journey as I thought.

"You were taught, with regard to your former way of life, to put off your old self, which is being corrupted by its deceitful desires; to be made new in the attitude of your minds; and to put on the new self, created to be like God in true righteousness and holiness." (Ephesians 4:22-24)

What about you? Do you notice any figure eight patterns developing in your walk with God?

"Therefore, if anyone is in Christ, he is a new creation; the old has gone, the new has come! All this is from God, who reconciled us to himself through Christ and gave us the ministry of reconciliation..." (2 Corinthians 5:17-18)

Figure eight patterns belong on the ice—not on our journey with God.

"...in all your ways acknowledge him, and he will make your paths straight." (Proverbs 3:6)

Pray Continually!

"Rejoice always, pray continually, give thanks in all circumstances; for this is God's will for you in Christ Jesus." (1 Thessalonians 5:16-18)

After many years of prayer, a dear friend's husband finally accepted Jesus into his heart. What a glorious day! My sister-in-Christ is a wonderful witness to the power of a praying wife.

"Wives, in the same way be submissive to your husbands so that, if any of them do not believe the word, they may be won over without words by the behavior of their wives, when they see the purity and reverence of your lives." (1 Peter 3:1-2)

Not only was this friend a beautiful witness to her husband, but she didn't give up praying for his salvation. Her persistence finally paid off. What hope this brings to each of us who are still waiting for our prayers to be answered. My friend could have simply kept this wonderful news to only a few, but instead she shared it with many. Her announcement of this awesome event helped me realize just how important it is for Christians to tell one another of God's mighty acts.

"Give praise to the LORD, proclaim his name; make known among the nations what he has done. Sing to him, sing praise to him; tell of all his wonderful acts. Glory in his holy name; let the hearts of those who seek the LORD rejoice." (Psalm 105:1-3)

We are so eager to share prayer requests, but we don't always remember to announce when prayers have been answered. Sharing answered prayer with others helps to strengthen and build the faith of all believers.

Perhaps you have desperately prayed for a loved one to give their lives to the Lord. I'm sure my friend would tell you to not give up. Keep praying! And when God does answer your prayer, share the good news with others!

"In the morning, O LORD, you hear my voice; in the morning I lay my requests before you and wait in expectation." (Psalm 5:3)

"I wait for you, O LORD; you will answer, O Lord my God." (Psalm 38:15)

As we wait for our loved ones to make a decision to accept Jesus for themselves, remember the wonderful words of Christian author Oswald Chambers, "You can never give another person that which you have found, but you can make him homesick for what you have."

Aliens on Earth

Even though my husband realizes aliens are not real, he still enjoys watching movie dramatizations of extraterrestrial creatures visiting earth from outer space.

The concept of aliens is not a completely out of this world idea. As a matter of fact, the Bible refers to this subject quite often. Before you think I'm crazy, take a look at the following passages:

"All these people were still living by faith when they died. They did not receive the things promised; they only saw them and welcomed them from a distance. And they admitted that they were aliens and strangers on earth." (Hebrews 11:13)

"Consequently, you are no longer foreigners and aliens, but fellow citizens with God's people and members of God's household, built on the foundation of the apostles and prophets, with Christ Jesus himself as the chief cornerstone." (Ephesians 2:19-20)

Christians are aliens living in a foreign land. This is not our real home. For this reason, no matter what wonderful things take place in our lives, we will never find complete fulfillment on this earth. Deep down in the depth of our soul, we have a longing for something else—something better. Our spirit cries out—*we were created for so much more!*

To know God personally and be near Him in every imaginable way—that is what our soul truly desires. The euphoria experienced by Adam and Eve in the Garden of Eden is our greatest need and heart's desire. We come close to attaining fulfillment here on earth when we seek God with all our heart. Yet, even this pales in comparison to what we will experience in heaven when we look into the eyes of Jesus.

> If I am to go on living in the body, this will mean fruitful labor for me. Yet what shall I choose? I do not know! I am torn between the two: I desire to depart and be with Christ, which is better by far; but it is more necessary for you that I remain in the body. (Philippians 1:22-24)

Until we reach our eternal home in heaven, we are strangers in a foreign land—aliens on earth.

Don't get too discouraged with life here on earth. *We aren't home yet!*

Run Your Race

"Do you not know that in a race all the runners run, but only one gets the prize? Run in such a way as to get the prize." (1 Corinthians 9:24)

When our son and daughter ran track in high school, my husband and I really enjoyed going to their meets. Most track events are judged on individual performance—unless of course you are running a relay race, in which case you are judged as a team.

Athletes seek to improve their personal times, being sure to do their very best in any given race. Of course, they hope to beat their opponents, but even if they don't win the race, they still take pride in knowing they've given it their all.

"Therefore, since we are surrounded by such a great cloud of witnesses, let us throw off everything that hinders and the sin that so easily entangles, and let us run with perseverance the race marked out for us." (Hebrews 12:1)

Our son was a sprinter, but his best friend was a long distance runner. Long distance running takes a lot of endurance. As the one mile race would near its end, teammates would gather alongside the track shouting encouragement to the runners, spurring them on to victory. I was always amazed to see how the exhausted runners would find a final burst of energy to propel themselves towards the finish line after hearing their teammate's cheers of support.

In First Corinthians, Paul makes the analogy that living the Christian life is a lot like running a race. If we want to get the prize, we need to go into strict training and give it all we got. "Everyone who competes in the games goes into strict training. They do it to get a crown that will not last; but we do it to get a crown that will last forever." (1 Corinthians 9:25)

Much like the athletes competing in a track meet, we sometimes need the encouragement of our teammates to propel us toward the finish line. The idea is not to finish ahead of everyone else but to run our personal best and to give it all we've got.

Do you see someone growing weary? Is their perseverance running low? Why not run alongside them for a while and cheer them on to victory. "Therefore encourage one another and build each other up, just as in fact you are doing." (1 Thessalonians 5:10)

Perhaps you're growing weary running your own race. Call out to your fellow Christians for some encouragement. Like any long distance runner, you too will find that extra burst of energy to finish your race strong.

"Always give yourselves fully to the work of the Lord, because you know that your labor in the Lord is not in vain." (1 Corinthians 15:58)

Directionally Challenged

I hate to admit this about myself, but I'm directionally challenged. My handicap is so bad that when I come out of a store, I struggle to find where I parked my car. If I get off the highway, I become disoriented and have a hard time finding my way back to the entrance ramp. For crying out loud, I even get lost in the mall.

The irony in all of this is that, at one point in time, everyone in my family had a navigational system in their car—except me. So, when I noticed my son's GPS system sitting on the dash of his car, I asked if he ever used it. He said that he didn't need to anymore because he had a navigational system on his cell phone. Since he didn't need his dashboard device, he gave it to me.

As Christians, our two-part navigational system (the Holy Spirit and God's Word) are effective tools for leading us along the straight and narrow path of life, but they are only effective if we know how they work. I can affix my son's *Tom-Tom* to the dash of my car, but I still need to read the instruction manual and turn it on. Otherwise, it's of no real benefit to me.

In the same way, we can accept the gift of salvation and own a Bible, but if we never read it or understand the power of the Holy Spirit in our lives, we are not experiencing the fullness of what God has to offer.

None of us are born knowing Scripture and how it applies to our everyday lives. We must put forth some effort to learn. As we study the Bible, the Holy Spirit will open our hearts and minds to a deeper understanding of God's Word.

"But the Advocate, the Holy Spirit, whom the Father will send in my name, will teach you all things and will remind you of everything I have said to you." (John 14:26)

"Send forth your light and your truth, let them guide me; let them bring me to your holy mountain, to the place where you dwell." (Psalm 43:3)

Are you feeling a little lost where your relationship with God is concerned? Are you ready to move forward but just don't know how to get there?

God will lead you down the right path, but be sure to spend adequate time reading your Instruction Manual (Bible) so you can better understand how to engage His Power.

Trust and Obey

Feeling nervous about driving home from an unfamiliar area in the dark, I was very grateful when I remembered my son's navigational system was in my glove box.

As I headed toward home, trusting the GPS was not something that came easy to me. Every time I was told to turn, I was suspicious about whether it was taking me the right way. The journey home was very dark, and everything looked different than it did earlier in the day; so I kept thinking that I was lost.

The lure to turn down a different road toyed with my mind a couple of times, but I resisted the temptation and followed the GPS instead. Within minutes, highway signs appeared in the distance, confirming that I was on the right track. Forty-five minutes later, I was pulling into our garage, safe and sound.

"So be careful to do what the LORD your God has commanded you; do not turn aside to the right or to the left." (Deuteronomy 5:32)

Sometimes I encounter similar resistance when it comes to following directions from God. The Holy Spirit tries to direct me one way, but I am still tempted to go another.

As I did with my GPS, we must learn to trust the guidance of the One who knows the way. Things may seem uncertain at the moment, but if we continue to accept the guidance of the Holy Spirit, following God's direction for our lives, we will arrive safely at our destination. *We simply need to trust and obey.*

"Whether you turn to the right or to the left, your ears will hear a voice behind you, saying, 'This is the way; walk in it.'" (Isaiah 30:21)

A Job Well Done

"Therefore, as it is written: 'Let him who boasts boast in the Lord.'" (1 Corinthians 1:31)

It feels good to complete a project you have been working on for a long time. There is a certain sense of accomplishment that comes with knowing it was a job well done.

Whether you're a student working on a school assignment, a housewife tackling laundry, an employee making a presentation, or a mom raising kids—we are called to give our very best. It doesn't matter if we have all the answers or know how something is going to turn out. We are merely asked to follow God's lead and do what He calls us to do. The rest is up to Him.

Sometimes we don't get to see the end result of our hard work. We must simply trust God to work out everything for His good plan and purpose. "And we know that in all things God works for the good of those who love him, who have been called according to his purpose." (Romans 8:28)

When I started this ministry, I had no idea what it was supposed to look like or how things were going to play out. All I really knew was that God was calling me to minister to women who were living in bondage to the lies of this world. God showed me the need, and I trusted Him to lead the way. Step by step, I continue to follow.

"You say, 'But He has been unwise to choose me, because there is nothing in me; I am not of any value.' That is why He chose you. As long as you think there is something in you, He cannot choose you because you have ends of your own to serve; but if you let Him bring you to the end of your self-sufficiency, then He can choose you to go with Him to Jerusalem." ~Oswald Chambers, *My Utmost for His Highest*

I am not the least bit qualified, by the world's standards, to be doing what I'm doing. But thankfully, God doesn't usually call the qualified—He qualifies the called.

> Brothers, think of what you were when you were called. Not many of you were wise by human standards; not many were influential; not many were of noble birth. But God chose the foolish things of the world to shame the wise; God chose the weak things of the world to shame the strong. He chose the lowly things of this world and the despised things—and the things that are not—to nullify the things that are, so that no one may boast before him. It is because of him that you are in Christ Jesus, who has become for us wisdom from God—that is, our righteousness, holiness and redemption. (1 Corinthians 1:26-30)

We may never see the full impact of what God does through our meager offerings in life, but that's okay. We simply need to give our all and fulfill each responsibility as it comes our way. In humble submission, we must continue to follow Jesus so that we will one day hear Him say, "Well done, good and faithful servant! You have been faithful with a few things; I will put you in charge of many things. Come and share your master's happiness!" (Matthew 25:21)

Afraid of Letting Go

L etting go is one of the most difficult things to do— especially for individuals struggling with eating disorders. Eating disorder behavior is directly linked to control. When everything else in life becomes unmanageable, the regulation of food becomes the method to regain or establish some semblance of control, or so we think.

Anorexics withhold. Bulimics purge. And compulsive over eaters gorge. Although each of these disorders manifests differently, these negative behaviors become a means for coping with difficult emotions, stress, and anxiety. Out of control feelings can cause some of us to head down a path of self-destruction. Before we know it we're trapped in bondage, unable to break free.

In her book *I'm Beautiful? Why Can't I See It?* author Kimberly Davidson shares a vivid illustration of getting trapped.

> Villagers that live in the forests and mountains of India catch monkeys by carving pots with necks as long as a monkeys arm and a base large enough for a banana. The monkeys can't wait to retrieve their prize. They put their arms down the

neck of the jar until they have the banana tightly grasped. However, they can't pull it through the narrow neck. So they sit holding their prize tightly for fear of losing it. Eventually, the monkey becomes immobilized, and they're simple pickings for the villagers.

I think that one of the reasons we fear letting go is because we are not entirely convinced that God will adequately manage what we hand over to Him. In other words, we don't trust Him. Trust is not something that happens overnight; it is built over time. God knows exactly why we have trust issues. He is not intimidated by our lack of trust. Saddened—yes. Intimidated—no.

When I minister to women, I assure them that God wants to earn their trust. I encourage them to give just one piece of their disorder over to Him and see what He does with it. Maybe you aren't ready to hand everything over to God, but could you try giving Him just a small piece? Try eating a 'fear food' today (something you are afraid to eat because you think it will make you fat). Keep that meal down this time.

Perhaps your struggle is something other than food. The same principles can be applied to any stronghold you are facing.

What is it that you're holding so tightly? Perhaps like the monkeys, you're immobilized with fear, unable to let go. God wants to help us, but He continues to respect our free will. He will not force us to let go.

"Submit to God and be at peace with him; in this way prosperity will come to you." (Job 22:21)

Two choices are in front of you. One leads to freedom, the other leads to deeper bondage. Remember the monkeys. Failure to let go led to their capture.

Freedom or bondage—the choice is ours.

"It is for freedom that Christ has set us free. Stand firm, then, and do not let yourselves be burdened again by a yoke of slavery." (Galatians 5:1)

Jesus Wept

"But you, O Lord, are a compassionate and gracious God, slow to anger, abounding in love and faithfulness." (Psalm 86:15)

I've been told that I don't hide my feelings very well. Apparently, everything about my demeanor: my voice, facial expressions, even my breathing is a dead giveaway of the emotions I'm feeling.

One afternoon when I was getting my nails done, the technician asked if something was wrong. I was kind of surprised by her question since we had barely spoken the entire time she worked on my nails.

"Why do you ask?" I prodded.

"Well," she responded, "you kept sighing while I was doing your nails."

I thought to myself, Wow! I really *don't* hide my feelings well. Even the nail technician is on to me.

My daughter is very perceptive when it comes to discerning my state of emotions. She's even able to distinguish my mood when I answer the phone with a simple hello. My son says that I'd never make it as a poker player in Vegas because my face says it all. What can I say? When my heart aches, it shows.

When we are hurting, sometimes it's good to share our heartache with a brother or sister in Christ.

An older woman from my church must have noticed my downcast spirit because she asked if I was okay. I immediately began to tear up. As this dear woman sat and listened to me pour out my heart, her eyes began to tear up too. I was extremely touched by her response.

It was a vivid reminder that sometimes the best thing we can offer someone who is hurting is our sincere, heartfelt sorrow. This woman didn't offer advice. She didn't offer up scriptures. She just cried with me. That said it all. Her tears showed she cared. She was sad because I was sad.

Jesus is the most compassionate man who ever walked the face of this earth, and He deeply felt the pain of others. The shortest verse in the Bible states that "Jesus wept" (John 11:35). These two simple words reveal Christ's heart towards our pain and suffering.

"When Mary reached the place where Jesus was and saw him, she fell at his feet and said, 'Lord, if you had been here, my brother would not have died.' When Jesus saw her weeping, and the Jews who had come along with her also weeping, he was deeply moved in spirit and troubled." (John 11:32-33)

Sometimes sorrow is so great that the only person with whom we can share our heart with is our Lord Jesus. There is no better place to go with a broken heart. Jesus will minister to us in ways that no human being ever could.

Are you hurting today?

Jesus is waiting to wrap you in His loving, compassionate arms.

"The eyes of the LORD are on the righteous and his ears are attentive to their cry." (Psalm 34:15)

"The righteous cry out, and the LORD hears them; he delivers them from all their troubles. The LORD is close to the brokenhearted and saves those who are crushed in spirit." (Psalm 34:17-18)

Circle of Trust

In the comedic film *Meet the Parents*, a young woman brings her new fiancé home for the first time. During a private meeting with the girl's over-protective father, the fiancé is educated about the family's sacred circle of trust. The fiancé's attempts to live up to his soon to be family's perception of the sacred bond, creates one humorous situation after another.

A circle of trust is an invisible boundary of sorts that encircles those closest to us. It includes family members and/or close friends, with whom we have the privilege of sharing some of life's more intimate moments.

Did you know that Jesus had a circle of trust? His close knit group included Peter, James, and John. These three disciples were part of Jesus' inner sphere of influence. They were often asked to accompany Him when the other disciples were left behind.

"He did not let anyone follow him except Peter, James and John the brother of James. When they came to the home of the synagogue ruler, Jesus saw a commotion, with people crying and wailing loudly." (Mark 5:37-38)

"After six days Jesus took Peter, James and John with him and led them up a high mountain, where they were all alone. There he was transfigured before them." (Mark 9:2)

"They went to a place called Gethsemane, and Jesus said to his disciples, 'Sit here while I pray.' He took Peter, James and John along with him, and he began to be deeply distressed and troubled. 'My soul is overwhelmed with sorrow to the point of death,' he said to them. 'Stay here and keep watch.'" (Mark 14:32-34)

Jesus understood the importance of having a group of individuals ready and willing to share the good, bad, and ugly parts of life with us. Peter, James, and John saw Jesus perform miracles that had been shrouded from the eyes of others. They witnessed Jesus' glorious transfiguration atop the mountain, and later they accompanied Him to the furthest point in the Garden of Gethsemane before He went on to be alone with His Father. As always, Jesus sets the example for us to follow in our everyday lives. God never meant for us to journey this life alone.

"A friend loves at all times, and a brother is born for adversity." (Proverbs 17:17)

"If one falls down, his friend can help him up. But pity the man who falls and has no one to help him up!" (Ecclesiastes 4:10)

Do you have trusted individuals ready and willing to share the good times and bad? Just like Jesus, we need a circle of trust.

Drowning out the Noise

To celebrate my birthday, I went with my family and friends to see two of my favorite Christian bands—Casting Crowns and Sanctus Real. Both bands contain incredible musicians who beautifully convey their passion for God through music.

Towards the end of the concert, I was struggling with my hearing. I'm not sure if it's my age or if the decibels had significantly increased throughout the evening, but the music became all jumbled in my head. As hard as I tried to hear, I just couldn't make out the words of each song. Looking for some relief, I cupped my hands over my ears and the most amazing thing happened—I could hear every word of the songs perfectly.

The instruments had become so loud that they were drowning out the vocalist. In my opinion, the lyrics are the most important part of a song, so even though I received lots of stares, I continued holding my hands over my ears so I could hear.

Do you ever go through life and feel like you're somehow missing the most important part?

Sometimes our lives are filled with so much reverberation we lose focus on what's most important. Days become so jam packed with to do's that we forget to simply be. We rush from one thing to the next and barely have time to breathe. "I have no peace, no quietness; I have no rest, but only turmoil." (Job 3:26)

In this day and age, everyday tasks can be accomplished in record time. With all the modern conveniences that we have available to us, you would think we would have more time to enjoy life. But do we?

"Be still before the LORD, all mankind, because he has roused himself from his holy dwelling." (Zechariah 2:13)

"[Jesus] got up, rebuked the wind and said to the waves, 'Quiet! Be still!' Then the wind died down and it was completely calm." (Mark 4:39)

When chaos abounds, Jesus is there to help us filter out the confusion of our lives so we can focus on what's really important.

One Step at a Time

Sometimes my brain is filled with so much information that it actually hurts. I call it brain overload. My mind is stretched beyond capacity. Focusing on the big picture of anything is extremely mind boggling for me, so I've decided to take some cues from my husband when it comes to tackling large, overwhelming projects.

My husband, Gerry, recently painted our living room. Under normal circumstances, painting a living room isn't all that big of a deal, but when you consider living room walls extending up to the second story—it *is* a big deal.

Since we aren't exactly spring chickens anymore, I tried to convince Gerry that this was a project we needed to hire a professional painter to do, but he insisted that he could handle it. I was skeptical, but after twenty plus years of marriage, I know my husband is a driven man. Once he's put his mind to something, there's no stopping him.

Gerry made sure he had the proper tools and equipment for the project. He gathered paint, rollers, drop cloths, brushes, and a very big ladder.

Next, he put a plan together. He didn't just jump ahead and begin painting at random. He took some time to decide which walls were best to begin and which were best to save until the end.

Finally, he split the project into more manageable pieces, tackling one wall at a time.

Sometimes we become so overwhelmed with a project because we are focusing on the whole picture rather than taking one step at a time. Each step, no matter how small, brings us closer to the finish line.

"If the LORD delights in a man's way, he makes his steps firm:" (Psalm 37:23)

Are you feeling overwhelmed? Take your focus off the end result, and concentrate only on what you can do today. Make sure you have the proper tools, put together a plan, and divide the project into smaller, more manageable segments. Before you know it, your overwhelming project will be on its way to completion.

"Commit to the LORD whatever you do, and your plans will succeed." (Proverbs 16:3)

"Many are the plans in a man's heart, but it is the LORD's purpose that prevails." (Proverbs 19:21)

Thief in the Night

"The night is nearly over; the day is almost here. So let us put aside the deeds of darkness and put on the armor of light." (Romans 13:12)

On our yearly camping trips with close friends, each family was responsible for bringing certain items to share. One of my friends was responsible for bringing her famous brownies. We all loved her tasty treats and couldn't wait to dig in.

Still feeling stuffed from dinner, we decided to wait before breaking into the pan of brownies. After we covered the desserts, we gathered around the campfire to let our food digest. With the firelight's glow illuminating our faces, we reminisced over previous camping expeditions. In between occasional bursts of laughter, the kids could be heard in the background, enjoying the freedom of playing outdoors after dark.

Raccoons only come out at night and usually have a healthy fear of people. However, in state parks, because raccoons are regularly exposed to people, their natural instinct to fear humans is diminished. Combine this little detail with the fact that we were a group of distracted campers and you have a disaster waiting to happen.

Someone heard rustling by the picnic table and decided to investigate. Moments later, we heard a shriek. With flashlights in hand, we hurried over to the picnic table. Hunched over our dessert pans sat an audacious little raccoon, devouring our delicious brownies. Lesson learned. Keep the coveted brownies locked up until you are ready to eat.

There is a point to my little camping tale.

> You are all sons of the light and sons of the day. We do not belong to the night or to the darkness. So then, let us not be like others, who are asleep, but let us be alert and self-controlled. For those who sleep, sleep at night, and those who get drunk, get drunk at night. But since we belong to the day, let us be self-controlled, putting on faith and love as a breastplate, and the hope of salvation as a helmet. (1 Thessalonians 5:5-8)

Lost souls hide under the cover of darkness to engage in shameful deeds. While that's not terribly surprising, I am astonished by the number of Christians who use the cover of darkness to engage in behavior they wouldn't dare take part in during daylight.

"Woe to those who go to great depths to hide their plans from the LORD, who do their work in darkness and think, 'Who sees us? Who will know?'" (Isaiah 29:15)

May we never forget that Jesus came to this earth and died for our sins so we would no longer have to live in sin and darkness.

"In him was life, and that life was the light of men. The light shines in the darkness, but the darkness has not understood it....The true light that gives light to every man was coming into the world." (John 1:4-5, 9)

"When Jesus spoke again to the people, he said, 'I am the light of the world. Whoever follows me will never walk in darkness, but will have the light of life.'" (John 8:12)

Because of our great love for Jesus and our gratitude for what He did on the cross, let us put away our deeds of darkness and live as righteous children of Light.

"I (Jesus) have come into the world as a light, so that no one who believes in me should stay in darkness." (John 12:46)

Displays of God's Splendor

"O LORD, our Lord, how majestic is your name in all the earth! You have set your glory above the heavens." (Psalm 8:1)

Louie Giglio gives a presentation called *Indescribable*, which highlights the expanse of the known universe and its unfathomable beauty. The images in the slideshow appear as though the LORD painted His awesome glory across the sky's magnificent canvas. Formations, colors, and nuances displayed across the great expanse of the universe are spectacular portraits of a world unknown to mere mortal men. God's created universe truly is incredible!

The Creation Museum in Petersburg, KY has a wonderful planetarium which takes you on an unforgettable tour of God's handiwork in outer space. As you watch the incredible images presented across the large domed screen, you can't help but contemplate the following words penned by King David thousands of years earlier.

"When I consider your heavens, the work of your fingers, the moon and the stars, which you have set in place, what is man that you are mindful of him, the son of man that you care for him?" (Psalm 8:3-4)

We have an amazing God who's not only mindful of us, but He knows us personally, right down to the number of hairs on our head (Luke 12:7).

Our LORD knows everything there is to know about us, and yet still He loves us. *Now that's incredible!*

The next time you have an opportunity to peer into the nighttime sky, look up and praise God for who He is and what He has created. Praise His name and thank Him for His great love.

"O LORD, our Lord, how majestic is your name in all the earth!" (Psalm 8:9)

Play It Out

My husband and I learned a new card game called Pitch. It involves quite a bit of strategy and is challenging because of the many unknowns. The ever changing variables keep the players guessing throughout the entire game. Our card game partners explained all the rules and the point value system, but it wasn't until we actually played through a hand or two that we understood the game to its fullest.

Experience is a great teacher. With each new hand I learned strategies and approaches that weren't fully understood through verbal instructions alone. During one particular hand, I took a big risk and lost the game for my partner and me. I felt bad for making the error, but I also realized that some lessons are best learned through trial and error.

"In the same way, faith by itself, if it is not accompanied by action, is dead." (James 2:17)

Faith is like a card game. We can read about faith and watch others live faith-filled lives, but eventually, you and I must put our faith into action.

As we experience the ups and downs of being a follower of Jesus, and as we step out and take risks in life, we learn comprehensive lessons to help us more fully appreciate what Christianity is all about. The most amazing experiences in life take place when we step out and put our faith into action. Minor defeats are not much fun, but they do better equip us to conquer future leaps of faith.

"You see that his faith and his actions were working together, and his faith was made complete by what he did." (James 2:22)

When it comes to true faith… we need play it out.

Therefore, since we are surrounded by such a great cloud of witnesses, let us throw off everything that hinders and the sin that so easily entangles, and let us run with perseverance the race marked out for us. Let us fix our eyes on Jesus, the author and perfecter of our faith, who for the joy set before him endured the cross, scorning its shame, and sat down at the right hand of the throne of God. Consider him who endured such opposition from sinful men, so that you will not grow weary and lose heart. (Hebrews 12:1-3)

Truly Blessed

Many U.S. citizens have grown complacent concerning the blessings and freedoms we have in this country. We've grown accustomed to the modern conveniences and perks, and sometimes, we even feel entitled to that which we've done nothing to earn or deserve. People who come to our country looking for a better way of life are often shocked by the waste and apathy they find here. We are the most blessed nation on earth, but do we really appreciate what we have been given?

"Give thanks to the LORD, call on his name; make known among the nations what he has done." (1 Chronicles 16:8)

It's time we recognize and give thanks for how truly blessed we are.

"Look to the LORD and his strength; seek his face always. Remember the wonders he has done, his miracles, and the judgments he pronounced, O descendants of Abraham his servant, O sons of Jacob, his chosen ones. He is the LORD our God; his judgments are in all the earth." (Psalm 105:4-7)

When we grow complacent, apathetic or have feelings of entitlement, we become blind to the blessings in our life. When we can't see the blessings in our life, we grow discouraged. Perhaps we could all benefit from a few reminders of just how blessed we are.

If you woke up this morning with more health than illness, you are more blessed than the million who won't survive the week.

If you have never experienced the danger of battle, the loneliness of imprisonment, the agony of torture or the pangs of starvation, you are ahead of 20 million people around the world.

If you attend a church meeting without fear of harassment, arrest, torture, or death, you are more blessed than almost three billion people in the world.

If you have food in your refrigerator, clothes on your back, a roof over your head and a place to sleep, you are richer than 75% of this world.

If you have money in the bank, in your wallet, and spare change in a dish someplace, you are among the top 8% of the world's wealthy.

If your parents are still married and alive, you are very rare, especially in the United States.

If you hold up your head with a smile on your face and are truly thankful, you are blessed because the majority can, but most do not.

If you can hold someone's hand, hug them or even touch them on the shoulder, you are blessed because you can offer God's healing touch.

If you can read this message, you are more blessed than over two billion people in the world that cannot read anything at all. ~Author Unknown

Bubbling Brook

"For the Lamb at the center of the throne will be their shepherd; he will lead them to springs of living water." (Revelation 7:17)

I love to explore creek beds. While I'm navigating the tributaries and stepping across large protruding rocks, I sometimes find stagnant pools of water isolated from the free-flowing stream. These murky patches look and smell foul and stand in stark contrast to the clear and fresh, bubbling brooks just a few feet away.

In biblical times, free-flowing water was considered living water. Living water was life-giving and continually fresh. For obvious reasons, it became necessary to build wells and cisterns to meet the needs of many people. But clean, clear, free-flowing water was always ideal.

"....The fountain of wisdom is a bubbling brook." (Proverbs 18:4)

Daily, we need fresh doses of God's living water to course through our spirits. Hearing God's Word spoken on Sunday mornings or through small study groups once a week is not enough. We need to be washed in the bubbling brook of God's wisdom each and every day. We need to drink deep from the life-giving truths in Scripture— truths that cleanse our hearts and fill us so completely that we overflow.

"Christ... gave up himself for [the church] to make her holy, cleansing her by the washing with water through the word..." (Ephesians 5:26)

Have you received your dose of living water today? Spend time sitting at the feet of Jesus and ask Him to fill your spirit and wash your mind with His living water.

"Jesus answered, 'Everyone who drinks this water will be thirsty again, but whoever drinks the water I give him will never thirst. Indeed, the water I give him will become in him a spring of water welling up to eternal life.'" (John 4:13-14)

What Do You Live For?

"The effect of the cross is salvation, sanctification, healing etc., but we are not to preach any of these, we are to preach Jesus Christ and Him crucified. The proclaiming of Jesus will do its own work." ~Oswald Chambers

In a recent Bible study, the author asked the following question. What do you live for? She went on to explain that the early church's response to this question would have been JESUS. It was all about Him. I felt a pang of conviction and wondered. *Is Jesus is the main focus in my life? Is He what I live for?*

I have to be honest. Jesus has not always been my main focus. At times I have allowed other things to take center stage in my life: family, friends, even ministry and church. Although these are all good things, they should never take precedence over Jesus.

Paul is someone who put Christ first in his life, but this wasn't always the case. In fact, before his intense encounter with Jesus on the road to Damascus, Paul spent much of his time and energy persecuting everyone who was a follower of Jesus. He thought he was doing the right thing until Jesus opened his heart to the truth.

Paul penned more books of the New Testament than any other author, and do you know what his central theme was? Jesus Christ!

> But whatever was to my profit I now consider loss for the sake of <u>Christ</u>. What is more, I consider everything a loss compared to the surpassing greatness of knowing <u>Christ Jesus</u> my Lord, for whose sake I have lost all things. I consider them rubbish, that I may gain <u>Christ</u> and be found in him, not having a righteousness of my own that comes from the law, but that which is through faith in <u>Christ</u>—the righteousness that comes from God and is by faith. I want to know <u>Christ</u> and the power of his resurrection and the fellowship of sharing in his sufferings, becoming like him in his death, and so, somehow, to attain to the resurrection from the dead. (Philippians 3:7-11)

In this passage alone, Christ is mentioned five times. Jesus became the center of Paul's life-message and preaching, and He should become the center of our life-message too.

Making Christ the center of our lives must be a conscious choice we make each and every day. I don't know about you, but I want to live for Jesus!

Whiter Than Snow

"Cleanse me with hyssop, and I will be clean; wash me, and I will be whiter than snow." (Psalm 51:7)

Although I'm not a big fan of winter, I do enjoy the beauty of freshly fallen snow, especially when I wake up in the morning to find a thick, white blanket covering the landscape surrounding our home. It's important to enjoy the beauty of freshly fallen snow right away because it doesn't take long before the glistening white turns a polluted grey. Cars and snow removal trucks definitely leave their mark.

"I write to you, dear children, because your sins have been forgiven on account of his name." (1 John 2:12)

When we first accept Jesus as our Lord and Savior and receive His gift of forgiveness, we feel as pure and unstained as freshly fallen snow. But as time goes by, new sin creeps into our lives and stains our souls once again. Christians should sin less, but we will never be sinless, at least not in these mortal bodies.

Jesus didn't just die for past sins. His mercy and forgiveness covers all of our sins—past, present, and future. We are called to acknowledge our sin and repent as soon as we realize our iniquity. God knows our need for His constant forgiveness—that's why He sent His Son Jesus to die for us.

"This is my blood of the covenant, which is poured out for many for the forgiveness of sins." (Matthew 26:28)

"Blessed is he whose transgressions are forgiven, whose sins are covered." (Psalm 32:1)

Don't let Satan deceive you into thinking that some of your sins are not covered by grace. If you have received Jesus as your Lord and Savior and have accepted His free gift of forgiveness, your sins are forgiven. Washed by the blood of Jesus—you are whiter than snow.

"In him we have redemption through his blood, the forgiveness of sins, in accordance with the riches of God's grace that he lavished on us with all wisdom and understanding." (Ephesians 1:7-8)

What should be our response to His merciful gift of forgiveness?

Progress—not perfection.

Facing Your Giants

"A champion named Goliath, who was from Gath, came out of the Philistine camp. He was over nine feet tall." (1 Samuel 17:4)

You and I may not be asked to battle a giant like Goliath, but our adversaries can be just as intimidating. The giants we face can appear in many different forms: a difficult marriage, broken or strained relationships, poor health, losing a loved one, unemployment, financial hardship, addiction and insecurity are just a few of the goliaths we face.

"In this world you will have trouble. But take heart! I have overcome the world." (John 16:33)

No one is exempt from difficulties, but our adversaries are no match for God's strength and power. "No, in all these things we are more than conquerors through him who loved us." (Romans 8:37)

We need to muster the kind of faith that young David experienced when he fought against Goliath. Scholars speculate that the young shepherd boy may have been only twelve years old when this event took place.

Regardless of his age, God's anointed (David) understood this important concept: the key to success requires placing the battle in God's hands. The shepherd boy knew full well that victory rested with the LORD Almighty—David had God-confidence.

"David said to Saul, "Let no one lose heart on account of this Philistine; your servant will go and fight him... The LORD who delivered me from the paw of the lion and the paw of the bear will deliver me from the hand of this Philistine." (1 Samuel 17:32, 37)

The proclamation David shouted as he approached his foe is the same one that you and I can claim when facing our giants. "You come against me with sword and spear and javelin, but I come against you in the name of the LORD Almighty." (1 Samuel 17:45)

David conquered his enemy because he placed his trust in the Lord. We will find victory over our giants when we do the same.

"So David triumphed over the Philistine with a sling and a stone; without a sword in his hand he struck down the Philistine and killed him." (1 Samuel 17:50)

Face your giants head-on and remember—the battle is the Lord's!

"You will not have to fight this battle. Take up your positions; stand firm and see the deliverance the LORD will give you, O Judah and Jerusalem. Do not be afraid; do not be discouraged. Go out to face them tomorrow, and the LORD will be with you.'" (2 Chronicles 20:17)

God's Favorite Color

Does God have a favorite color? I pondered this question one morning while staring out my living room window. The piercing blue sky provided an exquisite backdrop against the vibrant, green foliage of the trees. The combination of colors was breath taking.

God reveals Himself through His Word, but He also reveals Himself through that which He has made. Scripture tells us that even those who have never read a Bible can still come to know God through His creation. "For since the creation of the world God's invisible qualities—his eternal power and divine nature—have been clearly seen, being understood from what has been made, so that men are without excuse." (Romans 1:20)

Is it possible that God's favorite color is blue? After all, this color appears more than any other throughout His creation. The sky appears blue and surrounds the entire earth. Water appears blue and covers about seventy percent of the earth's surface, and from outer space, our world appears blue and is even referred to as the blue planet.

While contemplating these possibilities in my heart, God reminded me of a basic truth. Color is only visible when light is present. "But everything exposed by the light becomes visible, for it is light that makes everything visible." (Ephesians 5:13)

At night, both the sky and water appear black. The color blue is only discernible when light is present. The absence of light makes it virtually impossible to see color or anything else God created. However, with light we can see God's creation in all its glory.

In much the same way, we must allow God's light and Spirit to illuminate our path of understanding. The Spirit of enlightenment opens our eyes to all God's glory, even when we are walking in darkness.

Questioning God's favorite color may seem silly to you, but I happen to believe God delights in knowing we desire to learn such intimate details about Him. Knowing God's favorite color isn't the important thing. What really matters is that we know our Heavenly Father more intimately day by day.

"Call to me and I will answer you and tell you great and unsearchable things you do not know." (Jeremiah 33:3)

The color blue—*sounds like a winner to me.*

Straight Street

In one of my study groups, we were seeking new revelation while dissecting Acts 9:1-22—a passage which narrates the story of Saul's conversion. One of the members in the group pointed out the irony of the location where Ananias would find Saul—Straight Street. Surely, God has a sense of humor.

Before his encounter with Jesus, Saul was persecuting Christians. As a Jew and scholar of the Torah, Paul was zealous for God, but it just goes to show that a person can be on fire for God yet still be barreling down the wrong path.

Many in the world today believe there is more than one way to get to heaven. They are under the false presumption that being a good person is enough, or perhaps they believe that it doesn't matter whether you believe in Hinduism, Buddhism, Christian Science, or the Muslim religion—that all ways point to eternal life.

All ways point to eternal life all right—eternal life in heaven or eternal life in hell. There is no grey area here. It's one or the other. Just because a person believes something is true, doesn't make it so. Christians have the very words of God to back up what they believe—God's Word is truth.

According to God, there is only one way to eternal life in heaven—*Jesus Christ.* "For God so loved the world that he gave his one and only Son, that whoever believes in him shall not perish but have eternal life." (John 3:16)

"Jesus answered, 'I am the way and the truth and the life. No one comes to the Father except through me.'" (John 14:6)

Saul, who later became Paul, finally learned this truth and went on to write more books of the New Testament than any other author. He believed it. He lived it. And then he shared it with others.

"The Lord is not slow in keeping his promise, as some understand slowness. He is patient with you, not wanting anyone to perish, but everyone to come to repentance." (2 Peter 3:9).

Through His encounter with Jesus on the road to Damascus, Saul discovered the path leading to Straight Street. You and I are on the straight street too if we have accepted the free gift of salvation through God's one and only Son. We cannot earn it. We cannot pay for it. We can only accept it as a free gift. Once we accept this amazing gift, we have a one way ticket to eternal life in heaven.

Take the straight street to eternal life in heaven—
Jesus is the only way.

Overcoming Fears

"Who is going to harm you if you are eager to do good? But even if you should suffer for what is right, you are blessed. 'Do not fear what they fear; do not be frightened.' But in your hearts set apart Christ as Lord." (1 Peter 3:13-15a)

Each fall and spring, the Living in Truth Ministry team works the pledge drive for a local Christian radio station. The first time we participated in the campaign, I was quite nervous. The program director sent out a Power Point presentation to teach us how to navigate their computer system. After reading through the training documents, I was even more anxious, because I comprehend much better through hands-on experience.

The day we were scheduled to help, I sat down at my work post which consisted of a phone and computer. My palms were so sweaty you might have thought I was jumping out of an airplane without a parachute. I was practically immobilized with fear and couldn't bring myself to answer the ringing phone. My heart raced while a battle in my mind ensued. What if the person on the other end is impatient? What if I mess up and say the wrong thing? What if I enter the wrong information?

The program director must have sensed my anxiety because he came over to encourage me. "Go ahead," he coaxed. "After a few times you will feel more at ease."

"For I am the LORD, your God, who takes hold of your right hand and says to you, Do not fear; I will help you." (Isaiah 41:13)

Although I stumbled through the first few calls, the donors on the other end of the phone were very patient. By the end of the evening, I was actually having fun. In time, I grew so comfortable answering each call that I couldn't wait for my phone to ring. Afterwards, we all agreed that the experience was a true blessing and I told the program director to count us in for the next pledge drive.

Fear is one of the biggest stumbling blocks for Christians. More than any other command in the Bible, God tells us to fear not. *Why?* Because God knew it would be one of our biggest stumbling blocks. He understands that fear hinders our spiritual growth.

Every time we step out in faith and overcome our fears, we get stronger. In response God gives spiritual blessings and strengthens our faith for the next time. During that pledge drive, each time I answered the phone, God stepped in and gave me the courage to carry out my job effectively. If we never step out of our comfort zone, we miss wonderful opportunities to see God at work.

God would rather work through our weakness than our strengths, because through our weakness, He is glorified. When we are weak, He is strong.

The next time you are afraid of what lies ahead, like the Israelites who needed to cross the flooded Jordan River in order to get to their promised land, simply step your foot into the "Jordan" and watch God part the waters. The Almighty will help you overcome your fears—just like He did for me.

"So do no fear, for I am with you; do not be dismayed, for I am your God. I will strengthen you and help you; I will uphold you with my righteous right hand." (Isaiah 41:10)

Taming the Beast

"All kinds of animals, birds, reptiles and creatures of the sea are being tamed and have been tamed by man, but no man can tame the tongue. It is a restless evil, full of deadly poison." (James 3:7-8)

As a teen, I joined a 4-H club and began learning how to show horses for the county fair. Trying to manipulate an enormous beast with only a bridle and lead was a seemingly intimidating venture, yet I found the horses were fairly easy to train. These animals must not realize their power and size, for if they did, they would never allow humans to have such command over them. "When we put bits into the mouths of horses to make them obey us, we can turn the whole animal." (James 3:3)

It's interesting that man can have such control over a large beast, yet so little control over his tongue. The tongue is one of the most difficult things to tame. Flippant comments can spill out of our mouths without much thought or deliberation. Our words can be used as a weapon of destruction or a balm for healing—depending on the circumstance.

"With the tongue we praise our Lord and Father, and with it we curse men, who have been made in God's likeness. Out of the same mouth come praise and cursing. My brothers, this should not be." (James 3:9-10)

When showing horses, I would twitch my wrist slightly to the right and a creature five times my size turned immediately in response.

Why is it that we are able control a horse with the smallest inflections of movement, while our tongue seems to have a mind of its own? How many times do we wish we could take back something we've said?

Raw emotions often drive the untamed tongue. Hurt, fear, rejection, and anger can set our tongues afire, and before we know it, sparks fly out of our mouths.

Cursing is not the worst of it. When hurtful words spew from our mouths, they injure the spirits of others. That's where the real danger lies. "Can both fresh water and salt water flow from the same spring?" (James 3:11)

Do you know what happens when fresh water and salt water collide? The water becomes brackish and murky. It is no longer clear.

As Christians, our job is to point others to the living water of Jesus Christ, but we won't be very effective in our witness if that living water is clouded by our reckless words.

It's time to tame the beast!

> Create in me a pure heart, O God, and renew a steadfast spirit within me. Do not cast me from your presence or take your Holy Spirit from me. Restore to me the joy of your salvation and grant me a willing spirit, to sustain me. Then I will teach transgressors your ways, and sinners will turn back to you. Save me from bloodguilt, O God, the God who saves me, and my tongue will sing of your righteousness. O Lord, open my lips, and my mouth will declare your praise. (Psalm 51:10-15)

Taking a Detour

As I was heading to my weekly Bible study one morning, I came across a detour sign that blocked my usual path. Torrential rains from the night before had caused the tributaries to overflow, creating some local flooding.

I realize a detour sign is intended to keep people from danger, but all I could think about was how much of an inconvenience this was for me. For a split second, I was tempted to go around the sign and take my chances. That could have been a huge mistake—maybe even a life threatening one. And yet, because I was in a hurry to get where I was going, I was enticed to disregard the clearly marked sign and go my own way.

"Make level paths for your feet and take only ways that are firm." (Proverbs 4:26)

I wonder how many times I have disregarded the Holy Spirit's detour signs simply because I was in a hurry to get somewhere. Probably more times than I care to admit.

We need to remember that God sees the whole picture of our lives—the beginning, the end, and everything between.

"For I know the plans I have for you," declares the LORD, "plans to prosper you and not to harm you, plans to give you hope and a future." (Jeremiah 29:11)

Is God leading you down an unexpected path? What seems like a major inconvenience at the time, may actually become the very avenue through which God's tremendous blessings flow.

"Direct me in the path of your commands, for there I find delight." (Psalm 119:35)

Although our journey through life presents many roads of choice, we are wise to remember... not all of them are safe. God will direct our steps towards His good and perfect will.

As we seek the Lord with all our heart, may we heed the Spirit's warnings and stay on God's straight and narrow path. *It's by far the safest place to be.*

The Underdog

I find myself rooting for the underdog in any given situation: sporting events, singing competitions, horse races, you name it. My heart soars when the underdog swoops in from behind and claims victory. Something inside my soul shouts for joy.

What a difference it makes when someone believes in you—especially when you feel hopeless on your own. I know from personal experience that having someone believe in you makes all the difference in the world.

After God revealed to me that my eating disorder was getting in the way of my relationship with Him, I realized I couldn't keep it secret any longer. I finally confided in one of my best friends. Since that day, she has been one of my biggest supporters. She continually believed in me and kept me focused on the other side of healing, giving me something to hope for after I broke free. She kept saying that God was going to use every bit of my dim past to bring glory and honor to Himself.

I couldn't imagine how God could bring anything good from my many years of bondage, but my friend continued to speak truth into my life. She reminded me of the following promise from God in Isaiah:

> The Spirit of the Sovereign Lord is on me, because the Lord has anointed me to preach good news to the poor. He has sent me to bind up the brokenhearted, to proclaim freedom for the captives and release from darkness for the prisoners, to proclaim the year of the Lord's favor and the day of vengeance of our God, to comfort all who mourn, and provide for those who grieve in Zion—to bestow on them a crown of beauty instead of ashes, the oil of gladness instead of mourning, and a garment of praise instead of a spirit of despair. (Isaiah 61:1-3)

Jesus (the Great Physician) set me free and gave me the responsibility to point others to that same freedom.

"They will be called oaks of righteousness, a planting of the Lord for the display of his splendor. They will rebuild the ancient ruins and restore the places long devastated; they will renew the ruined cities that have been devastated for generations." (Isaiah 61:3-4)

God never leaves us empty handed. After we surrender all to Him, He uses every bit of our horrible past and gives us beauty for ashes.

I'm so grateful for the friend who believed in me. Do you know someone who could use encouragement today? Keep speaking God's truth into their life and let them know just how much you believe in them. Even more importantly… remind them how much God believes in them. *Keep rooting for the underdog!*

Broken Connection

Have you ever persistently tried to reach someone on the phone, but every time you called, you either got a busy signal or voicemail? It's easy to grow frustrated when we can't make a connection.

Sometimes I feel as though my spiritual connection to God meets similar resistance. I keep praying, but no answer comes. I leave message after message for God but receive no call back. After a while, I begin to question… *Did God even hear my prayer?*

"He will respond to the prayer of the destitute; he will not despise their plea." (Psalm 102:17)

When we feel that our prayers are not being answered, it's easy to grow frustrated or even discouraged, wondering if God actually heard our plea. Anytime we begin to doubt, we need to focus on truth.

"I call on you, O God, for you will answer me; give ear to me and hear my prayer." (Psalm 17:6)

God hears all of our prayers, but He answers them in His timing and with His ultimate purpose in mind. "The Lord is not slow in keeping his promise, as some understand slowness." (2 Peter 3:9a) "But the plans of the LORD stand firm forever, the purposes of his heart through all generations." (Psalm 33:11)

God sees the big picture. When we don't see things happening as quickly as we would like, we need to trust

God's higher ways. Oftentimes, God is working behind the scenes where our eyes cannot see, making needed preparations, so He can answer our prayers in the best way possible. We need to remember that God isn't just working for our good. He's working for the good of all those who love Him. "And we know that in all things God works for the good of those who love him, who have been called according to his purpose." (Romans 8:28)

When we don't see immediate results from our prayers, we shouldn't assume our connection to God is broken. We just need to be a little more patient while we wait. That's good advice for our relationship with God *and* our unanswered telephone calls.

Safety Net

‎◦⁓᠁⊙⁓‎

During our first year of marriage, my husband, Gerry, and I visited the Red River Gorge with some close friends. While my girlfriend and I were perfectly content to view the rich beauty of the scenery visually, our husbands had to experience the landscape in a more physical way—repelling off the side of a mountain. I must admit, we didn't fully comprehend all the risks involved with such a sport. When you're young you don't always think—you just have fun.

At the end of the day, Gerry decided to repel down the cliff one last time. He clipped onto the safety rope and began his descent. Once he was out of sight and the rope loosened, it appeared that my husband had made it safely to the ground. After several minutes of waiting, his buddy finally made an assumption that Gerry was at the bottom and untied the rope from its secure hold.

Almost immediately, the rope began to unravel with great speed, dropping over the side of the cliff. I screamed, realizing my husband was free falling. My friend, who was standing next to the coiled rope, got jerked to the ground when the line entangled around her leg. We grabbed hold of her so she wouldn't fall over the edge, but at that very moment, the rope stopped unraveling.

Realization set in. My newly wedded husband was at the other end of the rope. Questions flew through my mind. *How far did he fall? Was he okay?*

After several moments, Gerry yelled up to us that he was alright. Shaken and bruised—but alive.

"For in the day of trouble he will keep me safe in his dwelling; he will hide me in the shelter of his tabernacle and set me high upon a rock." (Psalm 27:5)

We later learned that Gerry had been resting on the side of the cliff, trying to catch his breath, when we untied the rope. When he pushed off the side of the cliff to repel the rest of the way down, he began his rapid descent towards the ground. Miraculously, he fell into the thick canopy of a tree which reduced the impact of his drop. The tree became the safety net that saved my husband's life. "For he will command his angels concerning you to guard you in all your ways." (Psalm 91:11)

God sent his angels to watch over us that day and provided a safety net when we grew careless.

The same God who saved my husband and friend from imminent danger watches over you and me each and every day. For that I am truly grateful. "Keep me safe, O God, for in you I take refuge." (Psalm 16:1)

Sliding on Ice

My husband and I were traveling down an old country road when our vehicle hit a patch of black ice and began to slide out of control. Thankfully, Gerry had some experience with driving on ice. Instead of panicking, he remained calm and held the steering wheel steady and straight. Avoiding the natural instinct to slam his foot on the brake, he gently pumped the brake up and down until the car slowed enough for him to regain control of the vehicle.

"Lead me, O LORD, in your righteousness because of my enemies—make straight your way before me." (Psalm 5:8)

Sometimes in life, we feel as though we're sliding across ice—everything is out of control. No matter which way we turn we seem to be going the wrong way.

Let's face it, there are things in life that we just can't control: illness, people, weather, tragic circumstances, and spiritual warfare, to name a few.

When life circumstances spin out of control, we need to resist the temptation to slam on the brakes. We need to keep our hands fixed firmly on the wheel and our eyes focused straight ahead. Allow the Lord to assume control over your situation, and He will slow things down.

When it feels like we are sliding on ice, the Lord will direct us back to secure and solid ground.

Master of Deception

My sister came away from her weekend retreat feeling completely filled by the Holy Spirit. With great enthusiasm, she shared how she had felt God's love and forgiveness more powerfully than ever before. Her time with the Lord had ignited passion in her spirit.

I told my sister how happy I was to know she was blessed by her time with the Lord, but I also cautioned her to beware of Satan's probable attack, knowing full well that he would try to bring her down from her spiritual high.

"Be self-controlled and alert. Your enemy the devil prowls around like a roaring lion looking for someone to devour. Resist him, standing firm in the faith, because you know that your brothers throughout the world are undergoing the same kind of sufferings." (1 Peter 5:8-9)

A few days later, my sister called and shared how she came to a particular passage of Scripture that had knocked her down from her spiritual high. The passage in question seemed to conflict with the message she had come to understand about God during her time at the retreat.

She was very confused, but because this particular situation involved Scripture, she did not recognize that it might be an attack from Satan. I quickly reminded my sister how Satan loves to twist God's Word. One of his tactics of deception is to cause us to doubt or misunderstand what God has said. The enemy has been using this method since the beginning of time. He even used it on Jesus some 2,000 years ago.

> Then the devil took [Jesus] to the holy city and had him stand on the highest point of the temple. 'If you are the Son of God,' he said, 'throw yourself down. For it is written: 'He will command his angels concerning you, and they will lift you up in their hands, so that you will not strike your foot against a stone.' Jesus answered him, 'It is also written: 'Do not put the Lord your God to the test.' (Matthew 4:5-10)

Even though Satan quoted Scripture, Jesus was not deceived. Like Jesus, we need to know all of God's Word—not just a few Scriptures here and there. Armed with the sword of the Spirit, we must put on the full armor of God and take our stand against the devil's schemes.

Satan is the master of deception—the father of all lies. He loves it when he can get us to doubt God. He can easily pull out a few passages of Scripture in an attempt to get us to build a belief system around his falsehood.

We must view all Scripture through the context in which it is written.

We must also view all Scripture against the backdrop of the entire Word of God. If something seems to contradict other passages, perhaps we don't fully understand God's original intent for the verse.

Finally, we must examine each portion of Scripture in light of God's character. If what we have come to believe or understand about a verse contradicts God's character, then once again, we do not fully understand the passage in question.

If we are still confused about a verse, perhaps we are being called to simply believe by faith alone.

"Now faith is being sure of what we hope for and certain of what we do not see." (Hebrews 11:1)

One day, we will know in full what we now know in part. But until then, we need to be armed with the sword of the Spirit and be ready to wield our weapon with confidence and authority.

Weakness or Strength?

At our daughter's bridal shower, the guests were asked to write a message on a note card with some marriage advice for the couple. Later each person had an opportunity to read their advice to the expectant bride. Some advice was humorous, some romantic, and others offered practical information, but my sister-in-law's advice was quite thought provoking. *"A person's weakness will often be their strength magnified—the reason you fell in love in the first place."*

So true! I'm even able to see this in myself. When my strengths are magnified, they become my weakness. I always try to focus on the good in people (one of my strengths), but sometimes, I place so much emphasis on a person's positive traits, that I overlook vital warning signs that indicate the relationship is no longer healthy for me.

Other examples of strengths becoming weakness may include a person who is really good with finances but becomes overly controlling with money or an ambitious person who over commits to the extent that his life is no longer in balance. Perhaps someone who is very nurturing can be taken advantage of, risking their own well-being.

We would be wise to look closely at our strengths and see how they might become potential weaknesses. Understanding our strengths and weaknesses can better prepare us for life and relationships.

Weaknesses or strengths aside, we have a God who is capable of bringing balance into our lives.

"He gives strength to the weary and increases the power of the weak." (Isaiah 40:29)

"In the same way, the Spirit helps us in our weakness." (Romans 8:26a)

"That is why, for Christ's sake, I delight in weaknesses, insults, in hardships, in persecutions, in difficulties. For when I am weak, then I am strong." (2 Corinthians 12:10)

When we are weak—*Christ is strong.*

Wrestling with God

"Then the man said, 'Your name will no longer be Jacob, but Israel, because you have struggled with God and with men and have overcome.'" (Genesis 32:28)

Have you ever felt as though you were wrestling with God? We might wrestle with God anytime we sense Him leading us to do something we don't particularly want to do, or if He asks us to give up something that we think we need.

When I struggled to break free from bulimia, I definitely wrestled with God. I wanted to be free from my eating disorder, but I wanted to accomplish it on my terms. I didn't want to gain any weight, and I wanted to be healed instantly. Sound familiar? I reasoned that if God could do anything, why not heal me instantly.

"Ah, Sovereign LORD, you have made the heavens and the earth by your great power and outstretched arm. Nothing is too hard for you." (Jeremiah 32:17)

Hindsight is 20/20. I couldn't see it then, but I can look back now and see why God's healing took place slowly.

"Little by little I will drive them out before you, until you have increased enough to take possession of the land." (Exodus 23:30)

God didn't remove my bondage all at once because He needed me to be strong enough to stand against any other form of bondage that might surface and take its place. "The LORD your God will drive out those nations before you, little by little. You will not be allowed to eliminate them all at once, or the wild animals will multiply around you." (Deuteronomy 7:22)

If we break free from our stronghold too quickly (without developing the tools to stay free), Satan will tempt us to enter into some other form of addiction or bondage.

> When an evil spirit comes out of a man, it goes through arid places seeking rest and does not find it. Then it says, 'I will return to the house I left.' When it arrives, it finds the house swept clean and put in order. Then it goes and takes seven other spirits more wicked than itself, and they go in and live there. And the final condition of that man is worse than the first. (Luke 11:24-26)

We must stop wrestling with God and learn to trust His higher ways. God is not interested in a quick fix. His desire is for us to find complete and lasting healing. God not only cleanses our soul, but He also fills us with His truth and Spirit so that nothing else is able to come in and take up residence.

Continue to trust God and seek Him with all your heart.

"'You will seek me and find me when you seek me with all your heart. I will be found by you,' declares the LORD, 'and will bring you back from captivity.'" (Jeremiah 29:13-14a)

Less Is More

We live in a culture that's obsessed with more. The desire for more food, more houses, more cars, more money, more free time, more education, and more technology and possessions has become a top priority for many. And what has all of this gotten us?

Well let's see… we have more disease, more debt, more stress, more headaches, more suicides, more substance abuse, more depression, more crime, more unemployment, and more unhappy people than ever before. *Perhaps more isn't all it's cracked up to be.*

In God's economy, sometimes less is more. The secret to true happiness comes from this simple yet profound statement recorded in the book of John, "He must become greater; I must become less." (John 3:30)

Could it really be that simple?

I can only speak from personal experience, but I have to say yes. I have a standing prayer to God that goes something like this. *Lord, may it be all of you and none of me.* When there is less of me, there's more room for God to work in my life, which in-turn makes me more fulfilled.

> I became a servant of this gospel by the gift of God's grace given me through the working of his power. Although I am less than the least of all God's people, this grace was given me: to preach to the Gentiles the unsearchable riches of Christ, and to make plain to everyone the administration of this mystery, which for ages past was kept hidden in God, who created all things. (Ephesians 3:7-9)

It sounds like crazy math, but less really is more when you are looking at life through the eyes of our Father.

A Praying Parent

"Answer me when I call to you, O my righteous God. Give me relief from my distress; be merciful to me and hear my prayer." (Psalm 4:1)

Do you have a long standing prayer, waiting to be answered? It can be hard to keep praying when it seems there is no change in sight. Weariness sets in and we find ourselves beginning to wonder if God is actually listening to our pleas.

Hannah was a woman who desperately wanted a child but was barren. The words used to describe her feelings express that she was *downhearted, deeply troubled, in great anguish*, and *grieved*. Even though Hannah felt such desperation she didn't give up praying. "In bitterness of soul Hannah wept much and prayed to the LORD." (1 Samuel 1:10)

Even in the bitterness of our soul, God hears our prayers. Perhaps you can identify with Hannah's long standing prayer. If you can, let her response encourage you and give you hope. Hannah didn't give up praying, and neither should you.

> Early the next morning they arose and worshiped before the LORD and then went back to their home at Ramah. Elkanah lay with Hannah his wife, and the LORD remembered her. So in the course of time

Hannah conceived and gave birth to a son. She named him Samuel, saying, 'Because I asked the LORD for him.' (1 Samuel 1:19-20)

The Lord answered Hannah's prayers and she gave birth to a son—Samuel. Hannah was so grateful for this precious blessing from heaven that she dedicated her son to the Lord. She didn't know if she would ever have another child, but she sacrificially released her son to God anyway. That took tremendous faith.

"'I prayed for this child, and the LORD has granted me what I asked of him. So now I give him to the LORD. For his whole life he will be given over to the LORD.' And he worshiped the LORD there." (1 Samuel 1:27-28)

Perhaps there is no greater heartache to be felt than that of a grieving mother. We too may come to a place where we must surrender our children over to the Lord. This doesn't mean we quit being a parent, but perhaps, God is asking us to let go of some things and trust His higher ways. In our hearts we must place our son or daughter at the foot of the cross and pray. *Not my will, Father, but Your will be done.*

"Hear the cry and the prayer that your servant is praying in your presence." (2 Chronicles 6:19)

A mother's prayers are powerful. We want so much for our kids, and yet they have a life journey all their own. Their path will sometimes be filled with bumps and bruises along the way. Life is a great teacher, but some of its lessons can be brutally hard to accept—especially for the parent who must stand by and watch.

We will never stop being their parent, but as our children grow and mature, like Hannah, we need to surrender them into the more than capable hands of our Heavenly Father.

"Be joyful always; pray continually; give thanks in all circumstances, for this is God's will for you in Christ Jesus." (1 Thessalonians 5:16-18)

Release your children to God—but never stop praying!

Let's Make a Deal

In the game show *Let's Make a Deal*, hopeful contestants come dressed in crazy costumes, trying to attract attention. The show's host then asks the audience for random items. If someone was lucky enough to have the requested item on their person, he or she would be the next contestant on the show. The participant would then barter with the host to advance further in the game. At the end of each round, the contestant would be allowed to choose between one of three curtains to determine his grand prize.

Bartering is fine for game shows and garage sales, but it's not a recommended practice for our relationship with God. And yet, we sometimes approach God this way, especially when there is something we greatly want from Him.

"Do not be anxious about anything, but in everything, by prayer and petition, with thanksgiving, present your requests to God." (Philippians 4:6)

God instructs us in His Word to present our requests before Him, but afterwards, we must trust Him with the outcome. Only God knows what is truly best for everyone involved. God is omniscient; He knows everything: past, present, and future. What seems good to us at the time, may actually be unfavorable for our future. We must trust God's ways and realize that they are above our own. "O Sovereign LORD, you are God! Your words are trustworthy, and you have promised these good things to your servant." (2 Samuel 7:28)

When I pray, I say something like this: Lord, I know You see the big picture of this situation, so if this is not something you desire to happen, then I pray You will help me be at peace with the outcome and trust Your higher ways.

God wants so much more for us than we could possibly imagine.

"Those who know your name will trust in you, for you, LORD, have never forsaken those who seek you." (Psalm 9:10)

Since God knows what's behind each curtain of our lives, let's allow Him to choose what's best for us.

"But I trust in you, O LORD; I say, 'You are my God.'" (Psalm 31:14)

Unused Gifts

"Each of you must bring a gift in proportion to the way the LORD your God has blessed you." (Deuteronomy 16:7)

My husband and I were instructed to bring a white elephant gift (something we no longer needed or used) for our small group's gift exchange.

The night before the party, I asked my husband to see if he could find a gift. He went down to the basement and came upstairs with his gift only minutes later. It was croquet set that we had received several years ago but never used. The game had been hidden away in our basement, still neatly wrapped in its original package.

Do you have any unused "gifts" lying around?

Romans chapter twelve explains that we have different (spiritual) gifts according to the grace given us. Unfortunately, sometimes our spiritual gifts never get used (at least not in the way they were intended). Spiritual gifts should be used to build the Kingdom of God. Scripture tells us to use spiritual gifts to serve others and to faithfully administer God's grace in its various forms.

Perhaps you are unsure of your spiritual gifts, or you simply don't know how to use them for God's glory. If this is the case for you, simply ask God to provide you with some enlightenment. "Ask and it will be given to you; seek and you will find; knock and the door will be opened to you. For everyone who asks receives; he who seeks finds; and to him who knocks, the door will be opened." (Matthew 7:7-8)

You also might find it helpful to take a Spiritual Gifts test. These online assessments can help identify our strengths so that we can hone in on and cultivate our gifts for building God's Kingdom.

Don't let another day go by without using your spiritual gift. Like the croquet set my husband found in our basement, it would be a waste to keep your gift tucked away never to be used. Discover your gift from God, and then, use it for His glory.

"Follow the way of love and eagerly desire spiritual gifts." (1 Corinthians 14:1)

One Size Doesn't Fit All

While watching some old home videos, I was reminded of a particular Christmas event that gave our family a hearty laugh.

With the presents evenly distributed around the room, it was time to open the gifts. Our, then, four year old son eyed his gifts with eager anticipation, anxiously waiting for his turn to be in the spotlight. When the time finally came, Ben chose a rectangular box from his pile—a package which conspicuously looked as though clothing may be inside.

Sure enough, after removing the colorful wrapping, Ben pulled out a pair of jeans and held them up. We all sat with confused looks on our faces because the jeans were a good six inches longer than his entire body. In a matter-of-fact tone our son reported, "I think we're gonna have to get a different size." We all started laughing hysterically. Apparently, during the gift distribution, someone mistakenly read the name tag that was labeled BEV and gave it to BEN. The jeans were supposed to be for my mother-in-law. Ben didn't need a different size—*he had opened the wrong gift!*

Sometimes a similar scenario takes place in our spiritual lives. We open gifts that were never intended for us. "Now about the gifts of the Spirit, brothers and sisters, I do not want you to be ignorant." (1 Corinthians 12:1)

My previous devotion talked about spiritual gifts and how they are to be used for growing God's Kingdom.

Some of the spiritual gifts are as follows: evangelism, teaching, speaking, leadership, mercy, discernment, prophecy, service, administration, faith, knowledge, healing, wisdom, and hospitality.

> Now to each one the manifestation of the Spirit is given for the common good. To one there is given through the Spirit a message of wisdom, to another a message of knowledge by means of the same Spirit, to another faith by the same Spirit, to another gifts of healing by that one Spirit, to another miraculous powers, to another prophecy, to another distinguishing between spirits, to another speaking in different kinds of tongues, and to still another the interpretation of tongues. All these are the work of one and the same Spirit, and he distributes them to each one, just as he determines. (1 Corinthians 12:7-11)

We may see someone using their spiritual gifts to effectively grow God's Kingdom and reason with ourselves that we could easily do the same thing.

For example, Jeremey has the gift of teaching. He really knows his stuff and is able explain what he has learned in ways that people can understand and apply to their own lives. When Tim comes along and sees the way Jeremey is doing his part to advance the Kingdom of God, he tries to emulate what he does. Unfortunately, Tim's spiritual gift is not teaching, therefore he ends up leaving his students bewildered and confused because he is trying to harness a gift that was never intended for him.

"There are different kinds of gifts, but the same Spirit distributes them. There are different kinds of service, but the same Lord. There are different kinds of working, but in all of them and in everyone it is the same God at work." (1 Corinthians 12:4-6)

We will be most effective in growing God's Kingdom when we use the spiritual gifts intended for us—not others. All the gifts in the body of Christ are equally important, and each one is meant to build up the church and bring glory and honor to God.

> Now if the foot should say, 'Because I am not a hand, I do not belong to the body,' it would not for that reason stop being part of the body. And if the ear should say, 'Because I am not an eye, I do not belong to the body,' it would not for that reason stop being part of the body. If the whole body were an eye, where would the sense of hearing be? If the whole body were an ear, where would the sense of smell be? But in fact God has placed the parts in the body, every one of them, just as he wanted them to be. (1 Corinthians 12:15-18)

Try to recognize your spiritual gifts and implement them in the arena where God has placed you—the field where you can be most effective for growing God's Kingdom. Like my son, be quick to recognize when a gift is not meant for you.

The jeans may have been too big for Ben, *but they were the perfect size for my mother-in-law.*

Knight in Shining Armor

I may not be a child anymore, but I still love a good fairytale—especially those involving a knight in shining armor who saves the day. Something resonates deep inside me when I see a prince rushing in on a white horse to rescue his fair maiden. Safe in the arms of her prince, the two ride off into the sunset, ready to enjoy their happily ever after.

Our hearts echo the joy of these enchanting tales because one day you and I will experience our own fairytale ending.

The Bible foretells that our Prince (Jesus) will come on the clouds riding His white horse, with all His glory and majesty, to rescue His beloved from imminent peril.

"At that time the sign of the Son of Man will appear in the sky, and all the nations of the earth will mourn. They will see the Son of Man coming on the clouds of the sky, with power and great glory." (Matthew 24:30)

"I saw heaven standing open and there before me was a white horse, whose rider is called Faithful and True. With justice he judges and makes war. His eyes are like blazing fire, and on his head are many crowns." (Revelation 19:11-12a)

Make no mistake. Jesus is coming back to reclaim His fair maiden—the Bride of Christ. And when He does, He will liberate us from this fallen world. Like a knight in shining armor, Jesus will sweep us into His arms and carry us off to His Kingdom where we will live happily ever after.

"Behold, I am coming soon! My reward is with me, and I will give to everyone according to what he has done. I am the Alpha and the Omega, the First and the Last, the Beginning and the End." (Revelation 22:12-13)

"Behold, I am coming soon! Blessed is he who keeps the words of the prophecy in this book." (Revelation 22:7)

Until then... live in God's truth day by day!

An excerpt from the book:

Nothing But Your Truth Will Help Me, God!

By Rae Lynn DeAngelis

T ry to imagine that you have just stepped into a courtroom. As you glance around the large open space, you are suddenly struck by the grandeur of the room. Beautiful hand carved wood adorns the walls and ceiling, and although the temperature of the room is cool, the rich dark tones in the woodwork have a warming effect on your senses.

You think to yourself. *If walls could talk, what grand stories these would tell.*

The musty smell of aged wood triggers an unexpected flow of memories. All at once your mind drifts back to childhood days spent playing hide and seek at grandma's house. It's funny how the sense of smell can generate such vivid images. Your thoughts linger there for a brief moment, recounting those simpler days in your mind, but the echo of your own footsteps shakes you back into reality.

Where is everyone, you wonder?

A quick look at your watch provides the answer. You have arrived thirty minutes early. Oh well, this will provide a few extra minutes to get ready.

You quickly find a seat to gather your thoughts and mentally prepare for the difficult task ahead.

Several moments later you are startled when two ornate doors at the back of the room open, allowing a stream of people to enter. All at once the reality of the moment hits your senses and a wave of nausea pierces your gut. The sudden noise and commotion only adds to your feelings of uneasiness.

You are intrigued, however, at how quickly the once quiet room comes to life. The prosecution, defense, and spectators enter, bringing with them an atmosphere of excitement and quiet apprehension. Moments later, the jurors file in with somber faces, adding a more solemn mood into the mix. As everyone prepares for the proceedings, the noise level intensifies.

The drone of idle chatter is quickly hushed when a loud, imposing voice bellows, *"All rise"*.

Watching now with great interest you notice a stately looking gentleman has entered the courtroom. As he makes his way to the front of the room, there is no mistaking his commanding presence. He is without a doubt the honorable judge.

He promptly assumes his rightful seat behind the raised mahogany desk located at the front of the room, and with a nod of his head, permission is granted for everyone to sit down.

During the preliminary proceedings, charges are brought forth, the prosecution and defense offer their opening statements, and careful instructions are given to the jurors. The time seems to drag on endlessly, and although you listen closely to everything that is said, your anticipation increasing with each passing minute.

Finally, the moment you have been expecting arrives when your name is summoned to the witness stand. It is not a surprise that you have been called as a witness for the defense. It is, indeed, the reason you are there. Yet somehow you don't feel quite ready. Realizing that there is no turning back now, you make your way to the front of the room.

Before you sit down, the bailiff walks over and instructs you to place one hand on the Bible while raising your right hand. The courtroom is silent as the bailiff poses this important question. *"Do you swear to tell the truth, the whole truth, and nothing but the truth, so help you God?"*

With the voice of confidence you reply, *"I do".*

I invite you to think about the question that is being asked when a witness is sworn to testify in court. *Do you swear to tell the truth, the whole truth, and nothing but the truth, so help you God?* Consider for a moment what (or more precisely), where is truth? I believe the answer to this question is under the witness's left hand.

Have you ever wondered why a witness places one hand on the Bible while being sworn to testify in a court of law?

The practice of using a Bible when taking an oath actually began in England hundreds of years ago, but why?

The answer is obvious to Christians. The Bible is truth, the whole truth, and nothing but the truth.

I am so thankful that God, in His infinite wisdom, has given us a reliable benchmark for truth through His Word.

The Bible is the handbook for life. It's a complete set of instructions and guidelines for us to follow in our everyday lives. As a matter of fact, the Bible is the only means through which we can truly discern truth from lies, right from wrong, and good from evil.

God has ordained everything contained in the pages of the Bible. What I mean by that is this. God gave the words directly to the authors who wrote it. I believe with my whole heart that God was completely involved in all sixty-six books, beginning with Genesis and ending with Revelation.

How do I know?

"All scripture is God-breathed and is useful for teaching, rebuking, correcting and training in righteousness, so that the man of God may be thoroughly equipped for every good work." (2 Timothy 3:16-17)

Many people say the Bible was written so long ago it isn't relevant to our world today. But what does God say.

"For the word of God is living and active. Sharper than any double-edged sword, it penetrates even to dividing soul and spirit, joints and marrow; it judges the thoughts and attitudes of the heart." (Hebrews 4:12)

God's Word is timeless! However, Satan, the father of all lies, has deceived many people into thinking it isn't relevant to them personally.

I have learned through first-hand experience that the enemy can be very convincing with his tactics of deception. For years he was able to deceive me with his lies.

Would you like to know why it was so easy for him to deceive me?

The reason is pretty simple. I just wasn't familiar enough with God's truths to even recognize the lies.

Friends, it is only against the backdrop of God's truth that we can truly discern the lies of the enemy. If you and I want to know truth, we must go to the source of truth— the Bible.

"Do not let this Book of Law depart from your mouth; meditate on it day and night, so that you may be careful to do everything written in it. Then you will be prosperous and successful. (Joshua 1:8)

It is also important to know God's truth so that we can witness our faith to others. Christians are given opportunities to witness the Gospel of Jesus Christ each and every day. Although the opportunities present themselves daily, how many of us actually act on them?

Speaking for myself, I'm ashamed to say, not very often. I usually only speak up when I'm confident the message will be received favorably.

Meditating on this thought, I began to contemplate the reason for my timidity when it comes to witnessing my faith. It was then that God brought to my mind the courtroom scenario I described earlier.

When you and I find ourselves in a position to witness our faith, we must never enter the courtroom of life without the proper tools. Just as a carpenter needs hammer and nails—we need God's Word.

Of course it is imperative for us to know what God's Word actually says, before we can use it as a tool to witness. Even more importantly, we must study His Word to understand and define exactly what we, ourselves, believe.

"Jesus said, "If you hold to my teaching, you are really my disciples. Then you will know the truth, and the truth will set you free." (John 8:31)

Sometimes I lack confidence in articulating my thoughts during challenging discussions with others. My mind is always racing, but somehow I don't feel I'm very clear when I try to put those thoughts into words— especially when I'm trying to witness my faith to someone. I'm a meditative thinker and am more confident when I have time to reflect on what I would like to say. Since I'm not usually given the time I would prefer, I have come to depend on God's Words to help me.

"If anyone speaks, he should do it as one speaking the very words of God." (1 Peter 4:11)

God is a Master with words. He is able to say so eloquently what I am stumbling and searching to say. I don't want to give you the impression that I go around constantly spouting Bible verses. I don't. However, I have found that sometimes God's Word simply says it best.

And unlike our own words, we can have full confidence that God's Word will never go void. That's a promise!

> As the rain and the snow come down from heaven, and do not return to it without watering the earth and making it bud and flourish, so that it yields seed for the sower and bread for the eater, so is my word that goes out from my mouth: It will not return to me empty, but will accomplish what I desire and achieve the purpose for which I sent it. (Isaiah 55:10-11)

Throughout this book I will be sharing some revelation and insight that I have experienced through the study of God's Word. Although I do not have a degree in theology or philosophy, I have spent the past several years of my life intently studying God's Word. The Bible tells us that when we seek God with all of our heart, He reveals to us hidden truths that are only visible when seeking Him intently.

> And if you call out for insight and cry aloud for understanding, and if you look for it as for silver and search for it as for hidden treasure, then you will understand the fear of the LORD and find the knowledge of God. For the LORD gives wisdom, and from His mouth come knowledge and understanding. (Proverbs 2:3-6)

Please be assured that I take very seriously the counsel found in Second Timothy. "Do your best to present yourself to God as one approved, a workman who does not need to be ashamed and who correctly handles the word of truth." (2 Timothy 2:15)

Perhaps you're wondering why someone like me would feel the need to put down on paper those things which I believe to be true. To answer, I would like to borrow the words of Christian author Oswald Chambers,

> If you cannot express yourself on any subject, struggle until you can. If you do not, someone will be the poorer all the days of his life. Struggle to express some truth of God to yourself, and God will use that expression to someone else. Try to state to yourself what you feel implicitly to be God's truth, and you give God a chance to pass it on to someone else through you.[1]

Eventually, each of us will be called to God's witness stand to testify the truth concerning the Gospel of Jesus Christ. Therefore, we must be ready.

"Always be prepared to give an answer to everyone who asks you to give the reason for the hope that you have." (1 Peter 3:15)

If we want to live in freedom from Satan's lies and be able to effectively witness our faith in this fallen world, we must first know the truth. Then, through careful study of God's Word, we need to grow in God's truth. And finally, we are called to sow that truth by sharing our knowledge with others.

"My son, pay attention to what I say; listen closely to my words. Do not let them out of your sight; keep them within your heart." (Proverbs 4:20-21)

In heeding these instructions from Proverbs, we can expect God to remind us of all we have learned from Him when the time comes to share that knowledge.

"But the Counselor, the Holy Spirit, whom the Father will send in my name, will teach you all things and will remind you of everything I have said to you." (John 14:26)

I love the Lord with all my heart, soul, mind, and strength. There is a passion within me to seek out the many truths hidden in God's Word. I am excited to share with you some of those I have found and will do my best to communicate how they have both shaped and defined my faith. God's Word is powerful!

My prayer is that after reading this book you too will have a hunger and thirst for God's unchanging truths, seeing all the more clearly how the Bible is relevant for everyday living.

Brothers and sisters, as witnesses for the defense, proclaiming the truth in God's Word, you and I will eventually be asked this important question. Do you swear to tell the truth, the whole truth, and nothing but the truth?

My answer will be… *"Nothing but your truth will help me, God!"*

You have just finished reading an excerpt from *Nothing But Your Truth Will Help Me, God!* This book is available online in both paperback and Kindle format. If you would like more information about this or other available resources written by Rae Lynn DeAngelis, please visit: LivingInTruthMinistries.com.

49761611R00215

Made in the USA
Charleston, SC
04 December 2015